THE ROAD TO BANJUL
KEITH AND GRAHAM'S AMAZING ADVENTURE

by
Keith Pugsley, Lord Mallens of Bedfordshire

authorHOUSE®

AuthorHouse™ UK Ltd.
500 Avebury Boulevard
Central Milton Keynes, MK9 2BE
www.authorhouse.co.uk
Phone: 08001974150

This book is a work of non-fiction. Unless otherwise noted, the author and the publisher make no explicit guarantees as to the accuracy of the information contained in this book and in some cases, names of people and places have been altered to protect their privacy.

© 2008 Keith Pugsley, Lord Mallens of Bedfordshire. All rights reserved.

No part of this book may be reproduced, stored in a retrieval system, or transmitted by any means without the written permission of the author.

First published by AuthorHouse 7/21/2008

ISBN: 978-1-4343-9499-6 (sc)

Printed in the United States of America
Bloomington, Indiana

This book is printed on acid-free paper.

This is for Diana Lewis
and everything she stands for

WARNING!
THIS NOTICE AFFECTS YOUR ENJOYMENT.

This is the true story of an epic adventure. It is my version of the exploits of Team Life Mechanics on the Plymouth-Banjul Challenge 2007. It's in two parts; Part One, *Getting Ready*, is an account of the preparations for the trip. If you're contemplating entering the Plymouth-Banjul or any similar Challenge, or just curious about my attempts to prepare for all foreseeable eventualities, read on. If such matters don't do it for you, motor on to Part Two, *Getting There*. In either case, enjoy the ride.

Keith Pugsley January 2008

Part One:
Getting Ready

I
THE CHALLENGE

I help people to stop smoking. That's what I've been doing in my studio in Ilfracombe for the six years since retirement from the legal profession brought me back from the home counties to my roots. I help people to stop smoking, lose weight, dispel their fears and gain self confidence. As a clinical hypnotherapist and life coach I meet and help a lot of people who want to effect positive change in their lives. Just such a one was Dave Trickett.

Dave approached me in February 2006. A lively and upbeat thirty something footballer and surfer, he had tried to quit the smoking habit many times before. He'd come to realise that, with some help, he could kick it into touch for good. So I met with Dave and took his case history. What he told me changed my life forever.

Dave, a professional landscape contractor, mentioned that he liked travelling to the Gambia with friends and would like to be more active in fund raising for good causes. When pressed for more information on this rather interesting side of his personality, he revealed that his trip to Banjul "with some friends" the previous year had been in an ageing and battered Honda Accord with a co-driver and fifty or so other eccentrics as part of PBO5, or The Plymouth-Banjul Challenge 2005.

My ears pricked up. I had been looking for an adventure for some time. Since retirement, holidays away from my beloved North Devon held no interest. But an adventure such as this could be life changing. For the next half an hour of what was supposed to be Dave's therapy session he regaled me with his experiences.

The Plymouth-Banjul Challenge, he told me, was conceived some six or seven years ago by Julian Nowill, Exeter based stockbroker, philanthropist and motoring enthusiast, as an affordable alternative to the Paris-Dakar Rally. Entrants are required to provide a vehicle, which should cost no more than £100 (a further £15 may be squandered to make it street legal and roadworthy!). The vehicle must absolutely be a left hooker (left-hand drive to those of us who are neither in the trade nor a specialist car enthusiast). Right-hand drive vehicles are reputedly illegal in the Gambia and you can be stopped and have the vehicle confiscated or pay rather a large bribe to stay on the road. The vehicle is to be piloted by a team of no more than two, one of whom should be able to blag their way in French, and the other to tell the difference between a dashpot and a hipflask.

The journey starts, notionally, in Plymouth on one of four dates between late December and early February. The suggested route is via Dover to Boulogne or Plymouth to Roscoff and then through France, across the Pyrenees into Spain, crossing the Straits of Gibraltar and into Morocco for Christmas or New Year in Marrakech (except the February departures). Challengers then cross the disputed territory of Western Sahara, travelling the beach road the entire length of Mauritania, escorted through Senegal, to arrive in Banjul, capital of the Gambia, approximately three weeks after departure.

In Banjul, all surviving vehicles are surrendered for public auction, and the proceeds distributed to Gambian children's charities and their Olympic Committee. In this way Julian Nowill has been instrumental in raising something like £50,000 per annum for Gambian charities since 2003. As Julian points out, the trip is no package tour. Once you leave Plymouth outward bound with the friendly RAC man behind you on the beach in Blighty, you're on your own with nothing but the wits and resources of your team between you, disaster and financial ruin. There's banditry and drug dealing in Mauritania, civil war and unrest and a minefeld to traverse in disputed Western Sahara. Disease, dysentry and moral turpitude are rife in west Africa and malarial mosquitoes entertain from Morocco southward. Officialdom is corrupt and bureaucratic, petrol and diesel tainted and dirty, accommodation in hotels either filthy or of dubious repute and British presence in Senegal regarded with suspicion.

The whole deal sounded like great fun! Three thousand seven hundred miles of often questionable, sometimes mythical, roads in a £100 banger with a couple of spanners and a healthy supply of positive mental attitude appealed to the sense of adventure building inside me. For the next few days I would be unable to contain my enthusiasm for the Challenge.

Dave eventually left, a successful and delighted non-smoker.

I sat back in the therapy chair, inhaled deeply and began to dream of Africa.

II
A MATTER OF FORM

Ten minutes later I'm gunning the engine and crashing gears as I climb the steep hill out of Ilfracombe, man on a mission, right foot hard to the floor, eyes gazing fixedly at the road ahead. My mind is already in Africa, and I'm willing the traffic out of my way. I charge across the Tesco roundabout startling some of the more sedate shoppers, who customarily drive around it. The sheep are apparently not so impressed and continue with their impassive chewing. I hurtle through the chicane at Two Pots as Terry Wogan warns me there may be trouble ahead. Careening around a left-hander at Lynton Cross, I swear one wheel leaves the ground, and I realise I'm becoming quite adept at this rally lark.

Through the double bend and onwards to Stapleton Farm, where, frustratingly, I have to stop for temporary lights while the highway authority effect some pointless repairs. Can they really not be aware of my superior mission? I trundle laboriously through the obstacle led by a spotty youth on a quad bike, and emerge into the open road at Berry Down. I open full throttle, and the car surges through both halves of Berry Down Cross on two wheels. Into the home straight and open country. The engine screams abuse for a mile as I tear along Long Lane, past Indicknowle Farm and the chipping store, and execute a perfect handbrake turn bringing the car to a grinding halt in a celebration of gravel and smoke in the front entrance to Long Lane Farm. I step out of the Nimbus, my trusty Reliant Robin. The engine sighs.

I'm not quite sure how to handle the next bit. I can hardly contain my excitement at the adventure in my head. But how will Gilly react? I decide to calm myself, act nonchalant, drop it casually into the conversation at some point. So I peg out my swimming trunks and towel to dry, and drift into the kitchen.

"Hello sweetness, I'm home", I call out, none too convincingly I think.

"Hello!" she calls back, over the drone of the vacuum in the background. "Have a good swim?"

"Yes, thanks. A bit crowded to start, but it thinned out towards the end." I'm at the table now, consuming a bowl of exotic fresh fruit salad she has lovingly compiled for my lunch.

"How was your smoker?" she enquires as she passes through, taking the iguana his share of the chopped fruit.

"Fine, thanks. A nice chap. I think he'll be successful."

"That's good. I've sorted the log burner and lit the fire. You can sit and read if you like. I must just clean the bath". She has a mop and bucket, a bottle of bleach.

"Dave's an interesting bloke. He travels to Africa for charity."

"That's nice. I fed the tortoise, but the donkeys need mucking out in the stock barn. I'll do that after the bath."

"OK. Yes, he drove there in an old banger. Last year."

"Sounds like fun. I'm going to help with the lambing down at Indicknowle this afternoon. Want to come?"

"Yes, thanks. Er, I'm thinking of going to Africa myself."

"That'll be nice. Pass me your bowl, I'll wash it up."

"In a car. For charity. Next year."

"You'll need some clean socks."

"Yes, I expect there'll be a lot to think about. I'll be away three weeks."

"Only three?"

"So you don't mind then? "

"It sounds like a better idea than your last one. What was it, unicycling in the Andes? Course I don't mind."

"Want to come?"

"No thanks. Do you want mash and sausage or chips 'n egg for tea?"

*

Application to take part in the Plymouth-Banjul Challenge has to be made on-line. I logged on the very next day at Ilfracombe Library's public terminal. It was disappointing to find the website for the current year's challenge not fully operational; unsurprising as it turns out, because in February 2006 when I made my first attempt the 2006 Challenge was actually in progress, the last cars limping their way over the finish line in Banjul. I had a couple of months to wait until formal application for the 2007 Challenge could be made. I studied the embryonic website avidly, took notes in a good old fashioned low tech note book and reported back to Management at Base Camp (Gilly).

Interest in the Challenge is buoyant, and places limited. The application has to be of good quality, imaginative and submitted on time for the selection process. Apart from the administrative details, a five hundred word essay justifying selection for the event is required. The fee on entry was £250, refundable in the event of an unsuccessful application. Some 2,500 expressions of interest in taking part were expected worldwide, and selected participants hail from the USA, Japan, Holland, Germany, Italy, Scotland and, well, everywhere really. Competition is tough. Coming from the Challenge's home county would mean diddly squat.

I returned to the library terminal in early May. This time I had prepared myself with some thoughts of the skills and attributes that I and my as yet fictitious partner might possess to justify selection as one of the lucky few. But I was not prepared for the playgroup that was using the library facilities, nor the queues of students and pensioners who waited patiently for their allocated hour. More surfers than Woolacombe beach on a bank holiday.

Eventually I sat before a screen, logged on and quickly found www.Plymouth-Banjul.co.uk and the application form. Now I'm not exactly a technophobe, but completing an application on-line including an essay of convincing fabrication and fantasy all in an hour was itself a challenge for me. I removed the two children from my desk, and the other one perched on my foot, and got stuck in.

The administrative details were simple enough. Asked for a team name I selected "The Life Mechanics", partly as a reflection of my own professional style and title, but mainly because my allocated hour was fast dwindling and I couldn't think of anything more imaginative.

The competition essay was more demanding. Of course, as far as my own not inconsiderable qualities, attributes and talents are concerned, I can wax lyrical, almost fulsome. But my partner for the proposed jaunt had not yet been identified. I made him up. I gave him the unlikely name of Jack Sparrow. A qualified accountant, architect, engineer and medical practitioner, Jack was fluent in French, Arabic and Gujarati. He had studied motor mechanics and gynaecology at the Sorbonne, politics and home economics at Harvard. He was an accomplished chef, navigator, rally enthusiast and tap dancer. Et cetera. I began to wish I knew Jack. Anyway, that's what I think I wrote. Because just as I was dotting the last "i" and crossing the last "t" on my masterpiece of invention the screen went blank. My hour had expired. My efforts and the inestimable Jack Sparrow had been relegated to cyberspace.

My third visit to the Ilfracombe public terminal was more successful. Jack Sparrow's qualifications and expertise lost something in the translation, and I still have no record of what I actually said about him. But the application was duly lodged, and my cheque for £250 followed by snail mail. I could relax and await the selection process.

Over 4,000 expressions of interest had been lodged worldwide. Just over 450 formal applications were made. Jack Sparrow and I, the original Life Mechanics, were informed by email in late May that we had been selected as one of the 200 teams to take part in the Challenge. We'd been placed in our selected Group 4, with a departure date of 2 February 2007.

I celebrated in silence. Jack Sparrow was also, I forgot to say, a Baptist missionary.

III
THE SEARCH FOR JACK SPARROW

Having secured my place on the Challenge, the enormity of its potential began to hit me. I must make the most of this experience. There was a lot to do, and detailed preparations would be the key to success. I blundered around for some days thinking what pyjamas would be suitable in Mauritania, and would I need a hot water bottle in Banjul. Then, galvanised into action by Gilly, we sat down and made a list of all the things, in no particular order, that I would need to take, prepare or do. Instantly the two major priorities, which above all would need to be in place for a successful outcome presented themselves. A mate, and a car. In that order, because I really didn't fancy trekking across the desert in a banger on my own.

Jack Sparrow had served me well at the application stage, and possessed some unique personality traits and skills that would prove invaluable on the journey. But somehow he lacked substance.

I had in mind a sort of person specification for Jack's replacement. My partner would have skills and attributes that would complement my own. He or she would be fit, durable, free of substance abuse, available without other commitment throughout February 2007, keen for an adventure with focus on the Challenge, an excellent driver with enhanced mechanical skills, good company and a sense of humour. Above all, there would need to be rapport between us; it's not advisable to live at close quarters for three weeks in basic conditions with a perfect stranger, even if they otherwise appear to possess all the skills and attributes required. I would have to be comfortable with my chosen partner if marooned on a desert island.

Gilly had an opinion on this aspect and added her own list of requirements. As well as having the attributes I had identified, my partner would have to be male, trustworthy and known to her personally. She didn't want me behaving badly in Africa with a stranger, and she had already decided that to become my partner herself in this venture would be to test our thirty five year marriage too far. We rarely make it to Barnstaple together in a car without some minor spat over driving protocols. So Gilly became my patron and my mentor. She offered to buy me a car and bankroll the entire trip, from hotels and accommodation to spending money and gifts for the natives. So long as my chosen partner was male, trustworthy and known to her.

The first aspect of the Challenge which she helped me with was the selection of my replacement for Jack Sparrow. We prepared a detailed person specification. Here it is:

PERSON SPECIFICATION FOR JACK SPARROW

ESSENTIAL ATTRIBUTES	DESIREABLE ATTRIBUTES
Male	Superhuman strength, stamina and energy
Known to Gilly	Fortitude and courage in the face of adversity
Trusted by Gilly to keep me in check	Skilled negotiator
Fit, healthy and able bodied	The grace and bearing of an ambassador
Mechanical ability at least superior to mine	Fluent in French, Spanish and Mandinka
Experience of driving over rough terrain on the wrong side of the road	Professional rally driver

Elaborate sense of humour	Insensitive to expletive, invective and political incorrectness
Family support for the caper	Not squeamish over bodily functions or major invasive kerbside surgery
Have rapport with me	An adventurous palate
Available throughout February 2007	Suit an eye patch
Really want to go	Own teeth and hair
	Skilled in boxing and/or the martial arts
	Able to catch fish with a spear
	Competent outdoor survivalist
	Adept with a fly swat

Six friends seemed to fit most of the criteria.

Neil Caley is a self employed vehicle mechanic (trading under the name Vetech Services) who has a rare combination of talents. Not only a superb mechanic of the old school, he knows how to fix virtually anything and everything. Neil is an experienced driver who had a taste of adventure as a young man in the '70s when he drove vehicles and equipment down to southern Spain to be used in the making of the Star Wars Trilogy. He is also blessed with a wonderfully upbeat personality and a "can do" attitude to life. I get on with him well on a personal and professional basis. He lives less than a mile away from me as the banger limps, and he services and repairs the four or five cars I keep on the road. A rare mix of caution and confidence made him an obvious candidate.

Keith Lamprey is a cousin by marriage. He lived at Trimstone, a few miles from Long Lane Farm, and makes his living climbing telegraph poles for British Telecom. A keen motor cyclist and steam enthusiast, Keith would be promising company on a traction engine or dirt bike. He once converted a redundant ambulance into a motor home, and I could rely on his practical and camping prowess. As a part time coach driver, I could expect marvels in the driving seat. He had also been a loyal and trustworthy addition to my extended family for years, so Keith would tick many of the boxes.

Graham De Meur, my very good friend from the Bedfordshire days, was another natural choice. With French Huguenot ancestry, the name itself might be a boon in the French speaking countries we were to encounter. An engineer by profession, Graham had spent a number of years as a long distance lorry driver in Europe, and had many miles and vehicles under his belt. He was once going to set up a Reversing School, to assist those of us who find forwards easy but hindwards more challenging. He had particular skills with animals and a fondness for tractors. I met him ten years ago when he showed me how to dig a hole and bury a pig. Recently divorced and with a new partner, I'd need to be sensitive to the demands of Graham's new, and very happy, relationship. But teacher Sally, whom I'd only met once, was known to me already as supportive, encouraging and with a pleasant and wry sense of humour, someone who might see the funny side of two middle aged old farts "finding themselves".

Graham lives in Gloucestershire, and worked in High Wycombe, Bucks. We would need to meet from time to time to make preparations, but most of the organisation would be down to me.

Paul Wilson is an Independent Financial Advisor turned Clinical Hypnotherapist, coach and trainer. A member of my writing circle, very good friend and collaborator in the performing arts, Paul once helped me stalk and capture a peacock that was terrorizing a chronic orniphobic in Leighton Buzzard. We trod the boards as Dobbin, the panto horse (I was the back end, because Paul has more front), in the village hall production of *The Wizzard of Oz* in 2000, and he just had to feature on the list of potential partners for this particular adventure.

As did Phil Carter, my longest remaining friend from the 1960's when we spent many a happy hour pushing his clapped out Ford Zephyr around the lanes of Bedfordshire in search of high jinx. Phil is a craftsman pattern maker, self employed for 15 years fitting out plush executive jets for wealthy Arabs. But his love is still for the large American gas guzzler of the 1950's, and his skill with all things mechanical put him high on my hit list.

Finally, **Derrick Hamly**, the jobbing builder who had become my very good friend. Tall, strong, genial, calm and unflappable in a crisis, always eager to please, Derrick is a consummate professional in all that he does. I knew that, whatever the circumstance, Derrick would come through with the goods. He'd traveled in Africa and worked on building projects for the needy before. He had to be a contender.

All of my prospective partners were big on personality, and although they differed wildly from each other and myself in background, I would have been more than happy to travel the African continent with any or all of them. Gilly and I measured them all carefully against the selection criteria.

Graham ticked most of the boxes. More importantly, he was up for the Challenge.

I had found Jack Sparrow.

IV
THE SEARCH FOR BLACK BETTY

The next essential for the Challenge was a vehicle. Only four rules applied here;

1. It should cost no more than £100.
2. A further £15 could be lavished on making it roadworthy and street legal.
3. <u>Must</u> be left hand drive.
4. The vehicle must be surrendered to Challenge Control for public auction in the Gambia, where proceeds would be donated to Gambian charities.

Rules one and two just asked to be broken. Most would recognise the unlikelihood of sourcing and provisioning a motor vehicle for this Challenge within such a meagre budget. So the figures are notional, and are meant to ensure that the Challenge is open to all who have an adventuring spirit and a little mechanical know-how. Rule four encapsulates the whole intention of the Challenge, which is to surrender something of saleable value, to be auctioned for good causes. Again, easy to comply with. It was only rule three that might pose a problem for UK participants. Finding a left hand drive car in this country is not as simple as perhaps it used to be, even though the object of my search, of virtually any age and condition, would be worth next to nothing.

I first considered our "fleet" of ageing and for the most part valueless cars; a standard Ford Escort estate, a Rover Metro (with personalised plates worth more than the vehicle itself), Gilly's Citroen 2 CV (affectionately named Jean-Paul), the Nimbus (my ancient Reliant tricycle with a music system worth at least twice as much as the car) and a prehistoric Land Rover. All were ruled out by the left-hand-drive rule and the only one readily convertible, the 1968 Land Rover Series IIA, would cripple me both financially and physically on a journey of 3,700 miles along coastal West Africa.

I broadcast the word to friends, family and clients, and had three local mechanics (including Neil Caley) on the look out for a suitable candidate. Diana Lewis of the North Devon Animal Ambulance (my chosen charity for sponsorship in the UK) arranged an interview with North Devon Journal reporter Kate Helyer. The Journal gave splendid coverage accompanied by stunning pictures of our photogenic donkeys Freda and Heidi, in an effort to tempt the offer of a car from the population of North Devon. Media coverage was not limited to the press. An interview for Spotlight South West on the early evening TV news did nothing to move on my search for a suitable vehicle.

Most people looking for a car of a particular type from the second hand market will eventually be drawn to Ebay. It was with some trepidation and reluctance that I succumbed to this route. I don't get on with the Internet or the way it seems to invade every aspect of modern life. However, as a source of left hand drive vehicles available for sale it seemed it couldn't be equaled. After some tentative fumblings with the process of registration, I soon found myself chasing one car after another, all totally unseen. I pursued a Honda Civic in Dorset, an ancient and lumbering Mercedes in Jersey (shipping costs to the UK an extra £100), a Peugeot 105 near Grimsby and a Vauxhall Frontera in a location unknown to me to this day. All my efforts surfing the Net were unsuccessful and I put this down largely to my own naivety with the rules of intergalactic bargaining. Ebay itself is simple enough to manipulate in its way, but the tactics of vendor and purchaser rigging bids, clubbing together in chatroom cartels to ensure success, getting one's friends to distort the bid process, all seemed a little, no, a big bit dishonest to me, and defied my open market ethics. I was never going to be successful on Ebay, but I am sure others are.

Robbie Herrick, an enterprising motor enthusiast friend of my schooldays, now teaching in Tenby on the Pembrokeshire coast, rang to tell me of a local businessman with a fleet of left hand drive Range Rover ice cream vans, painted corporate brown, and sporting the legend "Jones' Pembrokeshire ice creams—stop me and buy one". Apparently Mr. Jones was in the habit of disposing of one or two of his older vehicles at the end of each season. Obviously, a suitably equipped ice cream van, diesel and left hand drive, would fit the bill. Graham and I could arrive in Banjul in style, cool, refreshed, and perhaps make a small fortune selling 99's on the way. Unfortunately, on further investigation it transpired that Mr. Jones was only intending to unload one vehicle this season, and that was the van, suitably coloured and bedecked with banners awning and cone, that went down with all hands in Tenby harbour when surprised by an early and unusually high tide. Stuck in the mud, it appears the vehicle had to be abandoned by its crew of two who waded to the shore and watched in disbelief as the sun set over the loudspeaker to the tune of Greensleeves at dusk. So selling ice cream to the natives of Banjul was a lovely fantasy, but a short-lived one.

Next I tried the main dealerships in Barnstaple. My thought was that one of the main dealers would be bound to be sufficiently impressed with my remarkable bravery, astuteness, acumen and charisma in attempting this audacious challenge for good causes, that they would scour the countryside to provide a left hand drive version of one of the popular makes and present it to me gratis, together with full sponsorship and support, just because I had been cheeky enough to ask. Perhaps I was deluding myself. Perhaps my expectations and confidence in the successful outcome of my endeavour were outweighed by the ridiculous and unlikely nature of my request. Perhaps I shouldn't have shuffled and limped into their plush carpeted showrooms, unannounced, in shorts, sandals and T shirt, on crutches (suffering an acute attack of gout) with a couple of days stubble and my "windswept and interesting" look. But then I never was much at PR. What you see is what you get. Once again, I didn't really know the rules of the game. In shorts, my labours bore no fruit.

One morning at my local swimming pool, Jeff, a co-swimmer, suggested I try Milber Salvage of Newton Abbott, reputedly the largest car dismantlers in the South West. They're known to support banger racing, rallies and endeavours such as my own, he told me. I confess it hadn't occurred to me to try the breakers yards, and my search quickly turned down that avenue.

Milbers had nothing to offer. Left hand wrecks are, if anything, rarer than their roadworthy counterparts. But there are plenty of wreckers in Devon. Eventually my search through Yellow Pages found the most local car breaker, in Braunton, some five or six miles distant. By this time the response to my enquiry was becoming depressingly predictable, and, as expected, the local breakers had nothing to offer, indeed hadn't seen trace of a left hooker for over two years. I was about to hang up when the very helpful chap at the breakers asked me to hold on. I heard him call out, apparently across the yard, something about "did you want to get rid of that Jeep?"

The next voice I heard was young, enthusiastic and earnest. Lance had a left-hand-drive Cherokee Jeep. He was seeking to recover the money he had spent restoring her and would let her go for about £800. Was I interested? I took a sharp intake of breath. £800 was rather more than I'd planned on spending on my "banger" and, in any event I had no clear idea of just what a Cherokee Jeep is. I envisioned something like the Wally's Jeep of WW II and John Wayne fame. But as this was the first direct offer of a vehicle, in desperation I agreed to at least view her at the weekend.

The weekend came. Graham and Sally came to stay. We could've viewed the car but I'd been hearing mixed messages about Cherokee Jeeps; heavy on petrol, not secure if it's an open top, problematic suspension etc. I decided to give it a miss and to continue with the search for a chariot on Ebay. The current contender was the Frontera, and when this was lost to a higher bidder, I began to lose heart.

Next I resorted to the Cosmic Ordering Service. I placed an order for "a left-hand drive vehicle capable of getting me to Banjul in February 2007, and I want it by 31st July 2006". My order was placed in the letter box on the cosmic tree in our small wood on the fifteenth of July.

One week later I received a call from Lance Ginns, the proprietor of Freelance Motors, and the mechanic responsible for making Dave Trickett's Honda Accord ready for the 2005 Challenge. Talk about a small world, wheels within wheels, etc. The Cherokee Jeep was still for sale, and he needed to unload it as he would be emigrating to Crete in September. Was I still interested? I could have it for £650. It was partly out of courtesy to Lance, and partly a sneaking suspicion that my cosmic order might have been favourably received, that this time I would view the vehicle.

The breakers' is just outside Knowle. In one corner Freelance Motors occupied a neatly laid out and well kept workshop and yard. It looked a little incongruous amidst the piles of battered and broken vehicles, some stacked four high, in this rural setting. And at one end of the yard, between an ageing camper van and a Morris Minor, stood Black Betty. I fell instantly in love.

Black Betty is a Grand Cherokee Jeep Laredo, with a 4 litre straight six petrol engine, 2 wheel drive, central locking, electric windows, air conditioning, power steering and outrageously comfy seats. She's black. And beautiful. Originally produced for the American market (hence 2 rear-wheel drive), she was first registered (number H174 DMX) in the UK on 29 July 1997. Lance had saved her from the jaws of the crane moments before she was to be crushed to death, and lovingly restored her to her former self. The product of early neglect, a serious electrical fire and insurance write-off, he'd repaired her mangled roof and fitted a replacement windscreen, the original having popped from its frame when she was craned onto the back of the breakers lorry. I paid Lance his asking price of six hundred and fifty nicker and she was "sold as seen as scrap with original MoT to December 2006. No warranty".

I drove her the five or six miles back to Long Lane Farm with no tax or insurance. She was my first left hooker, and the first automatic I'd driven in nearly thirty years, so I was at first slightly anxious. But I drove her as Lance had instructed, aiming for the nearside cart track on the road, adopting a demeanour of quiet, calm nonchalance, and the habit came quickly. Those first few miles were like driving a cloud, with power, comfort and control. I already knew that I would miss her when I had to give her up in the Gambia.

It was 30 July 2006. The Cosmic Ordering Service had delivered, one day early.

V
A MEETING IN A FIELD

The launch party for the Plymouth-Banjul Challenge 2007 took place just outside Cullompton, East Devon, in June. All Challenge Teams were invited, as were the previous year's participants, as a sort of reunion.

Now I'm no longer a party animal, and I agonized over whether to bother driving the fifty minutes across county to take part in what I thought to be a dubious excuse for drunkenness and debauchery in a field full of strangers. The effort was worth while, however, and I was humbled to find people had flown in from the USA and New Zealand, and driven from all parts of Europe (including one couple from the Orkneys) just to take part.

As Gilly and I pulled onto the field that sunny Saturday afternoon, we were greeted at the gate by Julian Nowill and Drew, the Challenge Disorganisers. Julian, resplendent in pure white djelaba and red fez, smiled a welcome, handed me a mysterious black plastic sack, shook me warmly by the hand and gestured with his hookah that I should move on to his worthy assistant Drew. Drew is the techno geek, responsible for setting up and maintaining the Challenge website and for receiving participants. He registered the Life Mechanics and directed us to take up position in the corner reserved for Group 4.

Julian's mysterious plastic sack contained the launch pack (maps of west Africa, *Lonely Planets* of Morocco and Senegambia, door number signs with instructions on how to fit them, and a video of the first Plymouth-Banjul Challenge).

Leaving Gilly to enjoy the party atmosphere that was gradually beginning to rock and roll, I spent a couple of hours strolling between the groups, strategically encamped in the four corners of the field, with the Bamoko (Mali) contingent in the middle. I sat and listened intently to conversations with those I might be traveling with, and, perhaps more importantly, those who had boldly gone before.

Meanwhile, Gilly stayed dutifully by the car, watching the floor show unfold, bemused.

A VW camper, yellow with pink and blue flowers, lurched into the field in a cacophony of ABBA and exhaust. Its contents spilled out, four men in tight black mini skirts, gold lamé platform boots and long blonde wigs. The Dutch contingent had arrived. Four Hooray Henrys[1] in pith helmets, safari jackets and a battered and protesting Volvo tore around in the soft mud, intent on demolishing the solitary telegraph pole. Two Hells Angels in studded leather and shades erected their fastidious tent and left for a cultural visit to Exeter Cathedral, or maybe beer. Others blearily emerged from their afternoon tents, evidently recovering from last night's indulgence. There were, it seemed, two types of person involved on this challenge; middle aged adventure seekers, mature but a little mad, and the young, rich and rootless, also eccentric and making up in bravado what they lack in maturity.

The purpose in attending the launch party was, for me, twofold. Firstly, to gain as much practical advice as possible from the Challenge Dis-organisers and others more experienced than I. Secondly, to make some useful contacts within Group 4. Driving through the deserts of Mauritania, Western Sahara and southern Morocco is recommended in convoys of four or five. So I was looking for a selection of like-minded mature crazies that Graham and I could live with and render mutual support in these areas.

The information gathering was a success. I gleaned a deal of knowledge on what to take, what to leave behind, what to avoid and how to get through some of the more difficult border crossings. Pens and pencils, used T shirts, and anything electronic or electrical from used mobile phones to half a broken typewriter go down well with the

---

[1] A young middle or upper class man with an affectedly ebullient manner and an ostentatiously materialistic or self-seeking outlook. *Chambers Dictionary 1993 edition.*

locals. Passport and customs officials south of Morocco find whisky and pornography acceptable bribes, but you have to be careful and discrete with these two highly illegal commodities in predominantly Muslim countries. One unfortunate encounter with Simon the Zealot could mean a ten stretch in a Casablanca jail. There is a kerbside mechanic every one hundred miles or so to work miracles with your ailing car and he will reline your brakes with a roof tile, adjust your points with a baked bean can or patch your tyres with camel hide. The women in Senegal are amongst the most beautiful in the world. Some Mauritanian hotels are poorly disguised brothels. In Western Sahara credit cards are likely to be cloned, so their use is ill-advised. And don't open your boot (trunk in my case) in the presence of children. These were some of the gems I heard and noted amongst the growing village of tents that the launch party soon became.

The second purpose of my visit to this prestigious event was not realised. I could sense matters degenerating into an unseemly hooley when I spotted Gilly, half way up the telegraph pole with a can of Scrumpy Jack. So, when I could persuade her to leave her new found friends and partners on the Bamoko run, we left the party, still in the early afternoon, and made none of the contacts I'd intended for crossing the desert areas. This could be left until Spain.

Back at Long Lane Farm I continued the fact finding mission by watching the DVD of the first Plymouth-Banjul Challenge, depicting some of the conditions along the way and the horrors to come; traversing the minefield, breaking out of an enclosed compound in Mauritania and being washed away at high tide along the coast of Western Sahara. And what a lot of fun was actually awaiting us.

I joined the PB07 Group 4 chatline. Not a "chatterer" by nature on the internet, my motive was again information gathering, and in these early days I picked up tips about motor insurance, importing a French left hooker, how to get a visa for Mauritania and so on. The information on the PB07 Website was useful but not comprehensive, and that of course was part of the challenge. I picked up further guidance in books about Morocco, Senegal and the Gambia and spoke to friends and acquaintances who'd visited one or the other. But Mauritania and

Western Sahara are little known, less still written about, and hardly documented at all. Presumably because only the foolhardy visit these regions.

Putting all the information sources together I developed for myself and Graham a cunning plan.

VI
THE CUNNING PLAN

DOCUMENTS:
    Car insurance-green card
    MoT, V45, car tax
    Passports Mauri visa
    Driving licences IDPs
    RAC card Fiches x2x30
    Travel insurance—EHIC
    Ferry tickets Air tickets
    Yellow fever vac. Certs.
    Currency Credit/debit cards, international log book

INOCULATIONS
    Yellow fever
    Malaria
    Rabies
    Typhus
    Hep A
    Hep B
    Diptheria
    Cholera
    Polio
    Tetanus

PROVISIONS
- → Gifts (mobiles, watches, pens, t shirts)
- → Bribes (porn, whisky)
- → Clothes (socks, pants, hats, t shirts, chinos, Boiler suits, fleeces, pyjamas)
- → Food (tinned)
- → Drink (water)
- → Sleeping (tent, sleeping bags, mats, mattresses)
- → Hygiene (wash, shave, bog paper, wet wipes)

BLACK BETTY
- Service
- Check tyres, air con, temp gauge, oil, battery
- Radio? Satnav?
- MoT
- Spare hoses, tubes, tyre, bulbs, belts
- Fluids-oil, water, petrol, tyre repair, damp start, extinguisher, liquid metal, duct tape

FIRST AID
Needles-syringes
Suture kit
Ibuprofen
Steristrips
Plasters, bandages, antiseptic
Malarone
Insect repellant
Sun cream
Scissors
Tweezers-tick remover
Thermometer?
Dental kit?
Blood groups?

SUNDRIES
- ♥ Road book
- ♥ Medication-cholesterol and gout
- ♥ Maps-north Africa, Spain, France
- ♥ Books-Morocco, Senegambia, Journal, Reading
- ♥ Collapsible containers
- ♥ Spare specs
- ♥ Cameras-movie with films, stills with large memory, chargers
- ♥ Torch, batteries

ARRANGEMENTS
- ☐ mobile phone
- ☐ ferry to roscoff
- ☐ transport from Gatwick
- ☐ sponsorship (jeep uk, nfu, ndaa)

Mossie nets
Fly spray
Water purifier
Calomine
Rehydration salts/diocalm

FARM TASKS FEB.07
Pearl and Frederick, renew UVB's, heating oil, septic tank, Farrier, donkey feet, hot tub filter, dig grave, check cars-escort & metro.

VII
SISTER MARLENE

I've never been very comfortable with needles and injections, and would rather be taken by surprise than reminded, as the medical profession seem to like to do, that I will shortly be experiencing a "little scratch" as the needle machetes its way deep into the fleshy parts of my anatomy. My technique of dealing with this less than delightful experience is to roll up my sleeve, look away and ask my attendant to shout "NOW!" just as the needle's about to puncture the skin. Then I cough twice at the instant of entry, and count silently and quickly from 100 to zero, never actually reaching 94. I talked this procedure through with Sister Marlene, and she readily agreed to deviate from NHS policy and co-operate with my preferred protocol, in the interests of customer care.

Sister Marlene is the jolly character in starched blue based at my local Travel Clinic. Professional but friendly and approachable, she sees travelers abroad safely to their destination, with advice, suggestions and a ferociously accurate needle. My rapport with her was instant when I showed her a framed picture of her namesake, a delightful pet lamb we had adopted earlier in the year.

On my first visit, in August, she questioned me about the purpose of my trip and just what I would be getting up to in foreign parts. Then she studied my MASTA Brief and planned the sequence of inoculations.

MASTA (I never could find what the acronym stands for) is an organization providing advice and health care products for the traveler abroad. The advice, which comes in the form of a comprehensive, personally tailored and professionally produced health brief, is free. Talking to a mechanical voice on the telephone I'd listed the countries I'd be traveling through and, in each case, whether living conditions would be classified as tourist, moderate or "rural". I opted for the worst case scenario or "rural" in each country, as I really wasn't sure what conditions I might encounter. "Rural" denotes living with the natives, treating them medically or spiritually, or generally getting up close and personal. Whilst none of these was part of the specification for the Challenge, I put a high premium on my health and wellbeing, and on Graham's.

The MASTA Health Brief made for interesting, helpful, if daunting reading, for me and Sister Marlene. The only mandatory immunisation was for yellow fever, and I'd carry a Yellow Fever Certificate. Protection against polio was recommended, because of the possibility of contact with contaminated food and water. Hepatitis A virus, also transmitted via food and water, should be covered. As far as I could recall I'd never been protected from this little beast, which attacks the liver and can lead to jaundice and prolonged illness. Typhoid, which can lead to coma and death, doesn't normally affect the short stay traveler in "good accommodation". I couldn't be sure of my accommodation, outside of the confines of my own tent, so protection was again indicated. As it was against Tetanus, usually contracted following contamination of deep puncture wounds. I've had tetanus jabs after dog bites, a motoring accident on honeymoon and following a wrestling match with one particularly bold and aggressive house mouse in Lewisham. But my protection would've long since expired, and I'd need a booster.

My mother had Diptheria when she was carrying me, so my protection was probably innate. However, you don't take chances with this one, which is usually transmitted by close contact with the infected, and it was recommended for me. I was advised to at least consider Hepatitis B, transmitted sexually and by skin puncture with contaminated needles, as it leads to liver damage and failure. I had no intention of indulging myself sexually abroad, or of breaking my lifetime drug free habit, at least not voluntarily. Perhaps Hepatitis B could be left on the shelf? Rabies however, transmitted via the saliva of infected animals and usually resulting from dog bites, is invariably fatal and 20 to 30 cases of human rabies had been reported in Morocco in recent times. Better safe than sorry.

Cholera, again caused by contaminated food and water, is generally associated with slum areas, refugee camps and hospitals, military personnel in conflict zones and "travelers visiting rural areas". All travelers are advised to take extreme care with water and food hygiene, and I considered that a cavalier attitude to this risk would be churlish. My protection against TB as an adolescent would still stand me in good stead, and there was apparently no benefit in boosting it anyway. Meningococcal Meningitis, transmitted by close contact with the infected, appears to be connected with long stay travelers in certain geographical areas. The risk to Graham and me could indeed be treated casually.

Other hazards to health we might encounter in February included, in France, tick encephalitis and lyme disease, and in both France and Spain, tick typhus. All linked to scrub or farm areas where animals wander and rats roam, the risk to us would be low. Immunisation against these horrors wouldn't be necessary, but tweezers for kerbside tick removal and a stout spade to splat the rat should both feature.

Malarial mosquitoes bite from dusk to dawn, and since malignant malaria is present from southern Morocco, throughout Mauritania, Senegal and the Gambia, precautions for preventing and treating bites need to be taken throughout. The advice is to avoid bites by using insect repellants regularly, wearing long sleeved shirts and trousers, especially during the evenings. "Knock-down" fly sprays should be used at night, plug-in vaporizers and the ubiquitous net will suffice where air conditioning doesn't exist. A variety of antimalarial drugs was recommended and Sister Marlene would advise.

Finally, Montezuma's Revenge. My MASTA report advised of significant risk to travelers of diarrhoea. Great care with food and water hygiene would be necessary, and we should carry supplies of bottled water, even for cleaning teeth. I was warned to examine bottle seals for integrity, as it's not unknown for river water to be marketed in rural areas as "fresh from a mountain spring". High risk foods to avoid included salads, shellfish, raw or undercooked meat and unpasteurised dairy products. A crate or two of Diocalm would be on the agenda.

I sat nervously in Sister Marlene's consulting room as she studied the brief from beginning to end, making notes in the surgery diary. Eventually, she sat back in her chair and beamed.

"OK, we can start right now. Take off your coat and roll up your sleeves. Both of them please."

I shuddered, hoping that I was to be initiated into the Freemasons, or perhaps asked to deliver a calf. I presented both bare arms and looked pointedly away, as if to say OK, do your worst, but be gentle with me.

"Little prick!"

"I beg your pardon?" I stammered, but it was all over.

I'd been expecting excruciating agony, wracking pain. I think I was slightly disappointed with the dull ache of Hepatitis A and B as it coursed through my left arm, and the throb of the combined diptheria, tetanus and polio in my right.

But my respite was short lived, and I returned a scant week later for the second Hepatitis A and B (right arm this time, I imagine to ensure both sides were covered), and typhoid (left arm). This time I was given a month to recover from any after effects.

In September I returned to Sister Marlene for my third dose of Hepatitis A and B. For some reason, which she was at a loss to explain, the Hepatitis B vaccine normally has to be paid for, whilst Hepatitis A is free. But if both are administered together, both are free. Just as well really, because now matters had begun to become expensive. The yellow fever jab, also administered on this third visit, cost £40.

Cholera vaccine comes as a pleasant drink. Perhaps not so commonly encountered in British pharmacies, it had to be ordered, and then kept in the fridge until use. I had to withstand temptation for seven days after the yellow fever jab before I could treat myself to my first cholera cocktail. It came in a box containing two tiny phials of live vaccine and two sachets of something tasting like Andrews Liver Salts, which were mixed with water to make the live vaccine more palatable. Cholera cocktails are taken fourteen days apart, and I was told to programme in the final vaccinations, for rabies, at least one week later.

The rabies programme of three jabs has to be spaced out at 7 and 21 day intervals, which ultimately meant that my visit to the Mauritanian embassy with Graham had to be postponed by a week, because there's little tolerance if these shots are to be effective. Ironically, I hobbled into Sister Marlene on crutches for my second jab, having damaged the sciatic nerve carrying a sheep through a stream. I'm too embarrassed at my stupidity in sustaining this injury to expound any further, but the reader can imagine the Sister's surprise and amusement at my presentation at the surgery on the same day for painkillers and a rabies booster. Rabies, or at least the precautions against it, was to cost me a further £110, and the very thought of this caused me to emerge from the surgery frothing at the wallet, if not the mouth.

Sister Marlene advised me to stock up on the preferred, if more expensive, Malarone to combat the mossies. One tablet to be taken with food or a milky drink, one or two days before entering the first malarial area and daily thereafter until one week after return to the UK. By my reckoning, this would mean we should start malarial precautions in France. £120 to deter a gnat!

She also gave invaluable advice on the contents of our first aid box, which should feature steristrips (to seal large cuts), hypodermic needles and syringes (so we wouldn't have to share a frequently used local one) and suture material (to hold limbs roughly together until a more permanent job could be done). Her tasks with me complete, she wished me a happy holiday and looked forward to my reasonably safe, and crutchless, return.

Hobbling clumsily through surgery reception, my attention was grabbed by the winter 'flu vaccination warning they paste up for the elderly. It occurred that contracting 'flu just before the trip could be disastrous. I had visions of Graham driving from Plymouth through France, Spain and half of Africa with me languishing in the back of Black

Betty, my cushions plumped up and dosed to the hilt with Beecham's. I certainly didn't intend to abandon the trip at this stage for anything less than life threatening. So I enquired about the possibility of a 'flu vaccination for this retired and ageing solicitor, pointing meaningfully and with some pathos at my newly acquired crutches. The supplies of vaccine were regrettably low at the time, and mainly reserved for the elderly, infirm and pregnant. I didn't qualify, apparently, under any of these categories, despite the cushion stuffed up my jumper. So I had to be placed on the reserve list and await developments.

Fortunately, I was called in during early December to take the place of a cancelled appointment for the 'flu jab. I duly attended, at 4.30 p.m. one dark and dank Wednesday evening. The jabs were being administered with almost indecent haste in a cloud of Algipan and lavender water. I barely had time to give my instructions on my needle coping strategy, when I found the deed had been done.

I was, hopefully, immune from anything that circumstance and misadventure might bring.

VIII
BANDITS BOMBS AND BRIBES

The doctor's surgery and the indomitable Sister Marlene couldn't help with terrorism. There's no inoculation against bombs and banditry, and the MASTA report, if believed in every detail, gave quite a frightening picture.

France, it appears, shares with the rest of Europe, a threat from international terrorism. Attacks can be indiscriminate and against civilian targets. Care in town centres and near public buildings is cautioned. But most visits are apparently trouble free, and petty crime and road traffic accidents the most we should expect to encounter.

Spain's threat of Basque terrorist movements had lightened since ETA announced a "permanent ceasefire" the previous March, but the recent presence of Al Qaida in Madrid when 192 died and over 1400 were injured following bomb attacks on three trains might just flavour our choice of route. Theft and pickpocketing goes on amongst the tourists but this would only involve taking normal care of our belongings.

Gibraltar would be a little bit of old world Britishness at the southern tip of Spain. With a refreshingly low crime rate, we would only be likely to suffer violence at the hands of rogue Barbary apes. Over the straits, however, in Morocco, where the real adventure would begin, we could expect a high threat of terrorism. Serious attacks took place recently in Casablanca, which we planned to visit. There's also a poor road safety record, and accidents on busy major routes are epidemic. Theft at knifepoint in major cities and on the beaches we'd be traversing isn't infrequent, and our passports would be the principal prize sought by opportunist thugs.

Western Sahara, the next country on our itinerary, is disputed territory with, since the Spaniards pulled out in 1976, undetermined status. Public unrest (particularly after Friday prayers) is common, and we'd be well advised to avoid large gatherings of people and, surprise surprise, hostile demonstrations. There's a high threat of terrorism and thousands of unexploded mines to avoid. Off-roading is definitely contra-indicated. As part of a loosely organized group, we'd be advised to stay in convoy, as independent overland travelers are often turned back at the border. When I read this, my mind began to turn to the type and quantity of bribes that would be required to ease our crossing of this peculiar and apparently lawless region. It is claimed by Morrocco, Mauritania and its former Saharawi inhabitants, now living in refugee camps in neighbouring Algeria.

Further south in Mauritania, we could expect matters to worsen. With no British diplomatic presence, there's an "Honorary Consul" who should be informed if we intended to travel outside the main cities (there are only two of these—Nouakchott and Nouadhibou). Again, unrest after Friday prayers is common, and hostile demonstrations not unknown. There are only four paved roads in this vast desert country and conditions, for overland travel, are notoriously poor.

With Senegal a semblance of civilization is recovered, and travel is reputedly trouble free. Passport problems, pickpocketing and street crime in Dakar are the major likely hazards. Oh, and they look with great suspicion upon cars more than five years old, so an escort through this French influenced former colony would be necessary. The south west of the country, preferably avoided, is the stronghold of a number of separatist rebel groups, and there have been isolated incidents of banditry.

Once in the Gambia, hazards are really only those associated with driving or walking on roads at night, because of unpredictable driving standards, lack of street lighting and rum. Sounds like North Devon really, and arriving at this haven, this oasis on the west African coast, would, I thought, be rather like coming home.

I duly absorbed all this helpful if disconcerting advice on health and security from the MASTA report, and sent a copy to Graham so he could make his own arrangements for inoculation in Gloucestershire. I gave him a couple of days to absorb the security advice, and then spoke to him.

"What do you think of the MASTA report?"
"Bit heavy ain't it? In places?"
"Yeah. Got any ideas?"
"Yeah. I thought nail bombs would be good. Perhaps some incendiary devices. Couple of kalashnikovs. We could make some Molotovs when we get there, out of your old socks and a coke bottle. And an anti-tank cannon with armour piercing shells. I've got some bungee cords, we could lash it to the roof. And a couple of sabres for hand to hand combat."
"I thought maybe we could just talk to them. Use tact and diplomacy, maybe a little humour. Appeal to their better nature. Adopt a conciliatory posture."
"And if that doesn't work?"
"Well then we could be a bit more firm and persuasive, use subtle innuendo, sarcasm, perhaps some satire."
"And if that doesn't cut the ice?"
"Well then I'd criticise them, let have the full fury of my invective, you know, a diatribe, a tirade of abuse. I'd really tell 'em off."
"I think I prefer the nail bombs and incendiaries. The sabres might be a bit much, if we haven't had training."

We compromised on a couple of baseball bats and a Swiss army knife. Also I would check the child locks on Black Betty. At least we could hole up in her back seat for a while if the going got tough.

Then I focused attention on something infinitely more important. The paperwork.

IX
THE PAPER CHASE

If I ever get to the pearly gates, I'll be handed a celestial clipboard and pen and given a job inducting new recruits. As an erstwhile bureaucrat, I'm not proud of it, but I'm good at it. Completing forms, ticking boxes, interpreting rules. Traveling through Europe and down the west African coast, a region of countries with largely French and Spanish influence, there would be numerous outposts and crossings where it would be prudent to be able to prove credentials. Clean and convincing paperwork would ensure trouble free border crossing and limit delays and the size and frequency of bribes. Driving licences and my well used RAC card would get us to Plymouth. The next 4,000 miles would need a rain forest of paper.

PASSPORT: THE CHALLENGE STARTS HERE

I'd need a valid British passport—ours had expired in 1992 with just sufficient time remaining to permit a visit to my father in a Spanish hospital where he died on holiday. Gilly would need one too, so that she could come to my rescue or retrieve my remains. Obtaining passport forms from the local post office was easy. The form itself was quite simple, but the instructions for completing it as patronising as they were encyclopaedic, whilst not having the merit of being either comprehensive or accurate. I waded through the form and instructions, being careful to use black ink and to keep my print strictly within the boxes.

Three queries on the completion of the forms weren't dealt with adequately in the instructions. First, was this a "first new application" or a "renewal"? The significance of the difference lies in the detail of documents that would be required for a "first new application" (birth certificates, marriage lines etc.). Mine did not seem to fall within that category, as I'd possessed passports (or at least a joint passport with Gilly) before. But then this did not seem to constitute a "renewal" either, as the passport had been valid up to April 1992 when it simply lapsed, and I hadn't left the country since that date.

The second query related to who would countersign the application. I've countersigned countless passport applications for friends and family members since the government of this country has always, somewhat misguidedly, regarded members of my profession as fine upstanding honest pillars of the community. Clearly I'd not be permitted to countersign my own application, and I felt the passport office would probably not look too favourably on Gilly's application being countersigned by me, even though I have known us both intimately for considerably more than the required two years. I was in a quandary. I'm not known personally to other solicitors, accountants, doctors or other professionals in North Devon. As a life long free thinker, neither am I known, spiritually or temporally, to the clergy. I do not tread in those circles frequented by magistrates and councillors. My GP, with whom I have a nodding acquaintance, would probably expect a fee, which I resented paying for a service which I've supplied gratis for many years. Again, the instructions were less than helpful with my particular predicament.

Thirdly, I had a query on dispatch of the application. The expired passport was in joint names, and had always been so, Gilly and I appearing on the same document, a practice which has, I understand, long since changed. When applying for a "renewal", it's a requirement that all previously expired or current passports accompany the application. Now if our expired passport was to accompany my application, it could hardly accompany Gilly's at the same time. Again, the instructions weren't clear.

Rather helpfully, there is now a Passport Helpline, which those in doubt are invited to contact. Whilst it did grieve me, as a reasonably intelligent adult, to have to avail myself of assistance to complete a very simple form, my concern was to get it right first time and avoid the delay occasioned by error. A genuinely helpful young lady at the help desk, after seeking advice from her own superior, confirmed that this was indeed a "renewal" application, even though there'd been an intervening period of 14 years during which time we had possessed an "expired" passport, since the passport, though "expired", hadn't been "cancelled". Get your head around that one. Secondly, I could approach my bank or building society manager to countersign the applications, and he or she was likely to oblige without charge. Thirdly, though surprisingly never having been asked this question before, we could in fact enclose both applications in one envelope and send our "expired" but as yet not "cancelled" passport with them. Hopefully both applications would be dealt with by the same official, who'd pick up the fact that our old joint passport was intended to be read with both.

We yawned at each other.

Next stop was the photographers in the High Street, where in a matter of minutes I was provided with a set of 4 photographs in compliance with the detailed requirements of the passport regulations. Gilly's fringe was swept aside by the natty little photographer, who explained that her eyebrows must be visible for a passport photo. I was ordered to remove my spectacles, which are also "against the law" in passport terms. This latter instruction surprised me as with the "Instructions on completing a passport application" comes a leaflet showing examples of "proper" and "improper" passport photographs, and one of the "improper" examples shows a lady wearing spectacles. But the only reason for the photo's impropriety is the fact that the spectacles obscure the lady's eyebrows, not the fact that she's wearing them. The photographer advised me this was a new, recently promulgated rule. The published example was out of date. I pondered awhile whether the wearing of a monocle or use of a rimless pince-nez would be permissible. What about a lorgnette? And how would those deprived of, or never having sported, eyebrows fare? Is the eyebrowless traveler never to be permitted to leave these shores? Whatever. Despite the self-defeating complexities that now abound concerning passport photographs, we left the shop with a set each of four presumably legal and reasonably attractive representations of how we would look with our fringes swept away and devoid of our spectacles.

I next repaired to the building society, a few doors further up the High Street, where I sought the manager's countersignature to the applications and certification on the rear of one photo each to the effect that they represented a true likeness. He obliged by countersigning both applications, swearing on a stack of bibles he'd known us for a continuous period of at least 2 years, and certifying our photos as representing a true likeness, on the day of comparison. I was surprised, because I didn't recognize him, until Gilly reminded me he's the kind and obliging chap who opts for the chocolate éclair. On my birthday, that is, when I treat the staff as a gesture of thanks for outstanding service. Thanks again, Nationwide!

Somewhat conveniently, a post office capable of transmitting our applications is to be found only a few further doors up the same High Street as the photographers and the building society, and it's to this establishment that I finally made my way in this quest. The post office offers a service called "Check and Send", whereby, for a handsome fee, the passport application is checked in fine detail and dispatched by security postal service (if you pay another extra fee!) to the passport office for processing. In view of the importance of getting the application processed as quickly as possible, and in any event before October when the rules were to change yet again making the whole sorry affair even more complicated, I chose to avail myself of "Check and Send" and the security postal service, even though I was convinced I had taken every precaution to get it right in the first place.

"Check and Send" didn't prove a sound investment. The good ladies of the post office were clearly determined to find fault with my application. Indeed they told me as much! I was told that, in view of the lapse of time between expiry of our old passport in 1992, it would constitute a "first new application" requiring support by full documentation including birth certificates, marriage certificate, utility bills etc. Whilst the photographs were just within the permitted tolerances in that Gilly's eyebrows were just visible (they are, after all, blonde!) the application itself was faulty in that the building society manager had omitted the "Y" from "SOCIETY" in his description of himself as "BUILDING SOCIETY MANAGER" and the word "SOCIET" would not be recognized by the computer reading the application. Also, our applications would have to be lodged separately, and our old expired passport, which should accompany the first application, would have to be returned to us so that it could accompany the second application. Quelle horreur!

I remonstrated with the good but formidable ladies of the post office, insisting I'd taken up all the major points with the passport helpline, and would they please now dispatch the application as drawn. By this time I was frustrated with what had become a bureaucratic nightmare, and would take up any issues with the passport office direct. In short, I preferred to abide by the suggestions made by the Helpline, rather than the somewhat negative and jaundiced approach of the post office. The staff did however warm to me when I promised to supply all with fresh cream cakes in the event of a successful outcome.

And so it was, with a disclaimer of liability on the part of the post office, that our thoroughly checked applications were sent by security post to the passport office, in full expectation of a barrage of insurmountable technical problems. In fact the only issue raised by the office, in a standard letter, was the failure to enclose the expired passport with Gilly's application.

Gilly phoned the number given after 6.30 p.m., as requested. A lady with a broad Welsh accent answered.

"Hello, can I help you?"
"Is that the passport office?"
"Yes. Hang on, I must just turn my cauli down."
"I beg your pardon?"
"My cauli, look you. It's boiling dry. I must turn it down. Hang on, will you?"

Some minutes passed. Mfanwy returned. Gilly explained that the expired passport had been enclosed with both applications, as advised by the passport "Helpline". It seems we'd all failed to anticipate that on receipt of the applications in one sealed security envelope they would be separated, one passport official being allocated to deal with my application, the other sent to Mfanwy and her cauliflower in Swansea.

"There' silly," continued Mfanwy, "Not to worry. I'll sort it out when I get back from chapel. You should receive your passports soon now."

And we did. In record time.

And the good ladies of the post office received their cream cakes, although there is a postscript to this encounter with officialdom. When I delivered the cakes across the counter in an unmarked carrier bag, they were regarded with great suspicion, and a reluctance to handle what must have appeared to be an unattended package!

INTERNATIONAL DRIVING PERMIT

It was with some misgivings that I returned to the High Street post office a few days later, in search of an International Driving Permit. The PB07 Website information insisted I'd need such a permit, specifically for driving through Senegal, and possibly Spain. Reputedly, an IDP was readily available on application at a post office, with a modest fee of four or five pounds. Unfortunately the ladies of the High Street post office who'd been so helpful in obtaining my passport didn't agree. They'd never heard of this particular animal, and I was assured they're no longer necessary, if indeed they ever existed, at least "not for any of the countries I have driven through". I felt, intuitively, that argument or persistence at this counter was unlikely to prove fruitful. Unsatisfied with the contradictory and largely anecdotal response to my request, I took my custom elsewhere, namely to the main post office in neighbouring Barnstaple.

Here I was met with a smile and "we don't issue those very often nowadays", as the clerk reached for a batch of ageing and dusty application forms, together with the mandatory instructions for the uninitiated form filler. It was clear the only country where we'd be likely to encounter difficulties without an IDP was Senegal. The fee was an unexpectedly modest £5.50. But I would need passport photos to attach to the application, so it was back to Ilfracombe and the friendly photographer for fresh supplies. Although he'd produced four pictures on my first visit, and only two were needed for the passport application, the other two would be necessary for my Mauritania visa (more of which below), so I couldn't afford to lavish them on something so relatively unimportant as an IDP. A few days later, armed with completed application form, photo and fee, and my UK driving licence, I applied for and was granted an International Driving Permit by a mystified official at Barnstaple Head Post Office.

VISA FOR MAURITANIA

Mauritania is a vast, obscure and peculiar country, which many think is somewhere in eastern Europe. I would need a visa to pass through it. The advice on the PB07 Website was to obtain a visa in Casablanca, where it should cost the equivalent of 9 pence (!) plus whatever bribe those issuing it would demand (expect). Visas are also obtainable at the border, but baksheesh likely to be significantly more. If the Casablanca option is taken, you can expect to be delayed 24 hours while the hierarchical bureaucracy of that region decides how to split the booty. So for any number of reasons I decided to prepare myself with all relevant paperwork before leaving these shores.

The Mauritanian embassy is in Carlos Street, Mayfair. I reached it by telephone on only the third attempt, my first two messages having been apparently overlooked. Naively expecting an embassy official to speak in the clipped BBC tones of the 1950's, I was pleasantly surprised at the laid back Latinate timbre and phraseology. The Mauritanian official told me to write requesting application forms, which should be returned together with a fee of £42 each, passport sized photographs and our passports. No guarantee could be given as to return of passports. Alternatively, application could be made in person, at 11.00 a.m. on a Tuesday or Thursday morning if there's an "R" in the month. Helpful though this latter day Pancho Villa had been over the telephone, neither Graham nor I were prepared to entrust our newly obtained passports to either the vagaries of the post office or the whim of the Mauritanian embassy, and this rather ruled out postal application. We decided to venture into Mayfair and make our applications in person.

I duly wrote to the embassy, enclosing my stamped addressed envelope, and received two nearly legible photocopied application forms within a week. Much simpler than the UK passport application, we completed them one weekend when Graham and Sally had come to stay, and made arrangements for the next part of the Challenge--obtain your visa to enter Mauritania.

Actually getting the visas for Mauritania proved to be an adventure in itself. One Wednesday morning in late November I packed Black Betty with the boost starter, tyre compressor, clothing and provisions for a couple of days in deepest Gloucestershire and set off at noon. An intrepid explorer in the making, I'd thought it a good suggestion of Graham's to travel to his place in Bishops Norton in Black Betty, thus giving her a decent trial run. In fact Black Betty was to prove more up to this task than I. She performed magnificently on the 140 mile journey, taking rain, fog, motorway spray and hairbrained traffic in her stride. I should let my journal for these few days take over:-

"22 November. Getting ready for journey to Gloucs. I was, unaccountably, tetchy and nervous. Perhaps not looking forward to this adventure into the unknown in an unknown vehicle, alone. Still, all packed up on this drizzly and unpleasant morning, I made my departure from Long Lane Farm for the first time in five years.
Journey to Bishops Norton (140 miles) largely uneventful. BB drove excellently, if over inflated and bumpy on the tyre front. Mist over Exmoor gave way on the M5 to dry but dull steely grey day.
When I get to Bishops Norton (excellent directions from Graham and I find myself here in 2 hours 40 minutes) I receive a magnificent welcome, chat with Graham, Sally and her daughter, Emily.
Four bottles of wine and a wonderful dinner later I finally rolled into bed as early as 10.00 p.m.
Must get my eyes (and teeth?) seen to before depart for Banjul.
Goodnight Gibbo. Miss you, and the Chillun.

23 November. Arise at 6.00a.m., still pitch dark and damp. Cup of tea and an early start with Graham in his BMW as we head for central London and the Mauritanian embassy. Satnav works perfectly, and although we deviate from the suggested route, it always brings us back on course. Central London has changed, but it holds no charms for me. Park outside the embassy at 10.15 a.m., in good time for the 11.00 o'clock appointment, having paid the Congestion Charge at a Pakistani corner shop and put about £25 in the parking meter. Delightful receptionist at the embassy, she is surprised when I take her photo. Two chaps in the waiting room, also Challengers awaiting their visas. Chatted about Mauritania, Western Sahara etc. Apparently Marlboro Reds are the preferred ciggies for bribes on the way down, and we should avoid whisky and porn at all costs, lest we upset one of the more officious customs officers!

Our passports, applications and cash (the Embassy have insisted on cash) is collected by another beautiful official, and returned to us within 15 minutes, our passports duly stamped with our new visas. I am reminded that we cannot enter Mauritania until 15 February, and a quick mental calculation tells me that we have about 12 days to get there from departure. This should be OK. I am assured by one of the other travelers that a modest bribe, eg. twenty cigarettes, will probably overcome any problems with an earlier arrival. Mauritania sounds like a desperate place, so we shall not want to tarry either on the border or within.

Leave embassy and head for home, again via Satnav, which sees us out of central London. Stop at motorway services station for full English to celebrate our success. No more stops until Gloucs. Visit Syreford, where Graham lives, followed by where he shoots and beats to pick up Rosie, his little black sprocker, and meet Gary, colourful Aussie partner of Graham's sister Kate. Then back to Sally's for tea, cake, dinner, more wine and chatter. Good conversation but very tired, and drunk, to bed. Goodnight again sweetheart, see you after linedancing tomorrow.

24 November Home again! It's 4.30 p.m. and I'm in the study at Long Lane Farm writing this on a fast darkling drear evening.
Arose early and prepared quickly for the drive home. Cold lasagne for breakfast (delicious). Said my farewells to Graham, Sally and Emily. Black Betty's tyres let down to 30 p.s.i. and I set off in the early light. Damp, spray on the road and I made a mistake in the first few yards, or rather I thought I had, but in the rectification I realized I was correct the first time!
On the motorway soon and feeling nervous from the spray, wind and traffic. Black Betty is enjoying the exercise, it is ME who is nervous and I catch myself tensing up as I am buffeted about in the high wind.
Stop at Taunton Deane services and put £20 squirt in the tank, though I think I would have made it there and back on one tank, which means a satisfying 300 mile range is possible. Much more confident once the motorway is behind me at Tiverton. Arrive home at 11.40 a.m."

So the adventure within an adventure was over. We'd obtained our Mauritanian visas. Black Betty had performed a 280 mile round trip faultlessly and Graham and I got together and did some planning (not much really. We just drank whisky and wine).

FICHE WITHOUT THE CHIPS

I'd been advised to carry a "fiche" (French for "slip, file or reference note") giving personal details of the road travelers and their car to be offered at border crossings saving time and work for officials. The PB07 Website helpfully provided a template, which I downloaded and adapted. I added a digital photo to each, which I thought might go down well, and gave them the grand title "Fiche Internationale de Keith Pugsley/Graham DeMeur". They had a satisfyingly "official" look about them. I'd be taking 30 each, as advised by one of the previous years Challengers, at the launch party. The French love their pieces of paper. Here's mine.

FICHE INTERNATIONALE DE KEITH PUGSLEY

Nom (Name): Pugsley

Prénoms (Given names): Keith Mahlon

Domicile (Address): Long Lane Farm,
Combe Martin,
Devon,
England,
EX34 0PA

Date de naissance (Date of birth): 23.09.1949

Lieu de naissance (Place of birth): Ilfracombe, Devon, England

Nationalité (Nationality): British Citizen

Sex/Sexe (Sex): Masculin (Male)

Numéro de passeport (Passport number): 123456789

Date de délivrance (Date of issue): 24.07.06

Date d'expiration (Date of expiry): 24.07.16

Profession (Occupation): Avoué (Solicitor)

Nom de Mère (Mother's name): Clarice May Pugsley

Nom de Père (Father's name): William Frederick Pugsley

Marque de la voiture (Make of car): Jeep Grand Cherokee Laredo

Numéro d'enregistrement (Registration number): H174 DMX

Date d'enregistrement (Registration date): 29.07.1997

(Complete en-route)

Date d'entrée dans le pays (Date of entry into country):

Lieu d'entrée dans le pays (Place of entry into country):

Only the numbers have been changed, to protect the innocent.

TRAVEL INSURANCE: LIFE AND LIMB

Travel Insurance seemed a good idea, and not having traveled abroad for many a moon I approached the NFU. They agreed to cover me over the 24 days abroad for the standard risks (death, loss of limbs, sight, speech or hearing, permanent disablement, medical and legal expenses, hospital benefit, cancellation expenses, delayed departure, transport failure, baggage, money, personal liability) for the inclusive sum of £37.95. I declined the offer of special cover for "winter sports", since the closest I'd be likely to come would be sandboarding in the Sahara, and this didn't seem to qualify. Under the heading "hazardous pastimes", I boldly declared "None". I still have the tongue in my cheek.

For the further extremely modest charge of zippo, zilch and nothing, I obtained my European Health Insurance Card, entitling me to free medical advice and assistance in the European Union. A short telephone call on a freephone line, where you speak to a mechanical voice and give limited details (name, address, date of birth, National Insurance Number and favourite colour) and I received my free card within a few days.

Finally, I thought it prudent to be in a position to satisfy border officials as to my record of inoculations. The only compulsory one, for Yellow Fever, comes with its own certificate, issued by Sister Marlene's assistant. But, if challenged as to the many other precautionary measures I'd taken there was as yet no evidence. This was simply remedied. When attending for my 'flu jab I asked for a printout of my medical records since the beginning of the year (2006). This was provided at no charge, and I had the practice stamp placed on it, countersigned by the receptionist, who managed a creditable likeness of a doctor's squiggle for the purposes of authenticity. If the French love their pieces of paper, they are generally ecstatic for an official stamp.

A PASSPORT FOR BLACK BETTY

Black Betty's documents would need to accompany us to The Gambia, as evidence of our right to drive her in foreign lands. Evidence of ownership would be required at journey's end for the public auction. I had the logbook, and had registered her in my name. This vital document must, by international convention, accompany the vehicle when abroad. It seems that some of the more dubious characters in countries such as Mauritania and Senegal might insist on deposit of the logbook as security when the car is kept overnight in a camping compound, and then demand largesse for its return in the morning. Carnapping of this sort is apparently not uncommon. So the advice was to travel with a couple of accurate colour copies, which should pass muster in remoter parts. I set to one afternoon with my computer printer, some glue and official looking seals, and produced two creditable forgeries which looked rather better than the original.

Quite late in the day the PB07 *Roadbook* was issued by Email to all Challengers. This gives step by step advice from the Disorganisers on a whole range of issues related to the Challenge. It's updated yearly from practical experience of participants, and obviously essential reading. When I received it in December, Gilly and I scanned it in some detail looking for anything we'd missed. An "International Certificate for Motor Vehicles" (ICMV) was advised. This document, sort of an international logbook or certificate of ownership, is not essential, but recommended outside Europe when traveling in those countries where the translations of vehicle details may be more readily understood than in English. It was reputedly available on application to one or other of the motoring organizations.

I've been a member of the RAC for years, so my first approach was to them. They'd never heard of the concept of an "international logbook", and I must be thinking of the International Driving Permit. Of course I had obtained one of those months before. But it was clear that the vacuous wench I was trying to explain matters to at the RAC (talking far too fast, wrongly anticipating my requests, probably painting her nails as she spoke) had heard of nothing like an ICMV in all the many (four) years she'd worked there. I explained, as politely as I could, that perhaps she would like to research the matter, in the event that she might receive another such request in the coming years. Then I approached the AA, who would pop an application in the post the same day. They did, and I received it by first class post. So ICMV's do exist. Should I inform/advise/educate the RAC? I couldn't be bothered.

The form itself was simple, all necessary information to be found in Black Betty's logbook. All, that is, except the "Unladen weight of the vehicle". For this I approached Neil Caley, who promptly found himself in a "guess my weight" competition on the telephone. He guestimated, by making educated comparisons with other vehicles he had known and loved, at 1650 Kg. I returned the form, with a copy of the logbook and £7.50 fee to the AA's International Motoring Services division in Basingstoke. My ICMV arrived a few days before Christmas, valid for a year from our departure. It helpfully translated the basic vehicle and owner details found on a standard British logbook into French, Italian, Spanish, Portuguese, German, Russian, Arabic, and Persian. It looked awfully official and I was sure it'd be well received in some of the countries going south. In fact, by its own admission on the second page it's not actually valid in any of the countries through which I was to pass, including England!

Black Betty had been destined for the crusher, but was validly ticketed until December 2006. Our departure date being in February, meant she'd need a fresh MoT, if only to get us to Plymouth legally. Valid MoT certification would be necessary in Europe too, but in Morocco and beyond such niceties tend to be overlooked. Although some of our colleagues on the Challenge intended driving to Dover or Plymouth (and in one case half way round the world from the USA) without vehicle safety certification, and then chance it abroad, that for me was a risk left long behind in my youth. Besides, the motoring organizations certainly refuse to assist the driver of an unroadworthy vehicle, so without an MoT we might not make Plymouth. I resolved to book Betty in with Neil.

With work on the brakes (the rear brake shoes had crumbled away) she sailed through the test, and this without a rear view mirror and defective speedometer (neither legal requirements if you have door mirrors). Black Betty's last ever MoT was obtained and the certificate took its place in my growing portfolio of Banjul documentation.

Insurance for Black Betty was next on the agenda. Advice in the *Roadbook* and on the chatline was to transfer the insurance from your existing car onto your Challenge car for the duration of the trip, and then transfer it back on return to the UK. Alternatively cheap short term insurance could be found over the Internet, covering the journey alone. I had five other cars on the road at that time, and chose in the short term to transfer insurance from our antique Land Rover (third party fire and theft only, used for collecting animal feed and very little else). The change was effected, but at no little expense. The Land Rover was in Group 3 or 4 and Black Betty, a far more exotic, powerful and altogether voluptuous creature, in something like Group 37. But I grudgingly forked out the extra £270 odd and she was insured for the rest of the year, at home and abroad, including "green card" insurance for Europe. The standard insurance would cover me (and Graham as a named driver) in the UK, France and Spain. By special request it was extended into Morocco. Car insurance for countries further south (Western Sahara, Mauritania, Senegal and the Gambia) has to be obtained at the border. Even if insurance is obtained in the UK, the man from the Pru will be stationed at the frontier, clip board in hand, demanding we buy local insurance as a prerequisite to entry. So attempts to obtain insurance in the UK for countries beyond Morocco would be pointless. My fixation on being prepared for all foreseeable events was to be thwarted on the insurance front.

With the logbook, MoT, insurance and green card in place, I was able to tax Black Betty. Until now excursions had only been joy rides with friends across our own fields to our neighbours in the valley below. I waited for the end of August, so that six months road tax would take us to the end of February 2007 by which time the Challenge would be over. Probably not necessary outside the UK, and certainly not required in the remoter countries of the West African coast, by displaying a current road tax disc Black Betty would be street legal in the UK and the rest of Europe. I could use her on the road before departing these shores and gain valuable experience of driving a powerful automatic left hooker before confusing the innocent population of northern France in February.

BOATS AND PLANES (NO TRAINS)

We decided to cross the Channel from Plymouth to Roscoff in northern France, and opted for an overnight crossing, leaving us fresh for the following day. I booked a double berth (and of course space for Black Betty) on a ferry for the 2nd. February 2007. The tickets would be available for collection a fortnight before departure.

THE WHEREWITHAL

Finally, I thought it might be useful to take some money. But how much? We'd be out of the UK for about three weeks. The major costs would be petrol, accommodation and food. Other incidentals would include road tolls, ferry fares, camp site fees, motor insurance at border crossings, loose women and the ubiquitous (at least from Morocco southwards) bribes and "considerations". I daren't take into account the cost of major mechanical breakdown, as I thought this would be tempting fate. If Black Betty contracted something terminal, she might have to retire from the Challenge, and we'd proceed, either forwards or in reverse (depending largely on how far we'd progressed), under our own steam.

It seemed sensible to let plastic take the strain, at least for major recurring expenses such as accommodation, meals, petrol and anything "official", at least until northern Morocco and the end of civilization as we know it. This would conserve the cash supplies until Western Sahara, and Mauritania, which are known to be cash economies. In these relatively out-of-the-way countries holes in the wall are literally that, and notoriously unreliable. Travellers cheques would probably take an age to convert, and although the safest option in some respects, are going out of fashion and looked at askance in countries south of the Tropic of Cancer. Use of the credit card and debit card in these regions is inadvisable, even if possible, as cloning is rife and money changers notoriously corrupt.

With all the above considerations in mind, I considered a healthy credit card, debit card and £1000 in Euros should suffice. Euros would see us through France, Spain and the more cosmopolitan parts of northern Morocco. Small amounts could then be translated into local currencies (Dhiram, Ouguiya, West African CFAs and Dilasi). At Graham's suggestion I devised a simple conversion card to prevent confusion at the many border crossings and souk markets.

All of the documentation would travel with us in a portfolio, ready to hand under the front seat, with the sherbert lemons and the fly swat.

X
GETTING READY TO ROCK AND ROLL

Black Betty sat in our back car park at Long Lane Farm, taxed, tested, insured but barely used since I drove her proudly home from the breakers yard in July. On her rare excursions from home she'd performed magnificently well, and I was confident she'd take us safely to the Gambia. But cars need to be used, and having secured our trusty steed, some time spent ensuring she was as ready as could be for the 4,000 miles of varying terrain ahead would be well spent. The trip to Gloucestershire had instilled in me a certainty of success. It'd also thrown up a few glitches to iron out. And I still had the £15 repairs budget to squander.

She was well shod with four good chunky tyres and a decent spare, but the two on the right seemed to lose pressure at an alarming rate. Pumping them up from four or five to thirty five p.s.i. weekly had proved a dubious pleasure and a laborious task with a foot pump, particularly when the operator has severe gout in a right toe, or sciatica in a left leg. After a few miserable Sunday mornings when Gilly took a spell on pump shift, I invested in a small battery driven compressor to lighten her load. Having converted this machine so it could be connected directly to the battery with crocodile clips, rather than working through the car's inaccessible cigar lighter, this helped no end. The compressor would undeniably prove its worth under an African sun and on African sand, where deflating tyres to 10 .p.s.i. is advisable for better grip. But the mystery of the self deflating tyres clearly had to be solved, otherwise Graham and I might find ourselves in spiraling deflation mid-Sahara.

A visit to Kirkham Tyres in Barnstaple soon solved the mystery. Alloy wheels, such as those on Black Betty, are prone to corrosion, which causes the seal between the tyre bead and the wheel rim to fail. The solution was to have both tyres removed and the rims cleaned and sanded. I think Kirkhams charged me £15 for the job, and threw in a couple of new inner tubes to get us out of trouble should we spring a leak. The tyres held their correct pressures from that day on. I'd spent the repairs budget wisely.

Black Betty became more difficult to start as the weather deteriorated, and Gilly's patience and energy pushing her up our steep lane in a driving rain began to wear thin. Winter, which promised to be severe, would make the decision for me. I could postpone purchase of a new battery until shortly before departure in February, by which time the rogue battery would finally be exposed.

Other minor points included the rear view mirror, which wasn't fitted to the windscreen. I found it in the glove box. This was probably a relic of the time when Black Betty had been grabbed by the crane at the breakers yard ready to be dropped to her death in the crusher. The crane's jaws had popped the original screen, and though Lance Ginns fitted a new one, he omitted to refit the rear view mirror. This could easily be remedied , and I'd get the necessary adhesive kit from Halfords.

A gaping radio-sized hole in the dashboard was all that remained of what had probably been a quality stereo system, judging by the remaining quad speakers. Black Betty had once been quite an up market car, probably piloted by some wealthy suburban American. I still possessed the radio cassette player taken from Gilly's Citroen 2CV, Jean-Paul, when he died from terminal rust. Perhaps this could be made to fit, so we would be regaled with hits of yesteryear from my battered collection of tapes as we hurtled through the desert.

Black Betty had been constructed with the air conditioning available in 1991, which, though more than adequate and perhaps a luxury on this Challenge, had almost certainly never been properly serviced. We might have to forfeit this particular luxury, but the heater blower, which had also ceased to function during my short period of ownership, would be essential through a damp and chilly northern France and Spain (even if the rain stays on the plain).

Cosmetically, she just needed a good wash and brush up. She'd spent some time in less than salubrious quarters, namely the dark corners of a breakers yard in Braunton and, however briefly, the back of a lorry. There were also some signs of questionable goings on in the back seat. After all, she was to be a second (perhaps a first) home to Graham and me for three weeks or more. We might sleep in her if the camping conditions became too desperate and there were no room at the inn.

Diana and Mick Lewis of North Devon Animal Ambulance, my sponsored charity on the journey to Banjul, kindly offered to pay, out of private funds, for Black Betty to be sign written, sporting the logo of the charity and some suitable signage denoting the purpose of the trip. I had a most interesting time watching the entire process of customized signwriting together with many hours in the company of Guy Morton of Idam Signs, who designed, produced and applied the decals to the bonnet (excuse me, hood) and rear hatch. The decals converted a sturdy but rather tired looking sixteen year old vehicle into a car which any diplomatic mission would be proud to take to the UN. With the NDAA logo (a cat and a dog with a white cross) and the legend "Plymouth to the Gambia in aid of North Devon Animal Ambulance", Black Betty acquired a style and an image that would set her apart from some of the other cheap but less than cheerful paint jobs we could expect to see along the way. And with her vaguely "medical" look, she'd cut a dash across borders in remote parts which other vehicles (viz. ice cream vans, American police cars) might find more difficult. Her enhanced appearance certainly helped raise a few quid and eyebrows for the Animal Ambulance and Diana Lewis' sterling work in the field of animal welfare, whilst still in the UK.

Already mechanically sound, Neil Caley had put her through the MoT with only minor work on brakes and lights. Neil and I went over the car with a fine tooth comb, to iron out any residual or anticipated problems. We met at his yard one fine but very cold morning in December, when the rest of the country was languishing in fog. As Christmas holiday-makers writhed in frustrated queues in airports, Neil and I lay

Keith Pugsley

in a greasy puddle under Black Betty, contemplating her underside and the world at large.

Unit 4. Chivenor Business Park, Barnstaple, Devon. Ex31 4AY
Tel:01271 816466   E-mail: idamsigns@btopenworld.com

The private parts of a 1991 Cherokee Jeep, American spec., are really quite simple. As we lay together on our backs on a piece of damp carpet, droplets of oil congealing on my glasses and nose, examining the rear axle and differential, Neil was almost lost for words. But everything was in place and in order. He applied the grease gun to the propshaft universal joints, both of which in Black Betty's case boldly, if brazenly, sported nipples for the purpose more commonly associated with cars of a more distant era. I spotted a shiny new exhaust back box, so no expensive or noisy problems should be anticipated there. The automatic gear shift linkage was in plain view. Neil explained that, in the very unlikely event of the shift cable parting from its linkage, or breaking in operation, there was a way in which the gears could be selected from under the car. As I operated the shift lever from inside the cab, Neil deftly, and with the use of proprietary typist correction fluid, painted the letters P-R-N-D-3-2/1, denoting the gears. If, in the middle of a sandstorm, Black Betty were suddenly to snap her gear linkage, I'd now be able to leap out, dive under and, with Graham at the wheel and throttle, I could, with panache and sleight of hand, put her promptly in gear. We could proceed with style. At least this was the scenario as it played itself out in my imagination. Probably a manoevre best not executed with the vehicle in motion.

From my vantage point Neil showed me the automatic gearbox, (plenty of ground clearance, and a concealed rock would hit the front beam axle before puncturing the sump) starter motor and other essential components. Everything did look in good order, and, satisfyingly, were recognizable. I was pleased, after all these years, not to be in totally uncharted territory.

We emerged, a little oil and grease spattered, but remarkably suave and well groomed, I thought, considering the ordeal of the preceding few minutes.

Black Betty's engine bay was immense and intriguing. Designed to house a large and lumpy four litre straight six petrol engine, it seemed packed with gizmos, large mysterious plastic and metal boxes of unknown function, wires, cables, tubes and pipes leading to unidentified locations.

Neil simplified all this for me. The air conditioning unit for instance, having probably never been serviced, as they rarely are, would be beyond economic repair. So don't go there. Fluid levels were all correct, and Neil suggested I check these daily, after an average 400 mile trip. I should take with me supplies of engine oil, automatic transmission fluid which would double for the power steering, water, battery electrolyte, hydraulic fluid for the brakes and screenwash. We inspected the air filter, which we found as clean as a whistle, and the oil filter, which had also had recent attention. The distributor cap and high tension leads all seemed clean, dry and uncracked, but Neil recommended I take a spare cap and rotor arm. The leads and contact points should be marked with the now ubiquitous Tippex™, to facilitate change of distributor cap. An error here could be fatal.

The engine was, mercifully, of the good old fashioned push rod variety, with no overhead camshaft and belt to worry about. There was only the one belt on Black Betty, which seemed to operate water pump, generator, fan, what passed for air conditioning and probably other items. It appeared in good order. Not worth replacing for the sake of it.

The one piece of electronic wizardry that had given me some cause for concern, was her immobiliser. In a 4000 mile challenge across desert roads and with unforeseen obstacles ahead, it would be less than helpful to be immobilized by a malfunction of the immobiliser itself. Graham and I very much wanted her to be extremely mobile. Neil shared our concern. For the sake of a tiny piece of plastic concealing untold electronic gizmography, we could be stranded in the desert and Black Betty might never emerge to complete the Challenge. Neil leant sagely over the bonnet, screwdriver in hand, while I operated the ignition. Suddenly, the engine gunned into life, with the immobiliser still vainly flashing. Neil had discovered the device only immobilized the starter motor. With the deft and strategic application of a long screwdriver, dinner knife, even a bent paper clip, the contacts between the starter and its solonoid could be shorted, the immobiliser device by-passed, and the car started. We would not be outwitted in the desert.

Neil fixed the ailing heater blower in seconds. One of Black Betty's impressive array of fuses had simply blown. A timely reminder, however, that a selection of fuses should feature in our spares kit.

I'd learned that petrol and diesel supplies are few and far between, south of Morocco, normally only available from grocers' stores in cheap jerricans, and invariably contaminated. Keeping the fuel lines clear and the petrol flowing freely would be crucial, and Neil suggested he check or change any in line filters. He also agreed to order the more obvious spares, and to fit the fuel filters early in the new year.

So on that cold and becoming bleaker day Neil shut his garage for the Christmas festivities. As I left the yard I spotted an ancient and battered Mercedes. Always on the look out for spares for my journey, I asked if there were any bits worth taking. He promised to look at the radio, and see if it could be made to work in Black Batty. And from the boot he produced and gave me a red triangle, one of the two that are a statutory necessity if you have a mishap in Spain.

2006 was hurtling towards its damp and windy conclusion, and shortly there'd be but a month left in which to carry out final preparations. It had been my goal to have Black Betty ready by the end of December, leaving January to check everything was provisioned and prepared for the trip. So on the day following Boxing Day it seemed the time was ripe to treat Black Betty to that new battery and Gilly to a rest. Kirkhams sorted me out with a cheap and cheerful battery that would see us to Banjul and beyond, for it came with a two year guarantee. And for a modest few extra quid Kirkhams also removed the front left tyre and the spare, cleaned and skimmed the rims, so that I could be reasonably sure of holding correct pressures until the desert. The spare wheel, which had remained enshrouded in its plastic cover until this time, looked meaty and serviceable.

I drove home with a renewed confidence in Black Betty's mechanicals. Fit tyres, new battery, everything essential apparently working to perfection. She even seemed a little conceited as I reversed her carefully into our top drive, where she was to sit for the last month.

That confidence was to be slightly dented the very next day. As it dawned with a promising rosy glow, we decided to trial her into Barnstaple for a few of the outstanding bits and pieces we'd need, including fire extinguisher, mirror adhesive kit and instant tyre repair. I was also looking for pens, pencils and paper for the Gambian children.

As we approached the clock tower in Barnstaple the bright morning sun had changed to a gentle overcast drizzle, and the drizzle to an unremitting downpour. Black Betty started to hunt in the slow but busy traffic. Then she began to misfire. I began to get nervous. Gilly reached for the workshop manual.

It wasn't so much the prospect of breaking down that perturbed us. We'd done that many times before on the roads of Great Britain. It was more the embarrassment of conking out, in a car that proudly boasted "Plymouth to the Gambia on behalf of North Devon Animal Ambulance" a mere eight miles from home. But to her credit Black Betty did reach the car park of the discount store. As I parked, the engine spluttered, coughed and died.

Close inspection under the hood in a gale and a driving drizzle was no fun, believe me, but Gilly did spot the possible culprit. The crankcase breather pipe to air filter had worked loose and separated, so she promptly reconnected the two tubes, a push fit connection. Black Betty didn't want to start again immediately, so we left her to compose her thoughts and ready herself for the return journey. We repaired to Halfords, as planned, a short but wet walk away. Strangely the return journey, about half an hour later, was uneventful. I was due to revisit Neil Caley early in the new year, and this incident could await his expert advice and attention.

In the first week of 2007, I took Black Betty for what was intended to be her last pre-trip medical. Neil's priority on this occasion was to change her fuel filter, situated under the rear floor pan about amidships. Removing the existing filter and upending it, a stream of filthy contaminated petrol flowed out, mostly under pressure and mostly straight into Neil's face. The filter had clearly not received attention for some time. The old filter really wasn't worth taking with us as a spare, bearing in mind the parlous colour of the petrol it contained, a sort of muddy grey.

Next he showed me how to overcome the problem experienced on the day after Boxing Day. He believed it was probably due to a combination of the build up of unspent gases in the crankcase, and flooding of the engine by overenthusiastic fuel injection. The crankcase breather pipe, which had blown itself off in Barnstaple, was better left off, allowing the engine to breathe unimpeded. Pressure could then be released by separating the main fuel line from the injectors, a simple operation, allowing the engine to clear.

As promised, Neil had gathered together a set of the more obvious spares and fluids; a gallon of engine oil, brake fluid, automatic transmission oil, a distributor cap and rotor arm, bulb kit, selection of fuses (mostly 25 amp) wiper rubbers, a tube of liquid metal and a circuit tester. Grubbing about his yard I found a sturdy plank to stand the jack on in the desert, and an empty five gallon oil drum for spare petrol. The promised Mercedes radio cassette couldn't be made to fit or work, so in car entertainment might have to be a pleasure forgone on the roads of France and Spain. Graham and I would have to content ourselves with the view, our witty repartee and perhaps some club singing.

Black Betty was street legal and mechanically fit for the road.

We'd need basic tools and sundries that might, with some ingenuity, get us out of a fix. Rummaging through my workshop, sorting through the pile of nonsense I had kept "just in case", I set aside duplicate tools, battered, bent and often rusty, those I could most afford to leave in the Gambia. I had no intention of bringing them back, and anticipated that trying to board a charter flight armed with hammer, spanners, razor knives and other assorted mercenary looking ironmongery might not put me high in the popularity stakes.

So I oiled and repaired a rusting tool box, and placed in it a selection of old ring and open ended spanners that seemed to fit Black Betty's exposed bolt heads, some screwdrivers (cross point, flat ended, various sizes and shapes, including one electrical), a pair of pliers, mole grips, two adjustables and a plug spanner. A hammer and chisel, for major surgery in extremis or the event of a crash, seemed like a good idea, as did a glass breaking hammer for effecting exit from the vehicle in an emergency. I'd be taking (and hopefully bringing back) the electric compressor to reinflate the tyres after traversing the desert at half pressure, a tyre pressure gauge, the circuit tester Neil had provided, and a couple of razor knives. The brace and bottle jack which came with the car had never been used, and Neil's lump of wood would enable us to use it on soft sand. I'd checked the wheel nuts hadn't been over tightened, and the brace would function in its allotted task if required. I secreted an exceptionally long screwdriver under the back seat. This would enable me to hotwire Black Betty if we lost both immobiliser fobs, or they ceased to function.

To save embarrassment and a lot of hard labour in the sand, I put aside two short rolls of carpet from the loft, which I hoped would function as sand ladders, whilst retaining the twin merits of flexibility and ease of transport. They might even carpet part of the floor of an impoverished Gambian if they survived the journey. I'd bought from the recycling center in Ilfracombe, for the princely sum of 50p, a couple of child's beach shovels, which Graham and I could use to dig Black Betty out after a sandstorm. Time, weather and the inclination permitting, we could also have some fun with these constructing sandcastles in the Sahara. Graham bagged the blue one, I'd make do with the pink.

Security of the car en route would be vital, and it'd be important not to lock ourselves out inadvertently. With the central locking operating almost too efficiently from the driver's door panel, the whole car became impregnable at the flick of a switch. Black Betty came with only one key, so I had two duplicates cut. We'd carry one each about our person, and I'd wear the original around my neck with my dog tags.

Sundry items about my workshop which might prove their worth included a can of WD40, to dispel moisture from ignition components and penetrate stubborn nuts and bolts, half a jar of Swarfega to clean up with if we got into a greasy mess, some wet wipes, more genteel but essentially for the same purpose in public, a couple of ratchet straps to hold things together and prevent them dropping off, two red triangles and two fluorescent jackets (donated by a well wishing Stowford Park Meadows of North Devon, they're another legal requirement for Spain), a tow rope, to help my colleagues on the Challenge, and a set of jump leads in anticipation of reciprocal arrangements.

We decided against Graham's idea of rigging up a lavatory seat on Black Betty's towball since, though this might well prove invaluable in the lavatorially challenged Western Sahara, we felt the contraption might detract from our otherwise diplomatic mission style.

Graham recommended a jar of Radweld, which I recalled from my childhood motor mechanics days as a useful preparation to save the inconvenience of a leak in the desert. A raw egg will do in an emergency of course, but this wise and cheap extra precaution would save the time and ingenuity it might otherwise take to locate an obliging hen. Another of Graham's more practical suggestions was to take on board a general purpose tarpaulin, some rope, baling twine and a ball of string to tie things on with. And some sticky back plastic. In the rarified ecosystem of our Cherokee Jeep Laredo, I envisaged washing lines, ropes, pulleys and all sorts of other ingenious contraptions being set up as we traversed the desert.

I'd discovered on the map a potential petrol free zone of about 400 to 450 miles on desert roads. The Gloucestershire trip had shown Black Betty had a range of 300 miles on a full tank, but I didn't know how big the tank was. As a test I deliberately ran the tank very low, and the needle dropped well into the red zone. In the early January drizzle and mist one Thursday afternoon I drove the shortest route to Barnstaple to pick up the ferry tickets and treat Black Betty's complaining tank to as much nourishment as she'd take.

When I stopped, involuntarily, just outside the village of Muddiford, about four miles from home, I realized two things. First, Black Betty's fuel gauge was unusually accurate, and "empty" really did mean "empty". Second, how very unprepared was I, who had prided myself on my preparedness. I'd not had the foresight to attempt this foolish and experimental endeavour with the benefit of a can of petrol for emergencies. Fortunately I was carrying the brand new mobile phone arranged for the trip, and was able to summon the best help I know. I called Gilly, who is known for extricating me from the direst of emergencies better than any RAC or AA patrol can. I asked her, as calmly as possible, to hotfoot it to my assistance in Muddiford and to bring with her the lawnmower petrol.

Meanwhile, back on that wet and miserable but surprisingly busy road through Muddiford (so-called because of all the mud and the ford which goes through it at this time of year), two passing police officers came to my assistance. Rick, an off duty detective constable from Ilfracombe, in plain clothes and unmarked car, was helpfully directing traffic around Black Betty. A motorcycle cop, blue light flashing, had equally helpfully stationed his bike at her rear to fend off unwitting borders from that direction. So Black Betty had her first (albeit stationary) police escort, and still we hadn't left Devon.

It was with some surprise and embarassment that, a few moments later, I turned the ignition and she burst back into life. I headed for the nearest petrol station, with my police escort. I filled her up with something over 63 litres (about 12 gallons for those of us who still aren't metricated) indicating Black Betty had indeed been running on fumes. And in all of the excitement I didn't even have the opportunity to thank the two gentlemen in blue (well, one was in blue) for their sterling efforts in protecting me, Black Betty and the motoring world at large, from my own stupidity. If they're reading this now, well, thanks guys. Oh, and thanks are also due to you, Gilly, dear wife. I've got the petrol, and the ferry tickets. If you're still looking for me in and around the petrol stations of North Devon and Cornwall, you can come home now, and bring the lawnmower petrol with you. They need a cut.

The petrol adventure had demonstrated the fuel capacity of Black Betty. Banking on a 300 mile round trip to Gloucestershire, I could expect to get about 25 to the gallon. Less through towns and on sand. I figured to be on the safe side I'd need to take capacity for a further tank of petrol in the car, or 12 gallons, in cans, which should, with luck, see us across the widest gap in civilization. I'd already collected two large plastic containers that would hold, between them, 45 litres or 9 gallons. A third such container would suffice.

With these last preparations, Black Betty would be ready and as confident as I for the 4,000 miles ahead.

It was time to establish Banjul Base Camp.

XI
BANJUL BASE CAMP

As the new year got into gear and accelerated away from the lethargy of Christmas, the final preparations and plans were crystallized. The new year is traditionally a busy time. A time for good intentions and resolutions, made in the early hours of 1 January and soon broken. So whether it's simple weight loss, cigarette cessation, alcohol abuse or just the blues of returning to a mundane job after the Christmas festivities, new year is a busy time for the hypnotherapist. This year there were too many loose ends to tie and preparations to finalise. Commitments would be kept to a minimum.

On my bleary-eyed way to the bathroom one morning before dawn, I passed Banjul Base Camp. At least that's what the sign on the pale blue door of what used to be a spare bedroom declared. "Banjul Base Camp. The Life Mechanics and starring Black Betty." I was intrigued. I forgot the more pressing needs for the bathroom and ducked inside (it's a low door).

Inside had been organized like one of those WWII operations rooms you see in cheap post war productions of the 'fifties. Maps of Devon, Europe and West Africa adorned the yellow wash walls. A full sized ops table, sprinkled with miniatures of Graham, me and Black Betty, tracing our route down the coast. And on the bed were stacked supplies. An orderly jumble of boxes and bags, crates and containers. And a gas mask case, a genuine relic of WWII. Gilly had been at work.

Banjul Base Camp was to serve as headquarters and storage depot for supplies and provisions for the trip. She'd rifled through our own first aid provisions (ancient bottles of sticky cough linctus, smelling salts and surgical appliances from yesteryear) and the shelves of a local pharmacy to produce a comprehensive but compact first aid chest.

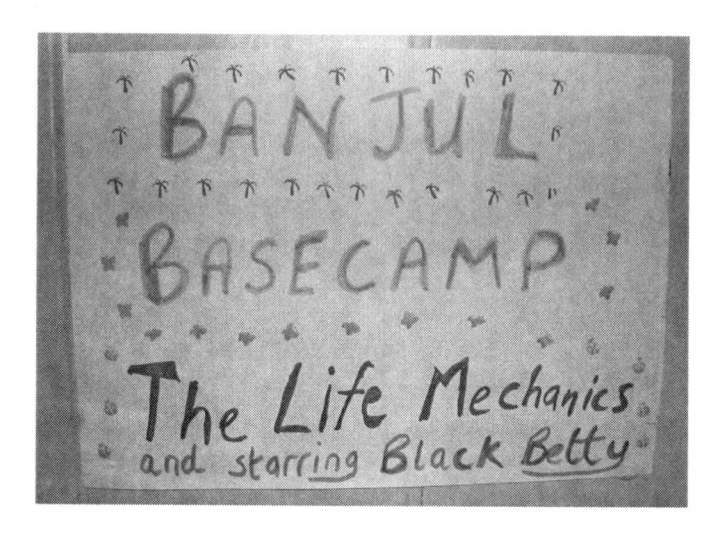

ESSENTIAL MEDICAL SUPPLIES FOR THE TRAVELLER IN AFRICA

- Sterile needles and syringes
- A suture kit for sewing up the larger wounds
- A sterile blood transfusion kit
- Ibuprofen for aches and pains
- Steristrips for holding more minor cuts together
- Plasters in all shapes and sizes
- Antiseptic spray
- Bandages, including a triangular one from which a sling might be fashioned
- Malarone tablets
- Insect repellant (lots of)
- Sun block (minimum factor 35. I hate this stuff, and would probably never wear it, but Graham might prefer it to his knotted hankie)
- A pair of scissors (for cutting bandages and performing ad hoc minor surgery)

- Tweezers (for extracting foreigners and foreign matter)
- A tick remover
- A thermometer (well actually we decided against a thermometer, partly because one cannot be carried on a plane, but mainly because neither of us would be in a position to determine the significance of a raised or a lowered temperature. Also, we couldn't agree whether the instrument should be placed under the tongue or in the anus. There's a subtle yet meaningful difference, particularly when you're sharing a thermometer in the desert.)
- Emergency dental kit, which wouldn't exactly permit one to perform delicate bridge work or major invasive dental surgery, but the odd filling could be temporarily replaced.
- Water purification tablets
- Calomine for bites and burns
- Rehydration salts for use after a bout of diarrhoea
- Diocalm to prevent need for the above
- An eye bath and patch. Stuffed parrot.
- Lamisil for fungal infections such as athlete's foot
- Throat drops
- A variety of indigestion purgatives
- Lipsalve for the dry desert winds
- Broad spectrum antibiotics (for which I had to obtain a private prescription. For use in the event of a wound or other injury including insect bite, snake bite, spider attack, crocodilian molestation or the common cold)
- Sterile gloves for dirty jobs on people or the car
- A mouth to mouth resuscitation guard (being very altruistic here, as I trust Graham's body fluids implicitly, though of course there might be other strangers about me who wouldn't, necessarily, trust mine.)
- Emergency foil blanket for shock and hypothermia
- A cold pack for muscle strains (of little use in the desert)
- Eye drops for flushing sandy eyes
- Oil of cloves for achey teeth.
- Personal medications of the old man variety

The only outstanding items were a knock down spray, to gently rid our tents of live mosquitoes and other uninvited guests at bed time, and mosquito nets, which were proving difficult to come by in North Devon in January.

Personal clothing needs would be minimal. Anyone who knows me will tell you I'm not renowned for my consciousness to fashion or my sartorial elegance. Indeed this trip would constitute an ideal opportunity to dispose once and for all of old, past-their-best, outmoded, ragged and, well, simply knackered items of clothing that most would've discarded years ago, but I continued to put in the wash basket and, much to Gilly's shame and embarrassment, to wear. I'd be traveling down in a reasonably capacious vehicle, but home by air with a limited luggage allowance. Anything that I could and was prepared to leave in the Gambia, would lighten the load homeward bound.

Quite where all the odd socks in my life came from I have no idea. They all started out as pairs, but somehow one or other of them lost their way, or simply changed career. Gilly found well over forty odd, worn socks, many with the toes or heel lost to oblivion. There were enough to make 21 disposable pairs. Like some ageing adolescent, I'd remove them at the end of the day and leave them more or less where they lay.

I was less fortunate with my underwear, and giving up on the obvious alternative option of taking some of Gilly's (I feared raised eyebrows of customs officials or medics en route and was not quite clear on the legal status of cross dressers abroad) I had to bite the bullet and take quite presentable trolleys. Fifteen pairs, with a couple of washes, would suffice. I would throw them away in Africa, if this seemed socially and environmentally acceptable. My third best swimming trunks would also accompany me, and these might be of interest to a modest Gambian swimmer, as they were in reasonable condition. Three pairs of chinos or cargo pants and ten long sleeved (because of the mosquitoes) shirts would make up my ensemble. The shirts could at a stretch be worn twice each, given the prevailing weather conditions in a north African winter, and then given away, unwashed, to the more needy inhabitants of the Gambia or Senegal, where they are, apparently, highly prized items.

The climate would change during the journey south from the bleak damp cold of Plymouth and snows of the Pyrenees, to the hot and arid

Western Sahara and Mauritania. Night temperatures, even in the tropics, in February, could reach sub-zero. I'd take a warm coat, my fishermans waistcoat, hat, scarves and a fleece, to cover all likely weather scenarios. For nightwear I would portray the traditional British image, and take good old striped winceyettes. My night shirt and cap might well cut a dash with its redolence of old Araby, but I was mindful of the ubiquitous mossie and the need to keep the nether fleshy regions covered, especially after dusk. I'd also take a washbag, stocked with shaving and washing gear, soap, toothpaste, and a small towel, for modesty's sake.

Keith and Graham's Amazing Adventure, as the Plymouth-Banjul Challenge 2007 was becoming known, at least locally to Long Lane Farm, could hardly go unrecorded. Personal items of equipment this ageing technophobe would carry would include a digital stills camera, with large memory card and a compact movie camera with five hours of mini tapes, together with chargers for both and a continental adaptor. Most of the trip would be recorded in note form in a journal, and I'd carry my Dictaphone with spare tapes and batteries for voice recording of points of interest in motion. I'd pack my spare spectacles, clip-on shades, and a lively novel to entertain.

Food supplies could be purchased in southern Spain, and we might lay in some iron rations there, or in Gibraltar, just in case the boiled camel's head or shredded sheep's face didn't appeal. A twenty litre water container would hold drinking water for Graham, Black Betty and myself in extremis, but we would exist otherwise on bottled water through Europe and North Africa, where it's in plentiful supply.

Basic cooking equipment comprised of a dinky portable gas ring and a couple of gas canisters, which I obtained so cheaply I could afford to leave in the Gambia with the boy scouts, if I could find them. With two mugs taken from home, a saucepan purchased from a charity shop for 50p and a tiny whistling kettle, I felt sure my culinary skills could cater for full English breakfast, with strong British army tea, mid desert. I also found, in an accommodating charity shop in Ilfracombe, a tin opener and corkscrew, which the kind volunteer let me have for 10p the pair. And we had enough knives, forks, spoons, bowls and plates to furnish the Gambian army (if it has one?). Graham and I would wine and dine in style, whatever the conditions. A bottle of washing up liquid (which could double in emergency as hand wash or shampoo) waterproof matches and a roll of rubbish sacks would be on board to make any camping experience quite a home from home.

As to home itself, I had spotted a bargain at the end of the summer. A local private supermarket staged a sale in August with banner headlines *"Now is the winter of our discount tents"*. For the modest sum of £45 I got a two man tent, complete with groundsheet, two sleeping bags, two air mattresses, and two foam rubber mats, all contained in a handy carrying case. We had our campsite in a bag. When, a few months later on another visit to the charity shop, I was offered a second tent in a bag complete with poles and pegs, for the princely sum of £1, I confess I couldn't resist. If Graham and I had a falling out, one of us could take to the annex.

Other incidentals on our list included lavatory paper. I'd heard public lavatories in West Africa, where they exist at all, range from unsavory through disgusting to downright abominable. Lavatory paper is never provided. We should be prepared by laying in, at least by the time we left Spain, copious quantities of our own, which could be either used, sold on the black market or given to our less fortunate and ill provided colleagues. I was by this time also envisaging another use for our sand shovels.

Lest we encounter a sandstorm (common in Mauritania, I'd been told) with our afternoon tea and petit fours, two pairs of swimmers' eye goggles might allow us to take tea in comfort and yet uphold the best traditions of the British Empire. Wearing these goggles in the local swimming baths had caused me severe headaches and other minor cranial damage, because with them on I'm quite blind and unprepared for the end of the pool as it races up (well, looms up) to meet me.

Essential reading for the trip would be the *Road Book*, written edited and published on-line by the Disorganisers. The *Road Book* would prepare us for the unknown, making a vital traveling companion. It gives dates and times for regrouping with other teams, tide times along the West African coast, and nuggets of information from pioneering Challengers.

To supplement the large scale map of Africa I'd received at the launch party, I bought similar quality maps of France and Spain. We could probably find Plymouth from North Devon even without a map. The *Lonely Planet* books on Morocco and Senegambia would make supplementary reading and give some priceless clues as to what might be in store.

I failed to locate a cheap or free radio for Black Betty. For entertainment beyond my and Graham's particular brand of banter and club singing, we'd rely on my cheap torch radio. It could operate on batteries or its own internal generator, wound up by a crank handle (one minute's winding equals ten minutes play, yes, it was cheap, remember?). This would have potential in mid Sahara where, if taken short, one could find one's way in the dark to seclusion in the sand and commune with nature to the strains of Handel's Largo, if Radio 3 transmissions reach that far, that is, and one's quick with one's communing.

The trusty and resourceful Swiss army knife which Gilly had thoughtfully bought me for Christmas was a must. I can only imagine that the doughty Swiss army must have frequented the desert, perhaps on manoeuvres, or perhaps during some long forgotten Mauritanio-Swiss conflict, so suited to life in that terrain is the Swiss army knife. Apart from the obligatory "thing for getting stones out of horses hooves", it contains every manner of screwdriver, things for cutting, hacking and sawing, opening bottles and cans, a compass, pliers, torch, gas stove, candlabra and thermo-nuclear device. Or at least that's what I think it is. In any event, if we'd forgotten anything at all, the good old Swiss army knife would be sure to come through.

The people of the Gambia have little by way of material wealth. They lack most of the simple trappings of civilization we take for granted. It would be good to take some gifts of entertainment or utility value. Judging by the evidence of those who'd traveled this way before, much of the officialdom we would encounter, at least from Morocco southwards, is benevolent but corrupt. Bribery is more or less expected at border crossings, and currying favour with local customs officials, the police and other minor governmental bureaucrats seems to be *de rigueur*.

I checked out the likely requirements for both gifts and bribes with a number of people including our local blacksmith Alf Doody, who spent some years in the Gambia teaching metalwork. Eventually we collected an assortment of more or less useful or decorative gifts that might appeal. Old mobile phones, DVD and CD players, digital and analogue watches, pens and pencils, clothing and a few pairs of shoes, a miniature TV set, some jewellery and toys. Cigarettes could be bought in Spain. Marlboro Reds are in favour at the moment.

One lady in North Devon who had made it her mission to adopt and sponsor a particular village asked me to transport a sewing machine to a family in the Gambia. Apparently a sewing machine, of the old hand operated type, is enough to make a family self sufficient. Cathy Karniewicz, known in the Gambia as "Mrs. Recycle", had been transporting all manner of items, together with her twenty five or so colleagues, for a number of years. But of course a sewing machine doesn't lend itself to secretion in hand luggage on a charter flight. So my mission would be to pick up the machine from Cathy in Goodleigh, North Devon, and transport it 4,000 miles to a young man in the Gambia, where his family would become self sufficient over night. I arranged to pick up the machine in my last week in the UK.

Nearly all the provisions for Black Betty and our personal welfare had been assembled by the first week in January. They were stored in Banjul Base Camp, where the bed was littered with items exotic and utilitarian, the nuts and bolts of our expedition.

XII
PUTTING MY HOUSE IN ORDER

With three weeks to liftoff I was so well prepared that I began to doubt myself, and whether my meticulous planning had missed something vital out of the equation. Black Betty sat quietly on the front drive, dehumidifier and electric fire gently humming on her back seat, in an effort to dispel the dampness of a wet winter and lack of use. Currency and ferry tickets were in place. I had registered Black Betty at the PB07 Website, as the rules of the Challenge required, so our documents would tally when we reached the Challenge Control Group in Banjul. Even transport back from Gatwick to North Devon had been arranged—Gilly and our good friend Derrick Hamly would pick us up from Terminal 2 in Graham's BMW, which would be staying at Long Lane Farm for the duration, and was insured for the purpose. Transport back from Gatwick by private hire car, taxi or train would, I discovered, have cost almost as much as the flight tickets from Gambia to Gatwick.

Everything was substantially in place for our amazing adventure, and what remained? It suddenly occurred to me that I'd spent little or no time at all preparing myself, physically, mentally, emotionally and, perhaps, spiritually, for the challenges ahead. Was I ready?

Physically

I was 57 years old with a lifetime of sedentary occupation and general dissipation behind me. Since retirement from the law I had begun to take fitness and well being seriously. A non-smoker, with a healthy diet although perhaps a tad too much alcohol, I felt fitter than ever before, despite the aches and pains that go with age and working with animals. I was swimming a regular mile thrice weekly, sometimes a mile and a half, and had gone for stamina rather than style or speed.

During the summer before our adventure I contracted gout (from good living, I'm told, and port wine) and seen this agonizing condition off in a couple of weeks. More pain was however in store for me as a result of my adventure with an errant sheep and Diana Lewis which had resulted in crippling sciatica and a slight weakness in the left leg. However, since sorting out the remnants of this injury with one visit to Jack the Back of Ilfracombe, several visits to a chiropractor and some weeks of light duties at home, I was back to the regime of three miles a week at the local swimming baths. Strength and stamina had virtually returned by early 2007, as had a little weight. So my physical fitness would be about as good as I could manage by February, and I would avoid ill advised antics with mad sheep, goats and donkeys in the meantime.

I did have some outstanding farm foreman tasks during January to perform, and promised myself to take extra care, because any injury sustained in these last days could have repercussions. The trimming of Pearl's (cockatiel) beak, and Frederick's (green iguana) claws should present no physical problems, being delicate tasks, performed indoors with the deft application of nail clippers. I'd check the fluid levels and tyre pressures in the cars left for Gilly to use in my absence. The drains would need checking and probably rodding before we left, and although I'd presented Gilly with a brand new set of rods for Christmas, I would ensure she was left with clear drains and no antisocial aroma to contend with. With care, I should sustain no lasting damage.

We spent one dry morning cutting up wood for the log burner, to lay in sufficient supplies for the duration. Here again, I wielded the chainsaw with care and the usual technical precision, while Gilly had the simpler, but more dangerous task of holding the wood steady on the sawhorse, and stacking the logs away in the store. This in the interests of preventing a visitation of the dreaded sciatica.

The jobs that generally cause the greatest aggravation and injury are animal related. I'd need to be particularly careful attending to the goats' and donkeys' hooves for their last bit of podiatry before departure.

Mistletoe the donkey can lose her sense of humour when her rear feet are lifted for treatment. A swift kick from a fractious donkey can easily break a human leg. If in any doubt at all, I'd leave this task to the capable hands of Uncle James, the farrier.

MENTALLY

As the day for departure approached I became noticeably more excited. But did I have all the skills necessary to meet the Challenge? My mechanical knowledge, and more recently acquired intimacy with Black Betty, would be enough, coupled with Graham's superior practical skills, to get us through most foreseeable and doable tasks. I know pretty well how most car things are supposed to work. Superficial maintenance on Black Betty would be a daily task for us both.

Again, I had the wherewithal and the basic skill to deal with minor medical emergency. Never exactly a first aider, I had, in the dim and distant, attended an Emergency First Aid course, and could practice the rudiments of resuscitation without embarrassment.

At school in the prehistoric sixties I'd been a modern linguist, but had hardly spoken French or German for almost forty years. Anticipating linguistic skills might prove useful when blagging our way through some of the border controls and negotiating cheap, bug-free accommodation, I bought a conversational French course on CD, produced by Linguaphone in association with the Daily Mail. Since the preceding August, when it arrived, my £5.99 reintroduction to spoken French had sat on a shelf in the bedroom. My good intention had been to play the CDs into the early hours of the morning, absorbing the French by osmosis direct into the subconscious mind as I slept. Yeah! Cool man! Well instead of that they just sat there on my shelf, and I couldn't bring myself to keep Gilly awake with what was, after all, schoolboy French. Then, at the beginning of January, a good friend gave me a number of redundant electronic gadgets to take to Banjul. One was a personal CD player. My French lessons began in earnest. I listened to one CD per day for the next 18 days, working my way through the complete set twice. The course quite cleverly revitalised my confidence with the French language in a pleasant and undemanding way.

My experience with a video camera was nil, and I'd borrowed one to record the trip and our experiences for posterity. We wouldn't be supported by a film crew, sound recordist, director or script writer. Graham and I would have to fulfil these roles, together with those of mechanic, driver, navigator, caterers, first aid, disaster management and post-traumatic counselling. So some time before departure familiarising myself with the camera's workings would be wisely spent. On one of the few bright afternoons of January I compiled a natural history epic of Long Lane Farm. Our animals appeared bemused when they spotted me creeping up on them unannounced, with comments for the mike such as "and here I am, at the foot of the Himalayas, in the company of one of the proudest and rarest of animals, a donkey. I can only tell you what a privilege it is to share this moment, blah blah blah… ".

Getting to know Black Betty was a priority in the last days before departure. Graham and I would be speeding across the desert sands, but also traversing a number of major cities in the 4000 miles between Plymouth and Banjul. So time at the wheel (very light steering) and handling her finer points (not many) would again be wise. I ventured forth, proudly showing off her new signage, and travelled the roads of North Devon with what I thought to be great panache. Getting to grips with her was great fun, though I did suffer a few more embarrassing moments. Like the petrol caper in Muddiford. And getting caught by a speed cop with a vascar gun in Ilfracombe, when my best negotiation (pleading really) skills helped me leave the scene without incurring fine or points. Of course, exclaiming "it's a fair cop!" to this blonde constable did less than you would expect to endear me to him. And the occasion when, overjoyed at having been donated half a dozen mobile phones, I was racing back home to show off the booty when I nearly lost Black Betty in a muddy ditch. Swerving to avoid said ditch the ever-so-light steering overcompensated and I found myself spinning uncontrollably all over the road, a mere 100 metres from home. Fortunately no vehicle was coming from the opposite direction, for Black Betty would surely have been relegated to history. Fortunately also, nobody but I was present to observe or record my foolish act of recklessness. So only I knew what a plonker I'd been, until now!

Emotionally

As D day, February 2, 2007 approached, my feelings swung between euphoria and excitement on the one hand and mild anxiety on the other. It was not so much fear of the unknown that beset me. It was more trepidation and the prospect of leaving my family at Long Lane Farm. Gilly and I had been together for over 40 years. We'd only been separated on, perhaps, half a dozen occasions and for a maximum of two or three nights. For the first time in our considerable history we'd be separated by 4000 miles, 2 continents and three weeks. I would miss my soulmate dreadfully, and although Graham would, I knew, be fun to be with and extremely capable, there'd be gaps he couldn't fill. The rest of my "family" of 54 is largely of the four-footed variety. I'd miss daily contact with the animals, all pets, and all of them contributed in no small part to the idyllic life at Long Lane Farm. And there was nothing I could do to assuage the guilt of leaving each and every one behind me, that something might befall one of them that would require my indispensable presence. Three weeks in February was almost bound to witness one death, but there was nothing I could do with these feelings. I resolved I would spend time with each of our charges in the last week of January, reassure them of my swift return, and perhaps take a picture or two of the star players in our little tableau with me to Africa.

As for Gilly, well I did invest in a new mobile phone, with which I'd be able to keep in contact over the continents. I promised at least two calls a day, more in the event of some dramatic landscape or event. For her part, I think she was keen to see the going of me. She would at least have Long Lane Farm to herself for three whole weeks, without her little Ayatollah to badger her along. And she had already had offers from many friends to come and stay, and leave their own Ayatollahs behind.

Spiritually

I'm not a particularly spiritual person, not one you'll find doing tantric yoga or meditation for relaxation. But I do Reiki and I suppose that's the limit of my spiritual indulgence. Reiki is based upon the theory that the free flow of positive energy through our chakras benefits us spiritually, emotionally and physically. As a healing art it can be used on animals. It can also be used on sewing machines, electric toothbrushes and cars. At least this is what I had been taught by my Reiki Master, as she opened my chakras and tinkered with my attunements.

In these last few weeks leading up to departure, I would revisit the Reiki principles, symbols and practices. If Black Betty needed any help along the way, or indeed any of my colleagues on the Challenge needed to get in touch with the feminine side of their cars, I could assist with application of my spiritual spanners.

XIII
THE FINAL COUNTDOWN

The preparations for the Challenge had taken place in a planned, but piecemeal, fashion, since the summer of 2006 when I located first Graham as my mate and co-driver, and then Black Betty as third member of Team Life Mechanics. By the time the last week was upon us there was remarkably little left to put in place, and the plan had diminished to a few short and undemanding "to-do" lists. The last seven days went something like this.

Friday   After an early swim I drive Black Betty into Ilfracombe to pick up the last bits and pieces. A second gas cylinder for the camping stove, replacement batteries for the Dictaphone and torch radio and a small supply of lavatory paper. Also, a selection of jubilee clips for securing errant hoses and pipes, bungee cords for the luggage, and two ratchet straps to hold petrol cans steady. On the way home I drop in on Neil for three mobile phones (two complete with chargers). Bribes for Africa.

Saturday   Search in workshop reveals two old but serviceable pairs of garden gloves, for digging us out of sand drifts. Faster and more effective by all accounts than shovels, which we could use for snow drifts (unlikely as they may be in the desert at this time of year). Also an old tarp to keep the rain out if we lose the windscreen. And a couple of old duvets in case it gets cold out there.

I listen to unit 7 of the French course for the second time, some useful stuff for booking accommodation and ordering meals etc.

Top up Black Betty with antifreeze.

Sunday   Check over cars for fluid levels, tyre pressures etc., so Gilly will enjoy trouble free motoring while I'm away. Leave her the workshop manuals, grease gun and footpump in case. Check over the Land Rover which she could use if all else fails.

Listen to unit 8 of the French course. More useful stuff on getting and giving directions.

Diana Lewis arrives with a goose for us to rehome. We name it Mahatma Gander and put him (her?) temporarily in the piggery next to Bunter Pig. Should be good company for each other.

Monday   Only a few days left now, and separation anxiety creeps in during the early hours. However, the last swim before departure finds me quite chipper and optimistic, particularly when I find that some of the pool staff have pledged money to my charity. Thoughts this morning are on how I should record this adventure. I should ration myself to, say, 5 stills shots and one quarter hour of video footage per day, so as not to bore my readers or watchers. Also the batteries should hold between opportunities to recharge. I should write the journal nightly, and supplement this with notes taken on the Dictaphone. I'll need to be flexible to cater for the highlights of Marrakech, St.Louis and Banjul Town.

I listen to the last unit of the French course for the second time. Something about stationery supplies and how to find your aunty's pen. It's surprising how my forty year old French has stayed with me, and only needed this boost to make me feel at least competent. Forty years on, la plume de ma tante has moved from le bureau de mon oncle and is now to be found dans son jardin.

I practice the basics of video cameramanship and visit all of the animals except Felix the cat, who apparently is out hunting. Include Gilly in this, to remind me of her technique for replacing roof tiles.

Tuesday   To Ilfracombe's Poundstretcher shop for a few last minute purchases, including some ball point pens and pencils with rubbers (go down well with Gambian children) and a continental adaptor for the camera battery chargers.

Wednesday This morning Gilly gives me a much needed haircut in readiness for departure. Pity that I "accidentally" give her blade No.2 to work with, rather than the usual No.4. The result being my resemblance to the Mitchell Brothers in *Eastenders* instead of the hoped for Albert Schweitzer or Ludwig van Beethoven.

Prepare Graham's will from instructions taken weeks ago and put it together for signature on his arrival.

With less than two full days to go it's time to start the packing. Everything that needs to be taken with us is either in Banjul Base Camp on the bed, floor and window sill, or in the workshop. I count among my strengths project planning, resource evaluation and sourcing the necessary. When it comes to the nuts and bolts of getting it all in and where, that's Gilly's department. While I've been dealing with the other pre-departure essentials, she's busied herself putting the items into a logical sequential order and packing them neatly into some plastic crates which can be stacked one-on-one for storage in Black Betty's rear compartment, leaving the contents substantially visible. Thus it is that when I first arrive on the scene, to assist with the packing, I find it nearly done.

Personal luggage and the all important documents folder are stashed in a capacious holdall. A smaller, sort of handbag, serves for valuables. One of the plastic trays contains first aid (supplemented by a flask of illicit brandy secreted for medical emergency against the rigours of a Muslim regime), the torch radio and fluorescent jackets. Another has cooking and camping equipment, the gas containers and matches. The tent, sleeping bags and air mattresses all fit neatly into their own bag. Another tray takes care of some of the gifts and bribes (I've been advised to refer to them collectively as "cadeaux"). Some of the larger "cadeaux", such as satellite T.V. systems, land line telephones, radar equipment and kitchen units might have to stay behind, I muse thoughtfully as Gilly shoehorns a four drawer filing cabinet into a carrier bag.

I reward Gilly for her sterling efforts by showing her how to change a fuse wire by candlelight, in case she needs to know.

Transporting everything to Black Betty can be left until Graham's arrival tomorrow.

Thursday With hardly anything left unticked on the plan, I award myself an extra and absolutely final pre trip early swim, travelling to the pool in Black Betty. She starts on the button, and I ride with comfort and confidence to the pool, where afterwards I bid farewell to my swimming buddies, who have taken quite an interest in my venture. On the way home I tank up to the brim with premium unleaded. I park Black Betty in the drive at Long Lane. She'll not be used again until tomorrow morning at approximately 11.00 a.m. when Graham and I will leave on the first leg, to Plymouth and the official start. The odometer reads 71,918 miles.

As soon as Graham arrives from Gloucestershire, we set about the business of packing Black Betty. This operation is a model of efficient teamwork. With more of us, we would set up a human chain to transport the many items from Banjul Base Camp and the workshop to Black Betty in the front drive. However, with lack of the necessary personnel, Gilly lugs the contents down two flights of stairs, over a stile and through a hedge to deposit them conveniently for Graham, whom I have delegated to pack the car. Graham's expertise with roping and sheeting gleaned from years as a long distance lorry driver in Europe comes into its own, and all four corners of Black Betty are soon filled. There's ample room for everything, to my surprise, and the packing is complete in an hour.

I sit imperially in the passenger seat, directing operations and ticking my clipboard. I am pleased with my efforts. We are prepared.

When the equine orthodontist appears in the middle of the afternoon to attend to Mistletoe's severe overbite, Graham and I are both able to break off and assist in this delicate operation.

Four sweating adults and a pouting donkey regard each other in the gloomy loose box. The orthodontist peers up into Mistletoe's clamped open mouth, studies the damage in the glow of her head lamp, prepares to grip the offending molar with a fearsome set of hook jawed pliers. I'm on Mistletoe's right flank, struggling to keep a hold on one lead rein while she glares at me through a malevolent eye. Graham's on the left flank, his left knee jammed into her guts.

"Hold tight now, I'm going to give it a yank."
"I've got her, I think."
"I've got her too. Keith, steady her with your knee, will you."
"OK. I'm there. Gilly, where are the rich tea biscuits?"
"Indoors."
"Well that's not very good organisation, is it? Go and get them, quick."
"I think we can manage without the rich tea. Give me the other rein Gilly. Now give me yours, Keith."

And so it was that Graham took over the reins.

Part Two: Getting There

DAY ONE
A GOOD SAMARITAN

The pale blue opalescence of the day we left for Africa will never leave me. Graham, Gilly and I arose to a morning cheerful and golden with early February sunlight filtering through the ash trees of Long Lane Farm. After a sodden January which had hampered and depressed with its relentless wind and rain, our departure was to be heralded with the first bright and beautiful day of the year. I was overwhelmed with excitement and anticipation. The start of an epic journey.

As we packed the last trappings into Black Betty, the farewell committee of friends and neighbours began to arrive. Gilly had arranged an official "start-line", at the front gate of Long Lane Farm. A sign on a wooden post, hammered into the ground on the A 3123, dramatically proclaimed "Africa!" with an arrow pointing, actually in the wrong direction, towards Woolacombe.

Neighbours Steve and Pam Parkin from Mattocks Down and the Wests of Indicknowle brought more largesse in the form of mobile phones, pens, pencils, jewellery and other items to grease our way through customs and spread amongst the deprived of the Gambia. Diana Lewis arrived with vet Norman Bussell and other colleagues and helpers to wish us well on our quest to take an awareness of animal welfare to Africa. Neil Caley turned up and Graham had a quick under-bonnet consultation with him on the anti-freeze situation. Graham had heard it can reach sub-zero temperatures in the desert at night, and his concern for the protection of Black Betty's cooling system wasn't misplaced. A quick taste of the tell-tale bitter sweet vintage anti-freeze put his mind at rest. Derrick Hamly, whose calming influence had been my mentor in more fractious moments was also there to wish us luck and trouble-free motoring.

At 11 o'clock precisely we boarded Black Betty, I in the driver's seat, Graham the passenger. With much wishing of good luck, a few tears and many shutters clicking, we left the front gate of Long Lane Farm and headed, broadly, for Africa, in accordance with Gilly's directions. To pass courageously and triumphantly through Barnstaple and the surrounding villages without incident was my fervent hope, and not to repeat the embarrassment of Muddiford.

The first few miles are blissfully uneventful. I settle down to a reasoned inner confidence that we will make our goal. As I drive through Barnstaple and on towards Torrington we begin to set the ground rules on which we'll base this three-week relationship as car mates. My preference is for sharing the driving more or less equally, one in the morning, the other in the afternoon, averaging perhaps four hour shifts, extended or reduced in the light of actual progress. With between 3,600 and 4,000 miles to cover in about three weeks, and factoring in a few rest days, breakdown time and delays at border crossings, we estimate that between 200 and 300 miles should be achieved daily.

But because of the necessity to muster with other challengers as a group in Tarifa in southern Spain, and in Dahkla in Western Sahara, we'll need to eat up some of these miles in the early stages. Graham's in favour of keeping ahead and buying miles in reserve rather than falling

The Road To Banjul

behind, making a rod for our own backs later in the journey when time might be of the essence. Our target for this first day is the ferry in Plymouth, which we board at eight and depart for the night crossing at ten. The target is set by the ferry times, at a soft 80 or so miles. We have plenty of time.

Musing thus on our good sense in preparing well for the event, and in the generous timing factored in for this first leg, I barely notice the slight misfire developing in Black Betty's ignition system.

With no in-car entertainment we amuse ourselves with tales of exploits past, our life and employment histories, jokes and the comical and unlikely stories of past acquaintances, places we have lived, experiences at home and abroad. Passing through Torrington, the seat of royalist fervour during the English Civil War, I hold forth on the merits and demerits of roundhead and cavalier politics and strategy, Oliver Cromwell and the unfortunate King Charles. Graham hungrily absorbs my potted history of seventeenth-century England, with rapt attention.

Just as his eyes are beginning to glaze over he becomes aware of the more immediate civil war that I've engaged in with the steering wheel. Conditions are dry, bright and pleasant, and yet the steering of Black Betty at these modest speeds has become unpredictable, even alarming. I'd ignored the early symptoms of oversteer to the left, putting this down to slightly over inflated tyres (for fuel economy) and Black Betty's characteristically over active American power steering. She's disconcertingly light on even the worst of roads. My first concern is to reach Plymouth and board the ferry without incident. But I have to begin to admit to myself that all's not well, and wrestling to keep on the correct side of the road, particularly on left-hand bends, is not a comfortable option.

"I think we've got a seized brake calliper on the front right," diagnoses Graham from the relative comfort and objective position of the passenger seat. Certainly, on the straight the steering is pulling, quite violently now, to the right, and significant effort is required to keep the car on the straight and narrow. And whilst right hand bends are trouble free, a bend to the left, particularly if it requires simultaneous application of brakes, results in an almost frighteningly balletic display of virtuosity on the part of Black Betty. Twice we're nearly in a ditch.

Just after Hatherleigh market I pull off the road to investigate. The front left wheel is perfectly normal. The front right burning to the touch. Graham's well-aimed spittle sizzles and evaporates in a microsecond. Indication of a seized caliper, as he predicts. About forty miles from home, with a potentially serious, even terminal, problem, the first real challenge of the trip has occurred whilst still on English soil. I confess my instinct is to plough on to Plymouth, board the ferry and try to get the caliper unseized, if that's the problem, in France.

"Problem is Keith, if we leave it, it's unlikely to free itself. At best we'll be driving with one brake applied, doubling fuel consumption, probably causing further damage. At worst, the bearing could overheat, dry out and seize. The wheel could fall off." Graham's logic is devastating, his argument convincing. Irritating, but convincing. This frightening scenario, and the prospect of terminal disaster somewhere in rural France or Spain, fire my enthusiasm to seek more local and urgent attention to our early plight. At the next sizable sign of civilisation we'll seek repairs.

Okehampton. A small town which boasts a castle and a working steam locomotive railway station, but not much else. Except, that is, for Okehampton Motors. Now I have some history with Okehampton. Nearly forty years ago, in my very early motoring days, I was passing through Okehampton in my first pride and joy, a 1951 Volkswagen Beetle, with my father and bride to be, Gilly, when the petrol pump suddenly and permanently retired from active service. The three of us spent a less than riveting day in 1960's Okehampton, waiting for the AA to send us by bus from Exeter, a replacement petrol pump for the Beetle. The ten hours spent in Okehampton on that historic occasion had been sufficient for me for the next forty years, and I'd studiously avoided contact with Okehamptonians out of a lingering superstition that, perhaps for me, Okehampton is mechanically contraindicated. However, today Okehampton and its residents must come to our rescue. We limp gingerly into the first available service garage on this Friday lunchtime, not really expecting anyone will be able or prepared to fit us in for consultation, let alone have the necessary parts or expertise to help. We're not disappointed in our expectations and are referred to Okehampton Motors, slightly out of the main town, who "might be able to help".

As we approach the large sliding doors of Okehampton Motors, a sturdy young man wearing blue coveralls and a beaming smile greets us. Graham eagerly describes the problem, where we're heading for both today and in the longer term, which is pretty clear from Black Betty's signage, and our plight - to board the evening ferry at Plymouth. Could he help us in any way with the caliper and, if possible, the misfire.

Gareth Davies seems to have no reservations or second thoughts, though he's clearly engaged on another task on a large and impressive Audi. The Audi's promptly rolled out of the way, I pull Black Betty into the workshop and in no time her front right corner is jacked up and the wheel removed. Gareth confirms Graham's diagnosis, and the likely consequences of carrying on much further with it. The issue is now, can the caliper be unseized so as to last another 4000 miles, or will it, and possibly its counterpart on the other side, have to be replaced, together with the pads, at enormous cost and not inconsiderable delay. The likelihood of locating new calipers for a sixteen year-old American specification Cherokee Jeep in under a fortnight are remote. My heart begins to sink.

Gareth deftly unbolts and removes the offending caliper, with some difficulty as it's effectively jammed on the brake disc. The first good news is it's not the operating piston within the calliper, but rather the reciprocating sliders which have become unfeasibly jammed in their passages. Gareth removes them with some effort, and discards the plastic protective tubes giving more room for movement. He then grinds about a thousandth of an inch from the girth at his bench and, having smothered them in high melting point copper impregnated grease, replaces them in the caliper. They now moved snugly but easily in their passages. The caliper is refitted and the road wheel replaced. The whole operation takes about fifty minutes, and probably saves the trip.

We're immensely thankful to Gareth for his skill, his professionalism and also his can-do attitude.

"What do we owe you?" I ask, expecting to be at least £50 lighter in the wallet for this instant attention to a serious problem.

"Call it my contribution to your challenge. Nothing." replies Gareth.

And that's when my faith in human nature, which has taken some rough dents recently when preparing for this Challenge, is effectively restored. I force a drink on Gareth, out of friendship. But this total stranger to us, to our cause and to Black Betty in particular, has taken us on trust. He's given of his best and saved what could've been a devastating problem in fifty minutes, and all for free. I vow I shall recommend Okehampton Motors and particularly Gareth to any of my friends and colleagues with a local mechanical problem. And I vow never to avoid Okehampton again.

The much less important problem of the intermittent misfire can't be so easily solved. A new set of sparking plugs might help, and these can be obtained from Kevin Cooper's in Okehampton town, Gareth advises. With a little helpful guidance for me on how to apply the brakes in future (as they mightn't be quite so efficient with Gareth's life saving modification) we're on our way. The brakes and steering perform perfectly.

At Kevin Cooper's we buy six sparking plugs. We've parked in the Waitrose car park while scouring the town for the motor factors, and returned to fit them. Graham extracts the existing plugs. All seem in good condition and burning to the correct mixture. However, new plugs installed, he checks the distributor cap and rotor arm, and gives the high tension leads a wipe with a rag. Any component of the ignition system could be responsible for the intermittent misfire, and whilst we've replacement rotor arm and distributor cap on board, it isn't worth replacing them until the sparking plugs have been eliminated from the equation.

Under the bonnet, sleeves rolled up and covered from fingertips to elbows in engine oil and axle grease, hair tousled and faces bearing an appearance of benign consternation, we must appear to the world, or at least to other visitors to Okehampton on this bright and spring-like February day, as amateur kerbside mechanics. In the matter of the thirty minutes it takes to change the plugs and clean the ignition system we're asked twice for directions into the town, once for change for the car-park ("have you nothing smaller... ?") and once for a full service and valet cleansing. Beginning to believe we've spent rather too much time in Okehampton, we put the tools away, clean up as best we can with Swarfega and cold water from the Waitrose conveniences, and hit the road.

Graham takes the wheel and we head gratefully towards Tavistock. The weather's fine and bright, if overcast, and Black Betty seems happier. She still has a slight engine misfire, which shows itself particularly when load's put on the engine to overtake slower vehicles. But the steering and braking are fine now, and the three of us are well pleased.

Tavistock in the early afternoon. The weather's returned to its glorious promise of spring. We pass Plymouth Argyle Football Club, heading for the town centre. The car park's full. I muse idly on how life and the obligatory Saturday afternoon football match must go on, regardless of the death-defying feat of human endurance we're embarked upon in this mission of mercy to the dark continent. And then Graham reminds me it's Friday, so the disrespect we're being shown is by shoppers, not football fanatics.

There's similarly no welcoming committee at the ferry terminal when we arrive just before three. "Please stop here - arrêtez ici s.v.p." reads the legend on the signpost overlooking Plymouth Sound. No sign of staff or any other life form.

With Black Betty overlooking the Sound, we joined the other illustrious travellers of yesteryear who departed from these shores for destinies and destinations unknown - Drake, Raleigh, Lord Lucan (?). Perhaps we could see, in the dwindling daylight of that sparkling day on Plymouth Hoe, our names, Pugsley and De Meur, emblazoned on those heroic monuments as a reminder for generations to come of our courage, valour and determination on this historic and prophetic trip. Anyway, we walked into Derry's Department Store to buy Graham a coat – he'd left his in the lobby at Long Lane Farm in the hurry and bustle of departure. We had yet France and Spain to pass through, not to mention the Pyrennees, before we could expect the torpor of the tropics. And when we returned with Graham's purchase we walked about the Hoe marvelling at the sites, the sounds and smells of this the last corner of England we'd experience for three weeks, as the sun set over Drake's Island. The redolence of fresh cut grass, shrill cries of skateboarders, joggers taking their early evening constitutional, the spicey aroma from the Wet Wok Chinese Restaurant. Black Betty was enjoying her taste of the English Riviera.

At five o'clock Graham's sister Kate and Brother-in-law Gary arrived with Rosie to see us off the premises. We walked Rosie on the Hoe, and repaired to the Waterfront Bar as the sun set for a couple of hours of entertaining conversation with Kate and Gary, the rangey Australian man of the outback. A most pleasant ending to an otherwise slightly fraught first day, particularly when we were invaded by a multitude of the most attractive debutantes on a girly night out.

At half past seven we left the bar, made our farewells to Kate, Gary, Rosie and England and joined the short queue for the ferry terminal. Passing through customs control, I was asked almost casually, whether we were carrying any petrol (had he noticed the three jerricans behind the back seat?), explosives, bombs, guns or other armaments. But we were welcomed on to the ferry with a smile. Struggling through labyrinthine passages, safety doors and bulkheads we eventually reached our cabin on deck 8. After a quick shower and change in our well-appointed but snug quarters (two foldaway bunk beds, desk, chair, an acreage of cupboard space and an unflattering full length mirror) we celebrated with fish, chips and brandy in the dining room, amused to find the bulk of the staff of Italianate extraction.

We took to our bunks at ten thirty, in the middle of Plymouth Sound. It'd been an eventful trip and tiring day. In the darkness of the bijou accommodation I fumbled with the new mobile phone. I'd check that Gilly was coping without me.

"Hello, light of my life, how is one faring?"
"I'm OK. Relieved you got to Plymouth. How's Betty?"

"Fine, fine. Just a minor problem with the brakes. I've got it all sorted now."

"Did Graham get a new coat? And has he found his passport? And his medication? I've searched everywhere."

"Yes dear, to all three. Benefits of being prepared you see. Honestly, you do worry. How are you coping?"

"Everything's fine. But where are the five amp fuses?"

"They're in a coffee jar. It's marked 'Soap Powder'. On a shelf in the dairy. Why do you ask?"

"Well, I'm up the ladder right now, trying to find them. And it's dark. All the fuses have blown, I think."

"Good. Apart from that?"

"Fine. Good. Everyone's OK."

"Good. Good. Goodnight then. Call you from France, tomorrow. Goodnight dear."

"Tit!"[2]

---

[2] A contemptible person (*vulg.*) a small, inferior, worthless or worn-out horse. *Chambers Dictionary 1993 edition.*

DAY TWO
LOST IN FRANCE

It was like trying to sleep in a washing machine set on "non-fast coloureds", the gentle undulation of the ferry in a February ocean, with the ever-present possibility of getting switched to "fast spin". Not at all unpleasant, for someone unused to rough waters. My last experience shipboard had been on the Oldenburg from Ilfracombe to Lundy Island in a moderate swell, when all on board had struggled to hold onto their breakfast, and most had failed. On this overnight crossing, where I lay recumbent in my snug bunk, the gentle motion of the ferry back and forth, back and forth, was almost hypnotic. Every minute or so the sensation was of plunging to unfathomable depths, quick, slick and dark. But sleep did not come to either Graham or myself. Perhaps it was the events of the previous day, or thoughts of what lay in store over the next three weeks. Perhaps it was just cold adrenalin that got us up at 6 a.m. and to the even stranger sensation of shaving and showering in a moving vessel. But distant experiences as a bus conductor for Luton Corporation nearly forty years previously had readied me for that particular manoeuvre, and in the shower I didn't even have my uniform and money bag to hamper me. Shifting balance from right foot to left, and then back again, I soon acquired sea legs albeit late in the crossing. Making the acquaintance of the lavatory was a less charming experience. It performed its own function perfectly adequately, but with a suction that would put a hyperventilating vacuum cleaner to shame.

"That doesn't hang about!" exclaimed Graham as he beat a hasty retreat from the ablution section of our tiny quarters.

Breakfast in the dining room on Deck 6. I had the continental, but Graham's heart was still in Gloucestershire. He opted for full English. We played briefly with our mobile phones as we fulfilled our promises to keep in touch at least twice daily. As we finished breakfast, the ferry docked noiselessly and the lights of Roscoff were picked out against a steely grey dawn. If I have one criticism of the Plymouth-Roscoff ferry, it's that finding the exit to the car deck was more complicated and circuitous than finding our berth on the preceding evening. We stumbled through heavy sliding bulkhead doors and along companionways, without any indicative signage, until at last, through bulkhead door G, several floors below where we had expected to find her, Black Betty winked demurely at me from her own berth. A scribbled message was tucked under the windscreen wiper, and I quite expected we'd contravened some bureaucratic regulation or other, or upset a fellow passenger. I shared it with Graham. From another PB07 Challenge team, it stated succinctly "Nick and Josh. VW Passat", and gave a mobile phone number. We vowed to make contact with Nick and Josh at the earliest opportunity.

We'd travelled a mere 81 miles by road from Long Lane Farm and several nautical miles overnight. Today's target would need to be bold if we were to make the projected rendezvous with our colleagues on the Challenge at Tarifa in southern Spain by 5th. February. We pulled off the ferry and into the early morning traffic of Roscoff, the small but bustling village that owes its entire existence to the port.

Instantly we're in France, and this is confirmed by the passing scenery and architecture - large rustic (decrepit) agricultural barns, cabbages, gentlemen on bicycles carrying strings of onions and wearing berets, the strains of a distant accordion and blue smoke and pungent aroma of the ubiquitous Gauloises. A red London bus, on its way apparently to Wimbledon Station, catches the eye momentarily, but gone are the battle scars of ninety years ago. The trenches have been filled in, or disappeared into history. This is my first experience out of England in fifteen years. I'm struck by the slight off key foreignness of everything.

Graham takes quickly to the concept of driving on the right. He's done a lot of driving of rather larger vehicles in Europe some years ago, and is a consummate professional with everything on two or four (or six or eight for that matter) wheels. We head for Morlaix and Guingamp on the E50 and soon find ourselves speeding along the excellent north French roads. Straight, well-maintained and surfaced, but with remarkably little traffic, and no litter at all, we hurtle along the main roads of rural Brittany taking in the lush green farmland on either side, the deep red soil and modest incursions of well-designed commercial and industrial life.

We pass through Guingamp and St.Brieuc where we join the motorway. In the centre of St. Brieuc Graham's cut up by an inconsiderate French driver. At least that's what I think Graham called him, it was certainly something appropriately Celtic. The Frenchman breezes on with a cheery wave and smile, clearly appreciating Graham's gentlemanly behaviour and superior driving.

Just before Rennes, we stop for our first petrol since leaving Long Lane. The weather has asserted itself and bold white clouds stud an otherwise perfect blue. The petrol station's an eye-opener. We'd expected the usual facilities to be available; petrol, edible materials of questionable quality and doubtful provenance, perhaps the odd stinking pissetoire. The truth is, we walk past well manicured lawns and perfectly coiffed bushes, through silent automatic doors into a sanitised pleasure dome. I pay for the petrol with plastic, conserving cash euros. We sample the conveniences, and find them spotless, modern and well, really palatial. The air gently fragranced with vanilla, soothing classical baroque melodies wafting through the atmosphere, charming and beautiful attendants with ready and welcoming smiles and immaculate uniforms. Not a sign of litter, graffiti or the other debris we have become used to in service stations at home. I'm both impressed and gently inspired. So impressed I decide to bury the first wishbone.

I should explain that, in the lead-up to leaving the UK, Gilly saved and painted seven wishbones, one to be planted in each country, as an omen for good luck, peace and safe motoring. Strung together on a leather thong they dangle from the rear-view mirror. I detach the

French wishbone and plant it, surreptitiously, at the base of a decorative jacaranda, just outside Rennes.

"Black Betty's taking a leak too, by the looks of it," Graham mentions, pointing at a little puddle of ominous dark fluid on the tarmac, mid-engine, just beneath the sump.

"What, here, in the car park, in broad daylight. Oh God, what's the problem now?" My heart's taking its time, but its jumping into my mouth at the very suggestion of mechanical failure. I flip the hood (you have to say that if the car's American. In other cases you just lift the bonnet). Graham's inspecting Black Betty's innards, his arms buried up to the shoulder in her mysterious depths.

"It's OK. Not coming from the radiator or hoses. I think it's the air conditioning, trying to make ice."

My heart jumps back.

Rennes is a river port, capital of the old province of Brittany, lying at a confluence of the Ille and Vilaine rivers, 190 miles west south-west of Paris. Once it was a commercial and railway centre, noted for its printing, weaving and tanning industries. The university, founded in 1735, specialises in Celtic studies. Among notable buildings are the Archbishop's palace (1672), the stately Palais de Justice (1618-1654) and the 18th century town hall. In 1963 it had a population of 154,000. At least these are the facts according to the encyclopaedia of my schooldays. I don't see any of it because in our hurry to traverse France in a day there simply isn't time to visit the sights and scenes of my historic school primers. But Rennes, or what we see of it when we inadvertently drive off the motorway at a roundabout on the ring road, seems a perfectly pleasant and typical northern French provincial town. When we find ourselves heading inland, for Paris, Graham makes a quick and not desperately legal adjustment, crosses the central reservation and heads south again, for Nantes.

Bright sunshine, clear sky, a lovely spring day. The roads busy up south of Rennes, Black Betty's performing well and eating miles of delicious French motorway.

The Road To Banjul

Nantes, at the head of the Loire estuary, is historically a great seaport and industrial town. Known in the past for its food processing, tobacco, ship and aircraft building industries, it sits on the Loire with St. Nazaire at the mouth as an outport. I remember it from my history lessons and the Edict of Nantes, signed in 1598 to end the wars between the Huguenots and the French Catholics. From our position, on the massive flyover which has been built sometime since 1598 and now crosses the estuary, my lasting recollection is of the vast timber yard on the Loire Valley. Hundreds of thousands of huge timbers floating majestically downstream like some manic tortoise, guided by nimble-footed lumberjacks as they leap effortlessly from trunk to trunk across an endless floating wooden bridge, poles in hand, jabbing here, poking there, keeping the moving platform on track and in place. In the past this crop timber was no doubt destined for the shipyards of Nantes. Now, perhaps for Ikea.

By one o'clock local time we're hurtling south for Bordeaux on the A83. Travelling south at speed, the weather is likely to be progressively more changeable, at least until we've left Europe. Still dry, but we're covered by a steely grey sky, glowering clouds and violent crosswinds that buffet us on their way to the Atlantic coast. Every mile or so windsocks remind us of the power and direction of these winds which, as we steer into them, become head winds. Black Betty's faltering ignition is upset by the extra effort required of the engine to plough ahead, and overtaking the occasional lorry becomes a slight embarrassment. Graham insists we look at the ignition leads at the next opportunity. I begin to wish we'd purchased a new set in Okehampton.

To take my mind away from the faltering ignition, and from the slight but ominous tension in my left thigh, which I hope does not herald the return of sciatica, I turn my attention to the topical question of malaria, and its prevention. Bizarre though it seems, that I should sit, huddled in a heavy overcoat hurtling through a bleak windswept landscape towards the foot hills of the Pyrenees, eking out our supplies of Malarone, yet these are calculations that have to be made. In a few days we shall be sleeping in jungle tents, under mosquito nets, battling with clouds of the verminous bitey little insects, in fear of imminent and painful delirium as the malarial virus machetes its way into the nervous system. Here in the cool breezes of rural France in the heart of the Bordeaux region is the time to make the essential calculation. We have 57 tablets between us. Our advice has been to take one tablet each daily, starting two days before reaching the swampy malarial regions, and to continue for at least seven days after return to the UK. 57 doesn't divide by two, so deducting one tablet as a spare, there are 27 tablets each. Taking all factors into account, we should commence the Malarone regime in two days time, when still in Spain.

Past Niort and the turning for La Rochelle we stop for petrol, about 85 miles north of Bordeaux. The sun's returned and displaced most of the gloom. Not exactly a cloudless day, but lovely like the late spring or early summer of an English May. Chilly cross winds have hampered us and increased my nervous tension, but Black Betty performs with skill and confidence and surprisingly reasonable fuel consumption for a four litre engine.

How clean, well kept and even attractive are the roads in these parts. Even on major motorways, a neat, well-maintained box hedge down the middle delineates north from southbound, giving shelter from the crosswinds. And the only refuse is road kill; two dead cats and an expired badger with a confused expression.

Passing through Bordeaux in the late afternoon, young vines, farmhouse sales of Bordelaise, the evidence of a region world-renowned for its wine production. Yet snow on the roadside verge remind us we're still in the throes of a European winter. We pass through the péage and long stretches of immaculate motorway without incident, and without a hint of the presence of historic Bordeaux to our right as we circle it on the EO5 on our relentless trek southwards. Across the mighty Gironde estuary and we veer right for Bayonne and the border with Spain.

Some miles before Bayonne (where the bayonets hail from, as I recall) on the Bay of Biscay, I decide we should take a well-earned break. Graham would willingly push on and probably not stop otherwise than for petrol and comfort, until we reach the Gambia. But he has to be told. The drive has been long and uneventful and I need a rest from the application of imaginary brakes. I feel it will not benefit us to race straight into the Pyrenees and over the border in the late evening. So we decide on Biarritz for our first and only night's stay in France.

Biarritz, seaside resort at the south end of the Bay of Biscay where the sandy coast of the Landes joins the base of the rocky Pyrenees. It reached its peak as a fashionable centre under the patronage of the Empress Eugénie. Bismarck and Queen Victoria both visited, and it was a favourite haunt of Edward VII. So it ought to be good enough for these two saddle-sore and intrepid travellers.

We pull off the main road and drive into out-of-season Biarritz at six o'clock. Once "fashionable", Biarritz made it into "chic". But by the time "trendy" was the word, the bloom of Biarritz was no more. Now few people holiday in Biarritz. It's not "cool". Still clean, tidy and respectable, with an undeniably cosmopolitan flavour in its choice of cuisine, Biarritz now is a bit of a faded anachronism.

I expected to find the place fair bristling with hotels of yesteryear, the faded Victoriana and a classic kitsch of a bygone era. However, the few hotels still trading in early February in the 21st century seem to have been mothballed. At least they were hiding from me as I trudged curiously around what I believe was the town centre, while Graham guarded Black Betty against whatever marauders she had to offer off season, at this time of the evening.

The Hotel Louisiane peaked shyly at me out of the shadows on my third circuit of Biarritz (I'd passed Graham or someone who looked awfully like him and had returned my wave, twice in the gloom). The restaurant Bâton Rouge, its more proud and boastful partner establishment, pouted at me from its "closed for renovations" doors. I thought I'd drawn a blank in my first bid for unbooked hotel accommodation. But something on my fourth circuit of the town (even Graham or whoever it was in the gloom, was becoming suspicious of my movements) tempted me to try the back door of La Louisiane. It was indeed open for business, even if the restaurant was closed. The reception was bright, professional and ably staffed by Madeleine, who took our passports and our booking for one night.

It was, unremarkably I suppose, in France that my revived acquaintance with the language paid most dividends. Booking a room with twin beds (not double, if you please, our friendship is not of that sort!) la plume de ma tante definitely was, still, dans le bureau de mon oncle. We took a pleasantly furnished up market ensuite with breakfast. Black Betty took a berth in the secure underground car park. Dinner, however, was not on the menu. So Graham and I left the insistent strains of cajun guitar behind, and hit downtown Biarritz.

A curious mix of the nouveau chic and the down-at-heel, Biarritz by night was busier than expected. Plenty of restaurants and more modest eateries in the main drag, numerous bars and clubs in the streets that ran laterally from it. Le Marocain boasted delights of west African cuisine that we were never to find in Morocco. Le Cubain looked promisingly exotic in a Hispanic colonial sort of way, but, like Le Muscovite, was closed. So we plumped for the modest but respectable "La Reine Mère" which sported a pretty good neon likeness of our late Queen Mum over the front façade. I suppose we thought there might be a degree of pro-British sympathy in an establishment so named. Anyway, the steaks were juicy and ample, and definitely beef, because I asked. Apparently horse meat is still eaten in France, but rarely in restaurants. You no longer need to specify "Bifteck", if that's what you require. Steak, chips and cold beer by candle light (there was a power cut). Not very adventurous, perhaps, for our first meal abroad, but it hit the spot.

We soon made our way back to La Louisiane and, after checking Black Betty in her snug berth, hit the sack.

We'd travelled 546 miles and the entire length of France.

DAY THREE
MEN OF LA MANCHA

Climbing out of Biarritz early on Sunday morning is a revelation. In the rush and concern last evening to locate what appears to have been the only open and habitable hotel, we missed the gentle splendours of this little alpine resort in the foothills of the Pyrennees. Delicate, crisp and precise, the half-timbered mock Swiss chalet style houses perch among the neat, well-manicured greenery in the hills as we pilot the incongruous bulk of Black Betty through the unsuspecting streets. Biarritz is still a discreet and rather well designed haphazardness of holiday homes. In the crystal clear powder blue of this multicoloured morning, I quite expect Heidi, complete with herd of jangling goats, to come prancing around the corner, crook in hand.

The Hotel Louisiane was comfortably appointed, lavishly supplied with all the little accoutrements that make being away from home bearable. Individually wrapped soaps, shower gel, shampoo and conditioner were arranged neatly in the pristine bathroom. As was shoe shine. A sachet of the stuff, propped against the mirror. Now I wore the same pair of charity shop trainers throughout the trip, rubber soles, plastic uppers. I certainly had no use for shoe shine. But I was intrigued at this remnant of a more genteel past—shoe shine in the bathroom—and I wondered indolently who would ever be bothered to avail themselves of this artefact during an overnight stay. Graham was not so curious or so introspective. As I pondered the mild curiosity, he busily lathered up in the shower, or at least tried to, with his complementary pack of shoe shine.

Breakfast was uninspiring but sufficient. We were clearly way out of season and shared the dining room with a family of three-mother, father and young son, French, and, like us, out of season. We ate in subdued silence, contemplating the day ahead, the silvery lights of the dining room chandeliers tinkling gaily on Graham's highly polished brow.

I hadn't used my newly revised schoolboy French much, as stops on the previous day had been few and far between, and conversation with petrol station cashiers limited. However, booking the room had been a breeze, and with my confidence restored I sent the dearly beloved a French letter on the back of a view of Biarritz. Madeleine edited my effort. Roughly translated, the message was:

"Wish you were here. Did you remember to rod the drains? See you in three weeks. Pug."

We emerged from the underground car park into a moonlit morning, heading for Spain on the A63 to San Sebastian Donastia. Our target for the day, carefully calculated by Graham with a route map and a rolled up morsel of paper, was Santa Cruz de Mudela, about 450 miles and over half way through Spain. But first we needed petrol.

Driving sedately out of Biarritz, the Gulf of Gascony on our right, we're overtaken at speed by a group of determined looking black lycra-clad cyclists taking their early morning exercise in the clear air of this pre-mountainous region.

"That'll be the Tour de France, I expect."
"No. Wrong time of year I think you'll find. Anyway, it doesn't come this far west."
"And there's no yellow jersey. More yer black lycra."
"Could be a brigade of Basque Separatists. We're in the right region."
"They're not wearing basques. Unless they're hidden under the lycra."
"And they're not separate. Quite cosy, I'd have said."
"D'you think they're armed?"

"Could be. Looks like they're toting small weapons."
"Unless they're just pleased to see us."

The cyclists speed away into this strange landscape of Swiss chalets. At the first petrol station, just outside Biarritz, we're stymied in our quest for fuel by the technology. The automatic till will not accept my plastic, and there's no human presence. Petrol's getting slightly low, and I'm slightly concerned. It's Sunday morning and we're in provincial France about to enter catholic Spain. Will the devout open for trade to these infidels on the sabbath?

We're soon on the motorway again, climbing the foothills. In front of us the Pyrennees, huge, snow capped, vainglorious, astonishing in the early morning mist. We pass through the San Sebastian toll, above the snow line. Without any warning at all, we're in Spain. But it's not stereotypical. Where are the gentlemen in sombreros and ponchos? Where the sleepy little bodegas, the exotic raven haired beauties thrusting hips and clacking castenets? Where are the tapas and tequila? We've made the Spanish border. Home is 643 miles away.

At the peage I'm told of petrol in a further 15 Km on this road, and we find it with some relief, as Black Betty's gauge is in the red zone. With the sun bleeding through the clouds and early mist, we hurry on towards San Sebastian Donastia, and all points south. Black Betty's again performing well, despite the slight intermittent misfire from somewhere in the ignition. When Graham checked the fluid levels last evening, he discovered we hadn't used a drop of anything since his last inspection, over five hundred miles before.

I take the wheel in the Pyrennees, the first time since our fateful stop in Okehampton. The roads are steep and winding, often taking us through tunnels, earily lit with an orange glow. I need to equal Graham's speed and progress, and I feel nervous, apprehensive of the road conditions and not particularly comfortable. My tendency is to hug the centre of the road, and Graham advises me more than once to shift position or risk collision. In short, my confidence in the driving seat doesn't match Graham's. I sense he feels the same. Is he genuflecting from respect for a catholic country, or out of real fear?

I prefer the passenger seat and we agree that Graham will make better time in this early part of the journey where it's of the essence. My role will be to deal with the administrative kerfuffle, the péages, border controls, hotel booking, navigation and translation. Also, to start the audio visual record, and take notes on the Dictaphone, so that a reminder of our amazing adventure can be compiled in the fullness. I effectively become, on this day, the Alan Whicker, or perhaps the Michael Palin in the passenger seat. Graham will stay at the wheel until Tarifa, on auto pilot, for mile upon mile of monotonous roads. This will ensure that our safety, our friendship and our underwear remain intact and unscathed.

In Spain the rules change. I'm asked for passport and other ID in support of credit card payment for the petrol. The French were much more relaxed. The Spaniards give warning of the distance to the next petrol station, which is a comfort denied in France. The scenery changes too. And the weather. And as we plunge through provincial Spain it appears to change quickly. Long winding tunnels snake through the Pyrennees and we emerge into cloudscapes of snowcapped mountains and mist. Rustic settlements cuddle the hillsides. It's picture postcard stuff, but in the microclimate of Black Betty we huddle in overcoats around the heater. It's sub-zero outside.

Victoria-Gasteiz is shrouded in fog. Or is it low cloud? Anyway we can't see much, and with no indication of what's the right way we charge ahead, past the casino and the swimming pool, flumes ghostly in the gloom. I'm relieved to spot the sign for Burgos and the A1.

Burgos, where the Generalissimo set up headquarters during the civil war. Capital of the ancient kingdom of Castille and home to the Cid. More importantly, for the Life Mechanics, the fog begins to lift and we can get a wiggle on. There's no fog in the tunnels, as Graham remarks, or snow. So if they were to build a tunnel all the way through Spain, unfavourable weather conditions could be dispensed with at a stroke.

Here the terrain's rugged and desolate. Scrub, tussocky grass, rocks. It's spaghetti western country. I expect Yul Brynner, on a horse, to gallop out of the parched landscape.

Now the fog has cleared, the plains of Burgos are bathed in sunlight. The fields are large, flat expanses of barley and wheat. But there are no houses. It's like Dartmoor in the sunshine. After Burgos it's the serious magnificence of the snow dusted Sierra de la Demanda that dominates the skyline before Madrid.

Madrid is mayhem. My vision, when preparing for this trip, was to do the grand tour. See some of the more famous sights and attractions of Europe. Soak up the culture. Here, I thought, we could take in the cathedral and the bullring, linger at one or two friendly bodegas. The reality is madness. We race along with the maniacal traffic, chased and hassled at breakneck speed with no real idea of the right direction. Another landscape, this time one of office blocks, industrial grade skyscrapers. Over flyovers, through grey underpasses, we go with the flow, hardly daring to step out of line. I'm so glad Graham's in the driving seat and appearing to enjoy this dodgem insanity.

The mayhem seems to stop as suddenly as it began. We're on the road to Cordoba. It's flat now, the mountains and the madness behind us.

La Mancha. No sign of the man, but we do see a sign to "Castille La Mancha" and three windmills on a hill in the near distance.

"Shall we have a tilt at those Gray?"

"How do you tilt in a Cherokee Jeep?"
"Not sure."
"Think we'll give it a miss then."

We stop just beyond Valdepeñas for petrol and consult the map. It's gone four o'clock and time to look for a suitable place for the night. We've achieved the target of Santa Cruz de Mudela. Graham's special measuring device was seven miles out. It starts to rain. The first rain in Spain and it is indeed falling mainly on the plain.

Descending from the mountainous regions and plateaux, it's undeniably warmer here, the vegetation more fertile and green. Rich loamy soil. The only animals, the large plywood black bulls that someone has erected, presumably to remind us we are indeed in Spain.

Andujar is a nondescript town, a provincial capital about as far as one can get from the coast. I have no idea whether it'll be suitable, but we've travelled over 500 miles. It's time for a break. We circle the roundabout and drive straight to the only visible hotel, the plush Del Val.

This is where I found how lacking is my Spanish. The Maître d'Hotel had no English at all. This was not a coastal resort. Now, I know the word for butter, and could, at a pinch, find my way to the station. Probably.

"Try 'Muchas gracias penis', suggested Graham helpfully, "I think it means 'Thanks a lot, cock'. I was going to learn Spanish before we left, but I couldn't get the operation on the NHS."

"Operation?"

"Yes, you have to have 5 mm snipped off your tongue."

We booked into a comfortable and spacious oak lined twin at the Hotel Del Val with some elaborate sign language, neat footwork and meaningful gestures. Black Betty was parked outside our ground floor window, where we could keep an eye on her.

Looking for somewhere other than the hotel to eat, we strolled into what appeared to be the centre of Andujar. A Sunday evening in Spain's Dunstable. The people were in a strange kind of pagan holiday mood. Children played around a bonfire in the middle of a shopping precinct, reminiscent of how post war British children used to play on bombsites. Adults walked, quite aimlessly, chatting, drinking, idling the time, celebrating Sunday in their way. However, Andujar didn't feel empathic to we men of La Mancha. Neither of us felt particularly safe. So we returned after a short and fruitless search for an eaterie, to the hotel.

A dinner of entrecote steaks. And brandy, vast quantities of the amber nectar, in goldfish bowls. The last I recall of this long and uneventful day is clambering onto Black Betty's roof in the dead of night, very drunk, to plant the Spanish wish bone in a tree top.

DAY FOUR
LITTLE BRITAIN

Castanets snap and crackle in my brain. The staccato step of a flamenco dancer, hot and heavy, clatters through my dream, bringing me to the brink of consciousness. Is this some strange and ethnic welcome? Have the local worthies gathered to celebrate our coming? I don't think so. It's last night's villainous Spanish brandy come back to haunt me. I feel sick. And disorientated.

Graham has dealt better with the alcohol. He's up, dressed and busily buffing his highly polished head.

"I've checked the levels in Black Betty. Absolutely no change again. I checked the plug leads too. One was slightly loose. Rattled a bit. Could have caused the misfire. It wouldn't have been helping anyway. So I've crimped it on the plug end. We'll soon know if it helps. You OK Keith? Look a bit green."

I'm not sure I can handle all this technical information, through the clack of the castanets. I drag myself from my pit, and after a cup of coffee (I can't face the rice crispies) we throw our overnight bags in the back and are off to Cordoba. It's a misty, damp and cool morning, but a very busy one with the early Monday traffic of Andujar.

Graham's at the wheel. With the plug lead tightened, the ignition problem seems solved. We reach the outskirts of Cordoba at quarter to nine. Weather still misty (early February, I am reminded), but visibility not bad. Heading south now for Malaga on the A45, a bit like the

Northampton bypass. Our first traffic jam. Probably the Cordoban rush hour.

Suddenly the mist clears, as if somebody has lifted a blind. A clear blue day, Spain is open for business and we head for Malaga and the south coast. Yesterday's target was exceeded, and we're more than half way through Spain. Here, in the south, the country's more fertile, and we've left most of the craggy desert behind. Olive groves and lemon trees, fields of young vines line the road.

En route we had many discussions to pass the time over the last couple of days. We set the world to rights on matters historical, linguistic, socio-political, religious and the immigration issue. Perhaps this is the best way for world leaders to settle their differences, sit in the front of a Cherokee Jeep and drive through France and Spain. World peace and prosperity would surely be achieved at a stroke. The pleasant reverie is shattered by a tirade of outrageous abuse from Graham, not directed at me, rather at the unfortunate local Spaniard who apparently hasn't yet understood his superior driving technique. Tangibly shocked at the emotional outburst, Black Betty's misfire returns, she labours to overtake the offending vehicle.

The countryside becomes more Spanish traditional and picturesque. Montilla village, a rainbow of adobe and spires perched on a hillside. By ten we're back on the dual carriageway, a two lane hardtop, thirty miles from Malaga with the imposing mountain Carmano Alto dead ahead. But generally it's much flatter than that experienced yesterday. The weather's changed yet again. Large scowling rain clouds blow over the mountain with a spattering of rain. It looks like we're in for a heavy storm. As we approach the coast it becomes suddenly mountainous again. Ten miles before Malaga we're speeding through a tunnel as I catch the first glimpse of the Mediterranean. The signs are to Algeciras, Torremelinos and Cadiz, places I've only seen in tourist brochures. We turn onto the coast road.

Malaga is classic Spanish seaside. Heavy traffic delays us again, but the weather's brightening. The sun glints off the sea and Graham's head. People are in holiday mood, even at this time of the year in this busy seaport and coastal resort. But Graham's unimpressed ("They're all arseholes!")

By eleven we're passing through Benalmedina, where my father died, on holiday, 15 years ago.

Our last petrol stop before Africa is in Marbella. It's a glorious day. The sun beats down on a sea sparkling with the proverbial azure blue as we ride the coastal highway at the western extremity of the Med.

Now we're on the Costa Del Crime, where the east London wide boys drip gold on the golf course, and their wives and girl friends, bottle blonde, bottle bronzed, bask by the pool at their mansions in the hills.

At noon precisely we round a bend and emerge through a cutting in the coastal hills. In front of us is the Rock. I recognise it instantly, though I've only seen it on postage stamps.

"It's quite big, 'aint it?"
"Bigger than on the stamps, that's for sure."
"Yeah, you wouldn't get that in a letter box."
"Can't see any monkeys."
"They're apes, in point of fact," says Graham, "And I don't think we're close enough."

We turn off the road to Algeciras and head for La Linea de la Conception, better known to the world as Gibraltar. But not to the Spanish, who hate the fact that it's there and steadfastly refuse to accept it exists. There are no signs to "Gibraltar". The clouds bank up ominously over the Rock on our approach.

We enter La Linea, a modest Spanish frontier town with Arabic influence. Africa's only nine miles away and palm trees line the streets of single storey pastel coloured adobes. It's as if Gibraltar's rock, thrusting dramatically out of the Mediterranean a few feet away, is invisible to the Spaniard.

Border control. 12.25, and we're in Gibraltar, the Rock on our left. Border staff are friendly and, without exception, very British. I feel instantly at ease. Immediately everything's in English, and I sense we're expected to follow suit. As I dig out our meagre sterling reserves, Graham drives straight into a multi storey and parks Black Betty overlooking the Rock. We take the lift to the ground floor and emerge through two sliding glass portals into......

Oxford Street. In the '60s. Dorothy Perkins. James Walker. Mac Fisheries. Tesco's and the Co-op. We're in Little Britain, by the sea. A man in his forties, swarthy, balding, mustachioed, hurries by pushing a sack barrow into Timpsons.

"Por favor, signor, " I venture, "donde esta la Post Office?"

The Road To Banjul

"Ee, lad, do I look Spanish? It's up this street, about fifty yards, between Barclay's bank and MacDonalds."

David's lived here for twenty five years. He wouldn't live anywhere else, he says. The residents are furiously loyal and patriotic, to Britain. Pay is good, and the living easy. We both feel ridiculously patriotic in reply, as perhaps Brits abroad are prone to do, while grumbling like fuck about the place when we're at home.

It's easy to find our way about. There are signs to "city centre", "coach terminal", "Europa Point" and "Post Office". We take a look around Gibraltar town, which is largely one main street with lanes running from it. Just before Parliament Lane (reminiscent, faintly, of Georgian England, three corner hats, coffee shops etc.) we duck into the post office (imposing porticoes, red double pillar box). We send post cards to the dearly beloveds:

"Whatho, Tub. Just popping down to the Gambia to visit the natives, and thought we'd drop in on dear old Gib. So here we are, don't you know old girl, pip pip. Splendid weather, hotels most accommodating, and the locals reasonably friendly, give or take the odd kerfuffle and broughaha with the driving fraternity. Cross the straits on the morrow. Toodle pip, see you on the return to Blighty! Pug."

Outside the post office I meet one member of another Challenge team, a Welsh lad. They're also front runners, in a twenty-year-old Shogun. They arrived yesterday.

Back in Black Betty, out of the car park, through passport control we leave Little Britain. Now looking for Algeciras and Tarifa, the ferry port and this day's target.

Our hotel is some 6 miles short of the port on the main coastal highway. It's called the Hotel Restaurant Meson de Sancho, and we must keep our eyes peeled. We've been warned by the Welshman (and the Roadbook) that hotel reception is on the left, but the car park and rooms for Challenge participants, on the right. Down the middle of the road is a continuous double white line which vehicles are absolutely forbidden to cross. The police are vigilant in enforcement of this safety regulation, as the road itself is fast and dangerous. To cross the road in a vehicle incurs a hefty penalty (100Euro or £70). One unfortunate and ill advised Challenge Team were caught offending yesterday.

Forewarned, we approach on the fast and winding road. I'm tense, alert, every nerve in my finely tuned body sensitised to catching the sign for the hotel on the left, the car park on the right. I spot the reception, and bark triumphantly at Graham,

"There it is, quick, pull over!"
"Where's the car park?"
"We've just gone past it."
"Shit."
"Fuck."
"Bollocks."
"Your turn."

The car park, brimming with Challenge vehicles, and the "Meson de Sancho" is fast dwindling behind us. Our colleagues waved cheerily as we glided by. We race on towards the port of Tarifa.

Now we're looking for a turning point or a break in this blasted double white line. We pass through two wind farms, sails sweeping majestically to attention.

Six miles later we reach Tarifa port. We attempt a turn here, before we reach the Med. We're helpfully warned by a frantic blast on the horn of an oncoming car, that to turn here is also a beheading offence, so we eventually find a quiet alley in Tarifa, Graham spins Black Betty in an angry three point turn, and we commence the long journey back to Meson de Sancho.

Back through the wind farms we hasten. Six miles. Now we're on the wrong side for the car park. Graham gives our colleagues a cheery wave as we pass. Several miles later (just before Gibraltar) we're treated to a roundabout. We return, slowly, and eventually swing into the car park. After our twenty mile sojourn to cross the road, legally, we find room for Black Betty beside the other Challenge cars.

Stay at this hotel has been arranged and prepaid by the Disorganisers, this being the first mustering point. Here we are to pick up our specially negotiated tickets for tomorrow's ferry. We've travelled a mere 265 miles on this last stage of the European experience, most of them in Tarifa.

To book into the hotel we had to cross the road, on foot, burdened with luggage, in traffic, on a blind bend, at speed. Because we missed the cunningly disguised subway tunnel helpfully placed for those without a suicidal disposition. We were fortunate to secure one of the few rooms remaining on the other side of the road. So we then transported our luggage to the room, taking our lives in our hands once more, because we still hadn't noticed, hidden amongst the bougainvillea and japonica, said subway. The room was adequate, quite pleasant really, but unheated and chilly.

We met some of the other Challengers and their vehicles in the car park at the Meson de Sancho as they tinkered under the bonnet and attached their Challenge door plates. A 2cv, two more Cherokee Jeeps, a Renault 4, a Volvo, a VW Beetle, a Sierra, and a Renault Trafic. There were teams from Holland, Wales and Spain. About thirty people in all, one with his wife, son and daughter-in-law in the same car.

The Life Mechanics got technical with Black Betty, getting her ready for Africa. I held the laminated door plates while Graham wielded the sticky tape. After all, we'd need to look authentic.

Satisfied with our work, we returned to the hotel under protection of the secret subway, discovered by following a couple of our colleagues through the undergrowth.

Dinner was adequate, if not sumptuous, and it was followed by an evening of carousing and merriment for the Challengers, sort of a celebration for completing the European leg and crossing the road. I was only interested in getting the ferry tickets, and when the agent arrived, I joined the scrum.

We retired early, leaving the bulk of the party to souse the night away on the obligatory beers, while we took to our beds in anticipation of an early start for Africa.

1399 miles away the sun set over Long Lane Farm.

DAY FIVE
A SHORT GUIDE TO CAMPING IN AFRICA

We awoke at six to the gong on Graham's mobile phone. A regular morning routine had established itself within the Black Betty travelling household. The usual ablutions completed in tandem, we took our first Malarone tablets and made an unbreakable rule that swallowing our medication for the next three weeks would be a first priority on arising.

Breakfast at the Meson de Sancho was served from eight o'clock across Death Valley. Although paid for in the original deposit, we decided to forego this particular luxury rather than risk life and limb on the road or in the subway. Our intention this morning was to make for Tarifa and the earliest ferry, thus taking the lead in Africa that we hadn't, apparently, in Europe. We threw our overnight stuff into Black Betty and made off.

A three quarter moon and the north star wink tantalisingly from a chilly indigo sky. The ghostly three armed structures of the wind farm loom in the headlights as we etch our cautious way along the six mile winding double white lined hardtop. In half an hour we're at the port and start to form an orderly queue, in good time for what we believe to be the first ferry to depart, at eight. Two Challenge teams have beaten us to the draw, but we're confident there'll be plenty of room. I'm cheerful and optimistic, pleased to have made it, unbruised, to the southernmost tip of mainland Europe.

Staff at the port were friendly, and told us the ferry would be leaving "in about half an hour". With luck and a following wind we'd be in Tangier for breakfast. Another day, another continent.

Gradually the queue lengthened and the day brightened. Some of the other Challenge Teams from the Meson de Sancho arrived and took their places in the queue, but most were sleeping off last night's beer, having no intention of getting on anything earlier than the eleven o'clock ferry. We would achieve our goal of staying ahead of the crowd. The next nine miles were free in terms of petrol, but expensive in terms of travel. The ferry ticket, at discounted rates, had cost 100 Euros, about £70.

At eight sharp the queue of cars snaked its way through passport control. Some were heading for Fes and the Rif mountains, some directly for Casablanca for Mauritanian visas and all stations south. Some decided to take the middle road to Meknes. We still hadn't resolved on our direction beyond Tangier, the primary concern being to land on the African continent today.

The gleaming catamaran sat in the harbour under a cobalt blue sky, the three quarter moon still visible amongst sparse mackerel clouds. Tarifa port felt faintly African, as did we.

With Black Betty safely stashed on the spacious car deck, we spent the crossing amongst new found friends in the plush and sparkling restaurant. I ate a baguette de l'omo (bacon and cheese roll). Graham selected the dish of the day, which appeared to be a sausage and custard croissant. The breakfast ensemble was completed with mugs of steaming coffee. Naturally social animals, in the relative safety of the ferry saloon we struck up a conversation with Team Two in a Four, Ian and Dan, who were making this epic journey in an ageing, but charming, powder blue Renault 4. They opted for the middle road to Meknes on leaving Tangier.

The ferry finally cast off at twenty past nine. We had in fact breakfasted in the port in Spanish waters, despite my romantic aspiration of egg and bacon in Rick's Café Americain. Ah well, as time goes by.

As we crossed the Straits we chatted to Ian and Dan. Both obviously love their job restoring clocks, and we listened intently to their stories, which appealed particularly to Graham who was contemplating a career change.

The crossing to Tangier was uneventful. We enjoyed clear weather, calm seas and friendly conversation. On disembarkation, in front of Black Betty stood a large Iveco van towing an old Abbey Norfolk caravan, and sporting the Moroccan national flag. Was there a Moroccan team on board?

Black Betty set first wheel in Africa at 10.40 a.m. on Tuesday 6th. February. For Graham too, a first step on the dark continent.

Africa hit us like a hammer. The culture change was instant and dramatic. We had stood on Moroccan soil (or rather sand) for less than ten minutes and were fleeced twice. The first mistake was to leave the ferry without stamped disembarkation cards or a visa for the car. We were unceremoniously hauled (or rather "guided") back on to the ferry by a gentleman whom I mistook for a philanthropist, a native befriending strangers to his land. In fact, it seems, my kindly Samaritan's intentions were more mercenary than altruistic, and I parted with I don't know how much in loose Euros for the privilege of being marched back in disgrace.

Thus was the first impression of Tangier. A queue of cars shimmering in the heat of a strong North African sun. A crowd of people in confusingly different attire, some in the pale blue uniform and high peeked cap of the border police or customs control, some wearing dark blue fatigues and a semi official bearing. Others sported the jaunty djelaba and hood or fez of the proletariat. And everyone wanted to hustle. It was quite impossible to distinguish between official and hustler, street vendor and customs officer, secret police and, if there were any, innocent passer by. It was also impossible to gauge just how much to part with, whether one was expected to pay or receive a bribe, pay a compliment or hurl abuse.

The hustlers weren't backward in coming forward. This chap at my window wanted a gift, and seemed content with a busted radio and a broken mobile phone. Then he wanted a gift for his very good friend, who had to content himself with a cheap ball point pen. Others on the Challenge were persuaded to part with 10 Euro notes, or just a cigarette. It seemed there was no logic in what should be the size of the gift, or what one might expect to receive in return. One of the more experienced and hardened travellers refused to part with anything, and seemed to get away with it, (although Graham subsequently noticed that he had one flat tyre and a dent in his head). One "official", clearly expecting a tip of some magnitude, I advised not to lift his dahlias before May. He seemed, at least on the face of it, both impressed and satisfied with this horticultural tip.

The sun continued to blister down on the endless and inexplicable queue. We shed topcoats and donned lighter travel wear. Our hosts clearly understood we'd arrived from a cooler clime. A street vendor presented himself at my window and tried to peddle copper bangles which, he assured me, would be good for my rheumatism. When I remonstrated with the man, explaining I had as yet avoided this affliction, he blew a cloud of stinking cigarette smoke in my face. Africa had suddenly happened.

Every 15 minutes or so the car would move forward one length. The running boards and bonnet were laden with street vendors, seekers after baksheesh, officials purporting to direct us to yet further queues, engage us in amusing conversation or just get a look inside. The pressure was unremitting. The most effective method of dealing with the situation seemed to be to engage your own partner in some pointless nonsensical but never ending conversation, and refuse eye contact. Also to carry loose change, which few of us had at this stage, not quite having reached civilisation.

Some of the genuine, uniformed officials would interview arrivals in the queue outside, using Black Betty as a temporary desk to fill out forms. I found this disconcerting, and had to draw the line when officer Mohammed Jaroo placed his in-tray, stamp pad and desk tidy neatly on the bonnet, next to his name plate and silver ash tray.

An hour later, still in the queue, a djelaba clad individual persuaded me I needed one of his forms, and he began to complete it in a laboured Arabic script. This cost 10 Euros, and whether I needed it or not I was by now really too tired and hot to bother. So I parted with the necessary and studied the proffered form. It was a Kingdom of Morocco "Declaration d'admission temperaire de moyen de transport". Black Betty had her own visa to enter Morocco. Quite what I was supposed to do with it I had absolutely no idea, but placed it with the portfolio of documents.

I phoned Gilly at noon.

"Hello love, we're in Africa."
"Hang on. I'll get off the dance floor."
"Have you started Graham's car yet?"
"I couldn't this morning. It's covered in snow. About four inches."
"OK. Gray says would you clear the snow off and put the battery on charge. You'll find the charger and spanners in the workshop. Take care. It'll be heavy."
"OK. I'll use the sack barrow. Are you having a good time?"
"Up to now, yes, but we've been stuck in this fucking endless queue for hours. I'm running out of patience. And pens. Anything happening your end?"
"Not really. Steve Parkin has put an axe through his head."
"Did he mean to?"
"I don't think so. Anyway, he was saved by his cap. Must go. I like this one."

The Road To Banjul

Kenny Rogers and Dolly Parton. *Islands in the Stream.* My mind lingered there wistfully for a moment. Then it was back in Black Betty, sat in the stifling queue of cars in Tangier being pestered for yet another gift. We got out of the car from time to time and compared stories with our colleagues in the hot house, always keeping tight to the car in front, never knowing what to expect next.

As we drew closer to the exit, the great outdoors of Africa asserted itself. I was ordered from the car and taken with other members of the Challenge teams. With no inkling of what was about to transpire, we stood at an open door and were interrogated by uniformed police. Passports were taken and examined in great detail, then stamped. We were frisked. Two were taken away and strip searched. I was spared that particular indignity, but we were all "invited" to contribute once again to what I imagine is some global West African benevolent fund. I got out of there a couple of cigarettes and a ball point pen lighter. Team Norfolk 'N Chance didn't fare so well. They were fleeced for a "fine" of 20 Euros because they were apparently under age. Nobody seemed to know what the proper age should be, but Graham and I were obviously over it.

After the body search and interrogation, we were escorted back to our vehicles. Black Betty had meanwhile been subjected to her own perfunctory search. Graham had struck a lifelong friendship with a fat, greasy faced and toothy non official, who was regaling him with stories of his family and life in Morocco. As the smoke from the Moroccan's stinking cigarette curled lustily about Graham's features, he wiped the sputum from his face and introduced me. Ahmed was delighted with the mobile phone I gave him, but did request further gifts for his friends, close relatives and camel. I promised him more gifts on our return.

"We shall bring gifts to Ahmed and all his friends and their children, and their childrens' children. We shall be this way again", I lied, rather convincingly I thought.

"Shukran, Ahmed. Ssalamu 'lekum. Bessalama. Fin yimkin I nkn bshklit?"

"Bugger me Gray, what was that?"

"Oh, just something I picked up."

Finally we emerge into the sunshine. We've travelled barely 13 miles since Tarifa. Now everywhere's truly foreign, and suddenly so. Arabic road signs, with only the major routes bearing a gesture to Europeanness. The architecture's quintessentially Arabic, most buildings in blue and pink. Palm trees line the baking mid day streets, and a faintly orange hue dresses the air. Perhaps that's why it's called Tangier, after the tangerine air, I muse. Djelabas and their inhabitants hurry about, dodging the furious and completely undisciplined traffic. We join the throng, scuttling twice around a roundabout frantically seeking signs for anywhere recognisable. When I see the sign for Rabat, I scream at Graham to head for it. We only discovered much later that the first stop is just before the roundabout where an ATM dispenses dhiram to the wise and travel weary. We have to make do with Euros and poor exchange rates for some time, but hey, we're free of the nightmare that Tangier port holds for the car borne.

We head for Rabat, the capital, the first place name we recognise, and for no more logical reason than that. This is a new driving experience for Graham, which he seems to take to quickly. I sit beside him in Alan Whicker mode.

On the outskirts of Tangier the traffic becomes a little less frenetic, and we can relax in the suburbs. Blocks of flats, a population sitting under the shade of trees and face veils, carts towed by motorcycles.

Scruffy sheep on rocky ground. Traffic, police, goats, whistles, subdued mayhem.

Exiting Tangier into grassland, lush and undulating. Field boundaries are of large and ferocious looking cactus. Small flocks of shabby sheep and lambs, each with its own shepherd guiding them to the next bit of pasture, making no effort to keep them from straying onto the road. Herds of goats too, each with a goatherd. We pass over the dust dry bed of the river Hasha, splashing through its few desultory puddles. Women work the fields with hand tools, on their knees or bending double. Boney arsed cattle wander aimlessly.

At the first petrol stop in Africa we encountered Morocco's take on fast food. A trestle table in front of the pumps bearing lamb and vegetable tajines which bubbled gently over charcoal and smelled delicious, fragrant.

We nearly did a runner, by accident. I bought four bottles of water from the service station shop, and understood the petrol was included. When we were chased across the forecourt by a dusky saracen bearing a leather satchel, credit card machine and scimitar, we figured perhaps something was amiss. Graham suggested we stop when the scimitar narrowly shaved my right ear and the credit card machine bounced off the windscreen. It was time to pay for the petrol. Later I realised how fortunate we'd been for Graham's initiative to stop and make amends. Doing a runner from a petrol station in northern Morocco is probably contraindicated. Visions of incarceration in a stinking Tangier jail did not appeal.

Back on the road. Larache is a conglomeration of concrete block houses painted white with windows, shutters and doors in pale blue, often with sheep and goats in an enclosed garden. A typical example of modern Moroccan life away from the centres. People sit around in the afternoon under trees, drinking mint tea with a purpose. We leave the motorway and head for Meknes, by a flock of sheep grazing in an orange grove.

At Souk-el-abhdu-rab, the road is much slower, traffic mainly donkey powered. Donkey rickshaws, people snoozing in the back, a souk market, cycle mechanics knocking bits of iron about on the roadside. Dusty people and shops. Trash and litter. A provisions lorry with stacks of passengers on the roof, some wearing djelabas and face masks against the dust, apparently all going to market. The verges are festooned with cactus bush. Unfeasibly laden donkeys and carts carrying people. Donkey foals. Donkeys drawing ploughshares, partnered with a horse, donkeys transporting goods and equipment. More donkeys. Donkeys, donkeys everywhere.

A sign to Meknes on a bunker, a remnant of World War Two. Perhaps the Moroccans learnt to build their houses in the European style, using the bunker as a model.

A large pottery market on the left is selling tajines, mountains of them. The stalls along the roadside seem unattended but are stocked with an amazing quantity and variety of pots and terracotta wares. Surely we have found the tajine mecca. "Tajines R Us".

Now, I'm under instructions from Gilly to take home a tajine, the pointy capped three part cooking dish of these parts. I negotiate with an elderly Berber woman and her sweet little granddaughter. With my well honed skills I achieve a real bargain on the tajine front. Probably. They pose for photographs, and I give the little girl a necklace and a ring. The tajine sits obediently on the back seat, wrapped in wads of newspaper. I wonder whether it will survive the next two thousand miles.

I take the wheel after "Tajines R Us". Within a dozen miles we pass many more tajine emporia, "Tajines-U-Like", "Tajine City", "Tajine-a-go-go" etc. But it's while I'm in the driving seat that I see an expiring donkey, having a heart attack in the shafts of its cart, the owner kicking it in an attempt to get it up again. The scene upsets me for the rest of the day. It haunts me now. I'm soon back in the passenger seat and resume my role as roving reporter.

Animals in general are not at their best in Morocco. Often abused and neglected, dogs seem to be treated more or less as vermin. Goats are meals on legs. Both travel the highway indiscriminately.

Sidi Kacem. A run down, grubby settlement of sheep goats and donkeys, carts, crops, and people doing nothing in particular. Ruts in the road as unpredictable as the drivers. It's Tuesday afternoon in Sidi Kacem. We're pulled by the police for disrespect to a stop sign. There's no stop sign that we can see (viz. Halt at Major Road Ahead!) even when it's pointed out. We get away with a stern look and a wag of the finger. No fine, no bribe. No incarceration. No sign either.

Five o'clock and eighteen miles short of Meknes. There are ibis and stork on the roadside. We're aware from the Road Book that to the south of Meknes is a campsite with plenty of space, electricity, flush toilets, running water, hot and cold showers, a restaurant and provisions shop, with secure off road parking. It seems a good time to be making plans to stop for the night, and try out the camping gear, rather than search for a hotel in the foothills of the Rif Mountains. Graham spots the Iveco in Meknes, and we follow it to the campsite. It's six o'clock. We've managed a meagre 181 miles since the late departure from Tangier.

We pull into "Camping Nationale d'Agdal". It is, encouragingly, provided with a security gate, though it's not clear whether this is intended to keep patrons safe or keep them in.

As the sun sets we find a large and very empty field, surrounded on all sides by mature trees. We pull off, through the trees, and Graham parks Black Betty in a corner, away from noise and interruption.

Now, here is the promised guide to camping in Africa. Take heed, if you intend to try Africa al fresco, for it is based on the experience of we two seasoned travellers.

A Short Guide to Camping in Africa. The do's and don'ts.

1. Don't.
2. If you are compelled by medical emergency or financial necessity to camp in Africa, do take a tent. And whatever you do, take it out of the cellophane and test it before you go. This will avoid your friends asking you, in a testily smug sort of way, "Have you tested this equipment?" and you having to reply, sheepishly, "Well, not as such."
3. If you think the tent you have acquired at a not-to-be-missed bargain price may be a little snug for two men, and either of you is a touch homophobic, be prepared, buy a second tent.
4. Don't buy it from a charity shop for £1.
5. If you have ignored 4 above, do at least check your purchase. Take it out of the bag, for instance, and look at it. This will help avoid the "Have you tested this equipment?" routine for a second time.
6. If you have ignored 4 and 5 above, you are not an eight year old wolf cub with a death wish and your second tent is also of the bijou variety, take courage. You can probably get in it if you adopt the foetal position.

We pitched both virgin tents, inflated the air beds with the compressor, and by seven o'clock were camped. As the muezzin called the holy to prayer (we gave this a miss) it was time to eat.

A swift circuit around the camp site revealed a complete lack of the promised facilities. There was no restaurant. If there was a shop it was carefully concealed and most definitely not open for business. The toilet and shower block did exist, as we stumbled across it in the failing light. But the toilets were of the Moroccan hole in the floor variety and running water, of any temperature, was distinctly absent. As was electricity or any other form of power or lighting. We came to a very quick conclusion that this would not be an ideal location to either eat or ablute. An early morning departure was yet again indicated, as was an immediate search for somewhere to eat.

Team Hugh Jarse had also chosen to overnight at this camp, but even with their far superior rig (the large Iveco, touring caravan, drinks on ice and fully stocked fridge) Tony and Harry decided to join us in the search for a restaurant. We soon discovered what passed for the site office, enshrouded in gloom and lit by one candle strategically perched in a saucer on the desk. In the shadows, a figure lying on a sofa covered with coats and blankets. This was the gate keeper, smartly uniformed as if a police officer, and as I peered through the twilight he raised himself to attention. In broken French I asked the fellow for directions to the nearest eating house. He turned out to be more than friendly, and without any demand for baksheesh came to the desk and drew a schematic map of south Meknes and the Royal Palace, part of which, he explained, housed a creditable restaurant frequented by himself and his colleagues in the force.

Meknes is the ancient capital of Morocco. It houses the summer palace, where the King stays when the weather is unbearable in Rabat. The palace is vast. Apart from the usual accommodations, it comprises its own gymnasium, leisure complex and an eighteen hole golf course, for use by the King and his retinue. We set off, following the policeman's map and directions, closely followed by Hugh Jarse.

We marched through a fabled landscape of massive fortifications. The yellow plastered walls that surrounded this vast imperial complex were quite thirty feet high and ten feet thick. For a couple of miles we walked in subdued wonder, through labyrinthine tunnels, under arches and along wide pavemented roads, until we rounded a corner where the restaurant should've been. But there was no sign of it. No flashing neon welcome, no highly coloured placard, nothing. Noticing some movement behind a modest little door in the side of yet another plaster edifice, I knocked. We were instantly welcomed and invited to eat at the Palais Didi.

With Team Hugh Jarse we shared a superior meal of tajines (mine was prime fillet steak and juniper berries) pastillas, soup and Moroccan mint tea. Our host Sakina, a charming, well spoken (English, French, Arabic) native Moroccan, showed us around the 17th. century guest house, a splendid Moroccan masterpiece worthy of the *Arabian Nights*. The entire house (we would refer to it as a palace) was adorned in marble, mosaic and sculpted woods, hung with coloured drapes and carpets. There were sunken baths, mosaic floors, five exotic suites and six sumptuous rooms. In the middle, a covered courtyard where a fountain gently played. Marvellous and spectacular terraces topped the palace. Its halls and passages led to the old Medina and the Royal Golf Course. It's surrounded by the most impressive remains of the imperial palace, through which, it seems, we had been walking for the last half hour.

The long walk home was uneventful, but we did marvel at our luck in finding the finest place to dine in the whole of Morocco almost by chance and with the help of a map drawn by candlelight by a policeman in the dark.

Back at camp I crawled into my child's beach shelter. I pride myself on my mental dexterity and physical flexibility in climbing into that tent. I managed to wriggle into my Superman pyjamas, and sleeping bag, and by adopting the advised foetal position dozed fitfully for a couple of hours, my ear pressed to the speaker of the wind up radio. This, to dull the senses and blank out the sound of the rhythmic synchronised snoring of Graham in his tent and the two Portuguese Challengers who had camped, in our absence, hard against our small encampment, in one corner of an otherwise empty five acre field.

As I tried to sleep I felt ever so slightly sorry for myself, with the awfulness of Moroccan radio, the cramp in my joints from the prolonged foetal position, the incessant snoring from my colleagues, the gentle drip of condensation from the unventilated tent, like Chinese water torture, on my head.

At five o'clock prompt, the muezzin began once again to call the holy to prayer.

DAY SIX
KIDNAPPED!

The incessant rain within my tiny quarters made it impossible to even attempt to doze.

"Keith, are you awake?" enquired Graham from the depths of his slightly larger accommodation.
"Not yet."
"Is it damp inside your tent?"
"Soaking," I replied, "but it's nice and dry outside".

We got up, yet again before dawn had properly broken, and before the muezzin commenced his dolorous wail, which would put paid to any last vestige of a hope or expectation of sleep. We broke camp quickly in the pre-dawn gloom, bailed out the tents and put them back unfolded, in the hope they might dry out after a day on the road. In fact, neither of us being particularly of the camping persuasion, we resolved to avoid sleeping al fresco for the rest of the trip. The tents were never erected again. For the time being they'd serve to conceal from prying eyes the more valuable of Black Betty's contents.

Neither of us could face a cold shower or shave in the dark, cheerless communal ablution block, less still the precarious operation of using a Moroccan lavatory in the gloom without instructions and copious assistance. So with no ablutions at all save for taking a pee behind a tree, I planted the Moroccan wishbone and we made for the gate.

I roused the security guard gently and helped him from the pile of coats and blankets in which he'd secreted himself from the arctic cold. We paid, by candlelight, for one night's stay at the opulent *Camping Nationale d'Agdal*. He unlocked the heavy steel gate and saw us on our way, clutching the pack of Marlboro Reds I passed him for his trouble.

Grubby, unshaven and looking like a pair of derelicts, we're on the road again, looking for signs for today's target, Marrakech. On the outskirts of Meknes, and before we plunge straight into the unknown, we stop to tank up with petrol and ask directions. Service station staff are, unaccountably, among the most helpful of all Moroccans, and this without demand or expectation of reward. We intended making for El-Hajeb and Azrou, continuing on the road on which we'd entered Meknes. From Azrou the route appears, on the map, uncomplicated, though we shall miss Fes, and my one opportunity to buy one. However, the triumvirate of pump attendants seem more doubtful, scratch heads, study us in mild amusement. A better route would be the motorway to Rabat (which we should also miss) and Casablanca (romantic but, according to the guidebooks, eminently missable). This will get us to Marrakech before dark.

The motorway's quite different from the country roads of yesterday where it was important to pay attention to a host of obstacles; dead cats, stray dogs, errant sheep and goats, dying donkeys, children, madcap drivers, potholes, more potholes, undisclosed railway lines, street vendors, more potholes and people who just seem not to want to live much longer. Whilst the motorway tolls will cost a few dhiram, we can certainly eat up the miles. Not yet dawn, we peer into the crossed beams of Black Betty's headlights, dazzling oncomers. I forgot to fit beam converters to the lights. I'm pondering the doubtful legality of our unconventional beams when we're overtaken by a car bearing no lights at all. A bicycle speeds by on the "hard shoulder".

Shortly after the bicycle we're overtaken by dense fog, and a feeling of the unreal. Looming out of the soupy murk in the pre dawn light, pedestrians stroll unconcernedly on the fast lane, amble on the hard shoulder. An entire family, mother, father, three children and a couple of goats shuffle across the central reservation, like a group of unrelated zombies.

In the early light the mist clears. The region appears quite fertile, with cereal crops, oats barley and maize in large quantities. We pass orange groves, the scenery becoming almost bucolic, the traffic, agricultural. The more mechanised farmers drive tractors with trailers, the less affluent sticking to the medieval donkey cart. In full daylight, with the sun rising steadily behind us, we overtake children on their way to school. Some glance up and wave.

We skirt Rabat, the modern capital, a large conurbation of concrete flats, houses and shops. The streets are hot, dry and dusted with a yellow pallor and the locals take to the shade of lime trees that line the avenues. Drivers stop, without warning, on the hard shoulder of what we still assume to be motorway, to chat with friends and acquaintances. Rabat seems a relaxed city, a city in repose. There's no sense of urgency. Suddenly, we're overtaken at speed by a tiny Peugeot carrying at least five large djelaba clad arabs, smoking cigars. A coach pulls up in front. The driver alights and we wait patiently for him to pee on the verge. Moroccan motorways, it seems, are often motorways in name only.

At Al Jasira's "Aire de Repos" (service station and restaurant) we stop to check Black Betty's fluid levels, reduce our own, and see about a bureau de change. The search for currency is in vain, but we can breakfast here.

"Try the mint tea Graham, it'll go well with the Malarone."

"No thanks, you're all right. I'll stick to coffee. Those little pancake things were OK though."

"They're crêpes."

"Oh, I thought they were OK. I could do with a bog right now."

"They're down there, to the right. (*pointing*). Not up to yer French standard, I'm afraid, but there is a choice of Moroccan or European."

"Do I need any dosh?"

"Don't think so. I didn't. If the attendant's there he might want a tip. Tell him not to wipe his arse on broken glass. He wasn't about when I went. Just walk in."

He leaves me to pay for the crêpes. But he's back in moments.

"Got caught by the bog police. He wants dhiram for paper. Got any euros?"

Our second offence on Moroccan soil.

Back on the road we veer left and inland at Mohammeddia, skirting the dubious delights of Casablanca. Although still on a motorway, the roadscape is medieval. An overturned lorry, a lone donkey tethered to a post, eating balefully out of a plastic carrier.

At El Jadida on the Atlantic coast, another, walking in circles drawing water from a well. Palms, municipal gardens and a pleasure beach, breakers crashing on the sand. The vile stink of a dustcart.

Heading inland now, southward bound for Marrakech. This time the smell is the familiar and friendly aroma of pigs. Most farmers here have a few cows, perhaps 25 or 30 sheep, sometimes a few goats and two or three working donkeys, maybe a horse. But we never see the pigs.

As we approach the High Atlas mountains, suddenly the land changes to arid and stony with rocky outfalls, little or no topsoil. It begins to resemble the Morocco I've read about. Twenty miles from Marrakech the roads are awful, and it becomes difficult to avoid ruts. We traverse a desolate landscape, a foretaste of the Sahara. A flat muddy river estuary on its outskirts is the prelude to Marrakech.

Marrakech punches with a suddenness that's shocking and a liveliness unexpected after many miles of languorous villages. We've no idea of the direction we should head in our quest for a hotel. Traffic hurtles this way and that, mainly cars and mopeds, but still the ubiquitous donkey carts. We've decided to overnight in Marrakech, though it's still early in the day, as civilisation appears to be sparse on our chosen route until Agadir. Marrakech might also be worth looking at with tourist eyes. My vision is of gleaming palaces, souk markets, idly wandering through the kasbah. Graham drives Black Betty around the main city, doing his utmost to appear as if we know where we're going, seasoned travellers, men of the world. I spot a little road where we can pull in and consult the map. So what is about to happen is largely my fault.

As we stopped in the side road a man emerged from the front door of what appeared to be, coincidentally, a lettings agency. I stepped from the safety of Black Betty and enquired, in my best broken French, as a stranger in town, where the hotels might be found.

"Look no further", he exclaimed (or at least that's what he appeared to be exclaiming) "For I am a lettings agent. Follow me and I shall find you a place to stay."

I couldn't believe our luck. We'd driven from nowhere, foreigners in a strange land, into the heart of a bustling city, and bumped quite fortuitously into the manager of the premier lettings agency in the whole of Marrakech, a man who was clearly going to tend to our every need and whim, and this from no motive of personal commercial gain but merely from the spirit of altruism and bonhomie between nations. My faith in human nature and in the residents of Marrakech was restored. Probably.

Mohammed, for that was the name of our saviour in Marrakech, promptly disappeared, and I reported back to Graham on our good fortune. He was clearly thrilled and most impressed with my quickly established rapport with the locals. As I explained to Graham, this man Mohammed was about to take us somewhere, what for I'm not sure, nor how long or what it'll cost, but isn't he a nice man and how accommodating are the town folk.

A few minutes passed. Mohammed reappeared riding a small and whining moped, with a passenger, riding pillion. "Follow us", the passenger, whom I later found to be Ali, gestured. And we did. Through the madness that is Marrakech, a melée of cars, carts, buses, donkeys, goats and aimless pedestrians, in the hot afternoon sunshine. We were having another adventure, and I thanked Allah that it was Graham in the driving seat and not I. Graham had by now adopted the principal rule of Moroccan town driving, that there are no rules. Focus on where you want to be and just go there. Wipe off any debris at the other end.

We hurtled through the streets in hot pursuit of the moped. Suddenly it disappeared through an opening in an ancient wall. We followed, and found ourselves in the Medina. A maze of filthy alleyways, barely wide enough for the moped, let alone Black Betty, and teaming with traffic of all descriptions; donkey carts, mopeds, bicycles, mangey curs, pedestrians, very few cars in fact. The alleys were strewn with rotting food, piles of undistributed gravel, and indescribable filth. Mohammed and Ali rode on, colliding briefly, almost casually, with a pedestrian in the impossible crazy turmoil that is the Medina. An angry exchange ensued, but soon we were weaving our way through the filth and the pedestrians again.

The Medina dates from the founding of Marrakech nine hundred years ago, and seems to have altered little since. A warren of alleys with an unbroken frontage to a hodgepodge of buildings. The alleys are eight feet wide at best, and you have to negotiate around piles of dirt and gravel, goats, pedestrians and anything else it has to offer. Traffic comes from all directions at the same time, so it was impossible and impracticable to predict what and where from traffic might appear next. Rather like trying to drive a car onto a tube train in the rush hour. Graham did magnificently well, having ditched his European road manners just outside the port of Tangier.

Eventually we arrived at what passed for a car park. A grizzled old man with grey stubble and a fez pushed another car out of the way to make space for Black Betty. We kissed bumpers as we pulled up.

By now I was getting a tad concerned as to what we were getting into. The moped pilot Mohammed disappeared into the Medina, and we never saw him again. Ali beckoned us into the Riadh J'DDI, Hotel and Restaurant Marocain. First impressions were not good. We followed Ali through a tiny, battered garage door. Past the façade was the faded remains of what had once been a fabulous town mansion. Through dim passages richly engraved with wooden mouldings we were led, and into an enclosed courtyard where a brightly tiled floor held a fountain in blue and white mosaic. We were shown about the house by Ali and the "manager", another Mohammed. The place was vast, with courtyards and terraces, winding passages, ornate bedrooms and tapestry hung chambers. The walls were bedecked with drapes and curtains, the floors with cushions and couches. But there was not a single window. We were entirely walled on all sides. The ceiling to the central courtyard could be withdrawn in the summer. I was entranced. Graham looked worried.

Shown to seats in the central courtyard, now used as an occasional restaurant, we were treated to the Mint Tea Ceremony.

A Short Guide to the Mint Tea Ceremony

1. First make the tea. Do not forget to warm the pot.
2. Roughly chop lots of mint leaves. Add to the tea and stew for some hours.
3. Take several glasses, about the size of a whisky tot, two or three for each person present should suffice. Add about two tbs. icing sugar to each.
4. Pour the well stewed mint tea into the glasses, from a height of at least eighteen inches. Be sure to splatter your guests liberally.
5. Return the tea to the pot and repeat 4 above, several times, increasing the height of the pot by three inches each time.
6. When the pot has reached between three and four feet, the tea is the consistency of cold treacle and everyone present is sufficiently splattered, it is ready.
7. Pour from a great height and serve in the same glasses. About half an inch is regarded as respectable.
8. Your guests must drink the tea with great gusto, and a satisfied grunt. To refuse is certain death.

I found the tea surprisingly refreshing. Graham wasn't fussed.

Over tea Ali explained that the house had been in his family for generations, over four hundred years. He'd lived all of his thirty four years in the Medina, working his way through college as a freelance tour guide. I never doubted him, but nor did I ever find out what he was a student of. I think I can guess now.

A tour had been specially arranged for us. Now neither Graham nor I were up for a tour, but we were in need of local currency, if only to pay for the overnight stay (we had been told £40, which seemed reasonable if it included an evening meal), so a visit to the nearest bank seemed like a good idea, and we reluctantly agreed to the tour, if it would take in a bank.

Ali led us back through the buzzing alleyways, out of the Medina, to the nearest bank, where we changed euros for our first dhiram, about £40 each. The tour continued. We wove our way through the Medina again, past the tiny and often filthy stalls that pass for shops. Butchers (fly blown meat, cattle hooves hanging up), greengrocers, leather goods, copper goods. It was a route march through anonymous and unsavoury alleys, but I felt curiously safe in his presence, as we passed the scowling shopkeepers. We weren't approached for baksheesh or by beggars, and I got the impression this was because we were in the presence of Ali, our guard and our guide, a known face within the Medina. So while I walked with one hand constantly on my wallet and the other on my camera, I didn't feel at risk of daylight mugging. We stayed close to Ali at all times. Had we lost him we'd never have found our way back to the Riadh, possibly not out of the Medina, and we could still have been there now.

Ali's special tour was to an "exhibition of traditional Moroccan crafts". It was actually a shop, owned by one of his many cousins. It was overstocked to bursting with carpets, balks of cloth, daggers, teapots, silverware, tajines, jewellery, all the tourist paraphernalia that we had no wish to buy or space to keep. It was clear they wanted us to buy, and clear that we were not about to. We endured the Moroccan tea ceremony once again (see above for directions) and looked for a polite way out. Graham very tactfully extracted us from this situation by reassuring Ali that we didn't wish to upset him or the management, but we really were not in the market for souvenirs. We'd not be allowed to take home a kukri with a nine inch blade or a hookah packed with hashish, and we really would like now to go to our room. Now. Please.

Ali seemed to lose interest in us at this point. The third part of the tour was back to the Riadh and our quarters for the night.

Our room was cavernous, quite forty feet long by sixteen wide. The ceiling was almost out of sight, at least thirty feet away. Furnished with a huge double bed at one end, and two couches (rock hard, with tight coverlets and no sheets) at the other, rugs adorned the walls. At one end a tiny shower room and toilet had been shoehorned, with the usual dubious plumbing. The vast chamber was lit by a single forty watt bulb high above in the vaulted ceiling. There were no windows at all. Access was via an ancient rustic wooden door in the wall of the courtyard. It could be bolted shut from the inside. Just about every health and safety requirement in the book had been flouted.

Ali specified the terms on which we'd occupy this mausoleum. The price quoted turned out to be "per person". It didn't include the evening meal, which would be about as much again, and there would, of course, be a charge for the "tour" of his cousin's shop. Ali graciously accepted all the dhiram in our possession, about £85, and we declined the evening meal in a vain attempt to make him feel guilty. The truth is, we were potless again.

Left to our devices in our gigantic hutch, Graham promptly bolted the door. I felt quite sick about the whole deal. We had our first wash since Spain, a mere lick and a spit. Neither of us could bring ourselves to shower in the dilapidated cubicle. Then we decided we should return to the car, check she was safe, and retrieve our evening meal, the tin of All Butter Shortbread Selection Sally had donated for the journey.

Weaving our tortuous way, unaided by Ali, back through the alleys of the Medina to Black Betty, the attendant gesticulated wildly, and

The Road To Banjul

we were caught in a shower of sputum. He wanted his fee, which we had, in our naivety, understood to be included. The situation, and the attendant, began to look ugly. Ali had told us if we had any trouble with the attendant or anyone else, to find him and he'd sort it. So the altercation, essentially about our right to retrieve our sustaining biscuits from the car, needed Ali's intervention. He was surprisingly easy to find in the Medina, indeed he found us, bumbling around on his moped. We explained the situation and he returned with us to the car where a furious and very nearly murderous argument ensued between Ali and the car park attendant. Blows were thrown. Much spitting and vituperative language later, Ali, younger and fitter than the car park attendant, seems to have summed up the arguments with a punch to the attendant's head. Dazed, but convinced of the rectitude of our claim, the attendant allowed us to retrieve our biscuits on promise of payment at the end of the week.

Back at the Riadh, Graham and I hunkered down again, feeling most uneasy. We were now more worried about Black Betty and her contents, under the not so watchful eye of a disenchanted and sadly abused car park attendant. We were concerned for ourselves, and whether we'd be allowed to emerge from this hell hole at all, or whether we'd be held to ransom. Nobody knew where we were. We had no receipt or other evidence of the money we'd already paid Ali. Secretly, I felt responsible for our plight and Graham's safety.

Late in the evening, and long after I'd written my daily journal with this sick feeling in the pit of my stomach, we ventured together into the depths of the Medina to check on Black Betty and the scowling car park attendant, who nursed his sore head in the darkness.

I phoned Gilly, and, summonsing my most confident and carefree voice and demeanour reassured her that all was well with the world. Graham did likewise with Sally, but cryptically dropped into his phone call the address and approximate whereabouts of the Riadh J'DDI.

We dined on All Butter Shortbread Selection and water, and resolved to make a dawn departure, yet again. Graham set his alarm for 4.00 a.m.

We tried to sleep, but the Medina, and the palace we were holed up in, were neither conducive to rest. Cries of children, the thump, thump thump of footsteps from above, the howl of dogs, the intermittent arguments and minor furies from without, the wail of the muezzin. We locked ourselves in with the slide bolt provided, but we left the light on, for without it the darkness was profound.

Two flies in a sticky web, we passed what remained of the night in a kind of silent terror, listening for the spider.

We'd travelled 331 miles and a thousand years from Meknes.

DAY SEVEN
ESCAPE TO TAN TAN

4.00 a.m. Graham's strident alarm jars me from a reverie. He's already alert, tense as he sits to attention on his bed. We've spent a restless and insecure night, and the knot in my stomach has yet to subside. The forty watts from on high in this stupendous chamber sheds an apology of light in the otherwise profound darkness.

"Have you got the Malarone, Keith?"
"Bugger. I left it in Black Betty."
"Let's go. Now!"
"You lead the way. I'll wind the torch."

Juggling the torch with my luggage and clutching the shortbread tin, I follow Graham as he gropes his way through the ornate wooden door and negotiates the maze of sinister passages. Our reliance on the torch is total. We find ourselves in the inner courtyard with its tiled floors, organdie hangings, restaurant tables set for breakfast, the dry fountain a reminder of past splendours. The whine of the torch and its pale glow cast an eerie dimension. We scuttle around a corner and eventually discover the heavy gothic back door.

"Oh, for fuck's sake!"
"What?"
"It's bolted and barred."
My heart sinks. Our path is blocked.

"Pass me that broom."

I work the torch furiously as Graham seizes the broom, jams it behind the padlocked baulk of timber and wrenches it from the door. It hits the floor with a muffled, splintering crash. Like some latter day Lord Carnarvon and Howard Carter before the tomb of Tutankhamun, we stand in front of the mangled door in fear and wonder.

But we don't hang about. We pull the massive door open and are outside in a trice. Racing down the alley, clutching bags, biscuits and torch, we take a left, and another, and yet one more, past dwellings dark and mysterious in the gloom. Eventually we hit the main thoroughfare through the Medina. It's wide awake, buzzing with life, people are working, sitting about, talking, smoking, begging. It feels like we're in a computer game.

Graham's sense of direction never fails. We're relieved to see Black Betty safe, unviolated, under the watchful eye of the argumentative fellow from yesterday. After a bribe (one cigarette) we extricate her from the car park, make a multi-point turn in the gloom, then burn rubber through the streets of the Medina. Graham finds the exit and we emerge into the relative freedom of the main thoroughfare. With two sighs, we head for Agadir.

The last twelve hours proved a steep learning curve and the experience was, if nothing else, not to be forgotten. Personally, I'd enjoyed the accommodation, if only for its architecture and air of mystery, an unusual place to stay. But we agreed our presence had probably been "unofficial", with payment up front and no receipts. We'd felt distinctly ill at ease and vulnerable. The night was broken by a cacophony of rhythmic and not so rhythmic thumping up and down stairs and in the corridors, the heaviest feet in Islam. Crying children, whining dogs, the wailing muezzin and other undecipherable noise had punctuated our troubled attempts to doze. The Medina itself was fascinating, if filthy, and could've been an enjoyable short term experience if one had not constantly been at the mercy of haranguing hustlers.

Today's plan, which formed itself after the scuffle and confusion of the Medina, was to make for Agadir on the coast. We'd then join the coastal road through Laâyoune in Western Sahara and head towards Mauritania.

On the road to Agadir that dark but starry morning, we licked our wounds and felt grateful to have extricated ourselves relatively unscathed from a dicey situation.

Lessons learnt from our stay in the Medina or

THE MARRAKECH PROTOCOL

1. I must stop showing the world at large the contents of my wallet.
2. I must stop trusting people so freely. The nicer they are, the more wary I shall be.
3. Malarone and other prescription drugs should be treated as valuables and carried in hand luggage or about the person.
4. We must not allow ourselves to be rushed, and insist on time to think.
5. We must be absolutely clear about what we are being charged, and what services are included, in total, per person, before we agree to anything. We should ask for this to be written down if the sum involved is significant.
6. We must ensure 5 above before parting with money or passports.
7. We must always view accommodation before accepting it.
8. We must demand receipts for any significant expenditure.

Calmer now, as we drive through the early hours, we reflect on our frightening experience. We may have overreacted, but, returning to Graham's expression, we felt like two flies trapped in a spider's web during those desperate hours.

By the time we get to Chihouaoua our routine has returned to normal. Graham's at the wheel, handling traffic, road conditions and obstacles, and sensing Black Betty's performance. I'm in the passenger seat, with the maps and Road Book, giving helpful advice and navigational hints, converting distances to miles with a pocket calculator (divide by 1.6, as Graham showed me), taking video footage, and recording progress on the dictaphone. There's nothing worth filming right now, except black holes in the dark.

At half past six, still in the pitch black, we record our 2000th. mile since leaving Long Lane Farm. We're half way to Banjul.

When the first glimmerings of daylight appear, we find ourselves in a convoy of lorries. These monsters proceed at a snail's pace on idler gears and burnt out brakes on the rocky declines. With the poor visibility we're unable to overtake on the winding road. Agadir seems a distant hope. To amuse ourselves we calculate precisely how much toilet paper is required for two men, passing normal to soft stools, twice daily, for fourteen days. This amount we shall purchase at Agadir, before we really leave civilisation behind.

Graham slipstreams the fumes belched out by the unfeasibly slow lorries for miles. Suddenly we're overtaken, at great speed, by a passenger coach heading for Agadir. Just as quickly it disappears into the fumes and the dawn. Twenty miles later, still dawdling in convoy, we pass the coach again. It's come to grief and lies indecorously on its roof in a large land drain, just off the hard shoulder. The driver and co driver sit smoking cigarettes on the wreckage, apparently unharmed and awaiting assistance. Mercifully, the coach seems to have been empty, apart from its resigned (and by now perhaps sacked) crew.

As the sun rises and we begin to descend towards the coast and the foot of the High Atlas, the convoy at last pulls over and forms a queue. Police are checking tachographs, which is slightly surprising, with the otherwise apparent lack of traffic regulation in this country. Black Betty is waved on.

The Atlantic Ocean beckons. We stop for petrol alongside it and pay the correct price, in the correct currency, for the first time on the African continent. Praise be to Allah!

We approached Agadir in a gradual descent through the High Atlas range with its stunted bushes and sporadic housing-hints of the desert terrain to come. We rolled into the car park of the vast Metro Hypermarket which caters for British visitors to Agadir and hotels in the area. It was stocked with all the basic provisions that'd see us through the desert *in extremis*. We travelled the aisles and chose from the many exotic delicacies on offer, including halal ravioli, camel crisps, cocktail sausages, pork and bean cassoulet, fruit cocktail (our five a day healthy eating plan) toilet paper (as calculated), coffee, mint tea, rice and mushroom soup, sugar lumps, water in copious quantities, and more shortbread (to replenish our dwindling selection). We could've purchased everything from washing machines, tractor parts, welding gear and plumbing requisites, to sanitary appliances and surgical trusses. However, pleased at the wisdom and eclecticism of our purchases, and with the good service we'd enjoyed at this veritable emporium, Graham packed everything carefully in the back of Black Betty, between the sewing machine and the tajine. This was the first comprehensive re-pack since Europe and Graham had clearly missed his vocation. He should've worked for Tescos.

By now the sun was high and the day blindingly hot. We didn't venture into Agadir, but could tell from the immediate surroundings that it was tidier, cleaner and altogether more European than the other villages and towns we'd passed through thus far in Morocco.

The road to Tiznit is under construction; diggers, graders and men at work in the hot sun. The clock returned to UK time somewhere between Marrakech and Agadir, and it's 10.10 a.m. in both countries. I phone Gilly.

"Good morning, light of my life, how is one?"
"I'm OK, but the dairy's flooded."
"How's that, pearl of my orient? What pray has occurred?"

"Washing machine packed up. But I cleaned the filter. It's OK now, but there's water everywhere. It won't go away. Think the soakaway's blocked. I'm just rodding it now."

"Good. Good. What's the weather doing?"

"Eight inches of snow. Country's at a standstill. What's it like there?"

"Oh, bearable, bearable. Bit hot. Well, must go. Got to help Graham choose his factor 15."

"Tit!"

When we repacked Black Betty, we placed the spare petrol cans right at the back. We figure we should carry spare fuel from here, as petrol stations south of Agadir could be few and far between and often run dry. It'll be important to be aware of the likely distance between them. We agree never to allow the tank to drop below a quarter full.

We reach Belfia and stop for coffee, mint tea and cake in the sunshine. Thirty six miles from Tiznit, 184 from Tan Tan, 375 from Laâyoune in Western Sahara. And yet it looks like Norfolk; greener and seemingly more prosperous than the interior. A long, flat road unwinds before us. A shepherd stands by his half dozen indifferent looking sheep, nibbling cactus (the sheep, not so much the shepherd).

Just outside Tiznit we experience our first police checkpoint since being pulled up for the non-existent stop sign. As intrepid adventurers we're waved on with a cheery smile. They're clearly more interested in the local lorry traffic.

Tiznit is blue. Completely enclosed in its pretty thirty-foot high blue castellated wall, its impact on the casual tourist is spoilt by television aerials and satellite dishes. We stop in the shade outside the town hall. Graham, weary after the early start and long drive in the dark, seizes the opportunity for a power snooze. We've been on the road for eight hours.

I took a wander around Tiznit. It was surprisingly busy for a town that appears to exist in a vacuum, sixty miles away from the nearest civilisation. I felt safe enough alone, as if strolling the streets of a busy provincial town in the home counties on a hot summer day. I scoured the streets with tourist eyes, and came across the only shop in the world to sell Valentines postcards, in French. Probably. I bought a couple for us to send. There were many well stocked motor factors, and I considered buying a set of ignition leads. However Graham appeared to have cured the intermittent misfire by tightening all the plug connectors. There were traders of all kinds, including plumbers merchants, building supplies and paint factors, but no souvenir shops. It was like Slough in southern Morocco. I did a circuit of some back streets and found an internet café where I managed to get directions to the post office. Being the only white face in an Arab town, I was conspicuous, perhaps, but I felt totally safe and uninvaded. Language was more of a problem as my broken French didn't pass muster this far from the tourist spots. Here, Arabic was *de rigueur*.

The post office in Tiznit, should you ever chance to be there, is opposite the tobacconist. A large, modern, air-conditioned concourse opened before me, and a helpful uniformed post official supplied stamps for England. I mailed a card to the dearly beloved, wishing her Happy Valentines and enquiring about the dodgy soakaway.

I negotiated the town unassisted, and even remembered my green cross code, in reverse. By the time I returned, Graham had finished his snooze.

We could, at Tiznit, have taken a much smaller road and visited the tiny Spanish relic town of Sidi Ifni, but an early finish beckoned. So it was on to Tan Tan, for an overnight stop.

Towns and villages in these parts are characterised by their gestures to tradition; the souk markets, the breeze block buildings with muddy yellow plaster and wash, and windows and doors in pale blue (the religious significance escapes me). Bouizakarne, at the foot of the Anti Atlas, is typical. Guelmim, with its castellated roofs and uniform appearance is a new village, but shares the same elements, and the same apparent lack of infrastructure, industry, commerce or agriculture. I start to wonder how people survive, so far off the beaten track.

At Guelmim we encounter the first traffic lights since Marrakech, and a shoe shine boy begs gifts at the window.

"I still don't need my trainers polished. How's your forehead?"
"I buffed it this morning thanks. Still nice and shiny."

So I give the lad a ball point, which he says he can use "a l'école". A water seller, complete with traditional pointed hat, drives a donkey cart laden with containers of water- puddle water, lake water, pond water and sewer water- all sold as drinking water. We give it a miss.

Just outside Guelmim, we're flashed by a driver coming in the opposite direction. We suspect he's indicating something's wrong with the car. When we stop we find part of the rear bumper trim and the foglight have come adrift. Graham rips them off and drops them in the back for later repair. Fog doesn't look imminent anyway.

We're in embryonic desert here. The beginnings of sand, rock and scree. A sign for "camels crossing the road" (triangle enclosing camel bearing supercilious look). Dust eddies, like tiny whirlwinds, presage the sand storms we've been warned about. Now, a circle of Bedouin tents. Donkeys, some no more than foals, dotted here and there. Deserted settlements of barrack like buildings. Abandoned petrol stations, the pumps long ago rusted out, unnamed villages that don't appear on our map, piles of boulders apparently marking field boundaries. It's looking less and less civilised, the further south we travel. There's nothing between us and Tan Tan but miles of straight, boring, featureless tarmac.

At four o'clock we reach Tan Tan, pull into the only petrol station, and fill Black Betty and all the jerricans. We're now carrying sufficient fuel to refill her from empty. She sits on her haunches, and the steering becomes suddenly even lighter. Graham decides from this point to conserve petrol by driving economically, keeping an average speed of between between 45 and 50 mph, only using the reserves if we really have to. To run out of either petrol or water anywhere between here and Senegal on these lonely desperate roads could be fatal. Pump attendants, ever helpful, seem sensitive to this and spend an age squeezing the very last drop into the filler pipe.

Rather than seek accommodation in this one-horse town, we pushed on to El Quatia. At least that's what it's called on the map. Locally, it's known as Tan Tan Plage, the coastal resort of Tan Tan, fifteen miles further and just off the main drag. Our spirits high, we were in holiday mood after our escape from Ali's clutches.

"This is Tan Tan Plage Gray, sounds suitably jolly, what?"
"Perfick. Look at that donkey Keith. It's carrying a bush, à la cart."

The Hotel "Le Marin" is described in the *Lonely Planet (Morocco)*, almost in passing, as "one block back, where rooms come with bathrooms and hot water". We thought we'd take a look. Tan Tan Plage is arranged in tiers, each parallel with and backing away from the beach. Each tier comprises a mess of single storey buildings, with no particular scheme or geometrical uniformity. Between the tiers are narrow alleys and back streets, sometimes just scrubby waste land. There don't appear to be any shops or commercial buildings, just a bunch of shabby beach huts trying to be a resort. We found "Le Marin" about three tiers back from the beach and parked in front of the façade. The frontage wasn't promising. We could only tell it was a hotel by its garish blue and yellow sign.

The proprietor scuttled from within, accompanied by his assistant, whose name I never discovered. Simo Mohammed bore a sallow, almost wasted complexion, small moustache and a shifty, greasy look. But he moved with an urgency and an energy which appeared, at first blush, to be an eagerness to please. He beckoned us inside, to this, "the finest hotel establishment in West Africa, perhaps the world". He asked for our passports and luggage, insisting there was not an establishment in the vicinity that could equal the luxury and the stateliness of "Le Marin". Simo and the assistant hovered close by, desperate to inveigle us within. But these two intrepid flies had learned their lessons. Straightaway we put the Marrakech Protocol into operation, determined not to be lured into another expensive web of deceit.

First we slowed the pace, asking him to show us our room before we parted with our passports. Then we clarified exactly what service we could expect, exactly how much the total cost would be for each of us, inclusive of evening meal and breakfast on the morrow. And to keep the car secure. I asked Simo to confirm it all in writing.

Simo was perhaps a little dismayed at our pedantry, but we were promptly shown the room. It was basic but clean, with unused bed linen. There were two single beds, a night table between that I could use as a desk, a built in wardrobe, and a separate shower room with toilet. This latter was tiny, with barely room for the worn and stained curtainless shower tray, the lavatory in the European style (we'd still succeeded in avoiding the Moroccan crouch!) and a wash hand basin. It was adequate, if not exactly the Ritz, and very cheap. The room was supposed to have hot water, and we'd yet to experience this particular luxury in Morocco. Graham asked, as much out of curiosity as with serious intent, to be shown some hot water. Preferably from the shower head. Simo, of

The Road To Banjul

course, insisted that within seconds it would be scalding to the touch, flaying the very skin off our backs with the intensity of its heat. So the shower was duly turned on in the presence of the assembled masses, and, sure enough, after about half an hour Graham indicated there was a sign that the chill might be lifting. Simo explained that, this being a Thursday, the day before Friday, the heat in the water might not be as impressive as normal, because of the necessary preparations for the holy day. It seems the concept of truly hot water escapes the imagination of the average Moroccan, unless it's in their blessed mint tea.

We agreed to take the room, despite the paucity of hot water. We felt we'd pinned Simo down to a contractual obligation, and that honour for the previous evening had been satisfied. We even paid up front, and obtained a receipt before parting with our passports. Our details were entered in the register and the passports handed back. They hadn't left our sight. Actually, I felt we'd been a little bullying with our demands and specifications.

"What would you like for your meal?" enquired the ever attentive Simo. I was warming to him with every minute. He really did appear genuinely concerned to please, now that the business formalities had been dealt with. Now, the Morocco we had experienced thus far could not be regarded as renowned for its culinary expertise. It's not a country I would visit in anticipation of rich and exquisite gourmet delicacies. In short, our choice had been limited to, well really one dish, the tajine, or meat and vegetable stew. The meat is generally chicken, lamb or goat, and the vegetables beans, potatoes, sometimes lentils. It's cooked over charcoal in a three part cooking pot with conical lid and circular base, also called a tajine, like the one I bought for Gilly. It's left to stew in its juices all day, before being served in the early evening. It can be very tasty and nourishing, depending on the ingredients, and because of the length of the cooking process is perhaps the safest option in remote Moroccan eating establishments. So we plumped for a tajine. Simo would have his speciality, lemon chicken tajine, ready at seven. This would afford time for a brief look around the hot spots.

We unpacked our few overnight belongings, and Graham took a luke-warm shower while I was collared by Simo for the usual mint tea ceremony (see DAY SEVEN above). For the umpteenth time I gargled the unfeasibly sweet green fluid while Simo regaled me with his past honours and achievements. Simo is the world's finest polyglot, fluent in some twelve or fourteen languages and a teacher of many of these too, though I could barely understand a word he spoke. However, he was a really nice bloke and something of a character. As we waded through our third glass of mint tea and he puffed on his twenty something cigarette, he bewailed the absence of a little wine to soothe his fractured life, here in this outpost of the Moroccan kingdom. His teeth were the worst stumps I'd ever seen in someone of his years, but, not a whit embarrassed by them, he would smile his stumpy smile and breathe his disgusting tobacco laden breath as long as I put up with it.

When a sufficiently polite amount of time had been spent at the tea ceremony, I found an excuse to leave Simo and his mate, and Graham and I took a look around Tan Tan Plage.

A lot of money was spent here, perhaps twenty years ago, and then wasted by neglect. It's a resort in name only, as no-one actually goes there. A large ornate fountain, complete with statue to some unknown hero in what passed for the centre, stood forlorn and dry, its tiles peeling off, its bowl filled with litter and filth. The statue mouldered under the sun. A vast walled playground languished, a tangle of twisted rusted iron. What had once been expensive playground equipment now projected from the ground in fearsome spikes and ghostly shapes. A tragic and bloody accident waiting to happen. Most streets were awash with litter, piles of sand and rubble, and the few residents who showed themselves had a listless dead-eyed look. Tan Tan Plage, the resort that never really happened.

We stood on the beach at sunset. The beach at the end of the world. Were I inspired to wax lyrical here I would tell you that gentle rollers lapped the soft sand of the deserted shore as far as the eye could see and that, in a brilliance of magenta and purple, the liquid sun melted into the golden river of the Atlantic. But I'm not that sort of chap, so I won't bother. Anyway, I caught it on two complete turns of my movie camera, including two workmen shifting a pile of sand by a brick shed. The sound track caught their curses as I condemned their souls to perdition. I spoke to Gilly. There was still snow in North Devon.

We returned for our meal, as promised, at seven. It was not quite ready, Simo called from the kitchen, and we should return at eight. We guessed he had yet to catch the chicken. We joined his assistant in front of the television in the saloon and watched a dreadful Morrocan soap opera, for as long as we could bear it, then took to our room. At eight prompt we returned, famished to the state of light headedness and really looking forward to the expected lemon chicken. Eventually, at 9.15, after an age during which much sluicing down of dishes and equipment could be heard from the kitchen, Simo emerged from the clattering cacophony, proudly bearing our starter.

The salad was excellently presented but we picked at it perfunctorily owing to a natural suspicion, as well as copious warnings about food washed in anything other than bottled water.

I'd been engaging Graham in pointless conversation for what seemed like hours in an effort to divert him from the goings on in the kitchen, and what the quantities of dubious water were being used for. But it was impossible to ready him for the promised tajines. The chicken, which bore a sickly yellow colour, must have died of old age, slowly. The toughest chicken on Allah's earth, probably stir fried, and with the head still attached to its shoulders, stared malevolently up at us out of its lemon garnish. We wrestled manfully with it, as we sat, the only guests for dinner, in fact the only guests in the hotel, with the Moroccan soap blaring in the background.

Tired after his battle with the chicken and a long day's drive, Graham took to his bed, leaving me to contend with dessert. Fresh fruit salad and strawberry yoghourt in a knicker bocker glory glass was served both to me and the absent Graham. Utterly delicious it was too, even decorative enough to pass muster as an ornament. I bolted mine hungrily and joined Graham, leaving his fruit salad to its own devices.

Hours later there was a light knock at the door. Simo, concerned I imagine for Graham's welfare, brought Graham's abandoned fruit salad to his bed. Stunned at this act of pure humanity, but unable to manage the dish at this late hour, he placed it in the otherwise empty wardrobe. It's probably still there, unless it's been rediscovered and removed from its place of honour on the hat shelf.

DAY EIGHT
LITTLE BEIRUT

We'd hurtled through France and Spain at breakneck speed, hurried down the west African coast, been ripped off in Marrakech and made dawn departures all the way. If we carried on at this pace we could've reached the Gambia in another week, but this was a challenge, not a race. So when I was jerked from slumber at five thirty by Graham's insistent alarm, I rolled over in my snug berth and dozed a while. Today would be quite soft in its demands, and a leisurely breakfast would set us right for the long haul down the coast.

For breakfast Simo excelled himself and our expectations. Moroccan bread (round, unleavened, dusky brown and absolutely delicious), saucers of olive oil, green and black olives, honey, jam, maple syrup, soft cheese, real butter, coffee (rich and aromatic), fresh fruit juices, fried eggs (two for Graham). The experience was novel and we ate heartily and slowly, as daylight broadened in the saloon at Le Marin. Our host scurried about in the most outrageous black and gold oriental silk pyjamas, complete with dragon motif, swathed in tobacco smoke and dripping ash as he went.

We reorganised Black Betty once more, moving the twelve gallons of reserve petrol to the foot well of the rear seats, for better balance and weight distribution. Hopefully this would correct the light steering encountered the previous day. With luggage, tools, petrol and gifts reorganised once again, we were seen off the premises by a laughing Simo, who made a last bid for a tip for the car park attendant. What car park attendant? I enquired. Why me of course, gestured Simo. We declined, pointing out that we were operating under the Marrakech Protocol. I'm not sure that Simo understood the allusion, but we did leave Le Marin without further expense.

The target for today, Laâyoune, capital of Western (formerly Spanish) Sahara, shouldn't be too taxing, about 200 miles along this seemingly endless coast road. We found a signpost giving the right direction, almost by accident, but to be honest it'd be difficult to get lost in Tan Tan Plage. There are only two directions out of it, and we'd arrived from one. The signpost indicated 282 Km to Laâyoune and 470 to Boudjour, also on our route. This would be easy, the softest target since Plymouth. We joined the main road with the sea on our right. The Atlantic Ocean was to remain in sight for the next three days, and we trundled by the Atlantic rollers in the hot sunshine on a baked road at a conservative pace.

The road is surprisingly good, if long and lonely. On the beach, concrete huts house the fishing population, pimples on the otherwise flat landscape. Stone, rock, scrub and the odd sparse weed makes up the hammada of these parts, it's desert, pre Saharan, under a relentless blinding sun and a sky that's so blue it's white. Piles of stones mark boundaries of what would be called fields, if there were any grass. It's hard to imagine anyone making a living from this land, yet every four or five miles we come across a shepherd tending a flock of perhaps twenty sheep or goats, leading them from one poor patch of marram to another. Thirty miles outside Tan Tan Plage we overtake a sole moped rider, a brace of fishing rods strapped precariously to the handlebars, projecting several feet fore and aft. Further on, a man dressed in flowing white robes and carrying a plastic carrier. Where has come from, and whither is he bound?. Asda, perhaps? The desolation is as startling as it's absolute.

As we pass an enclave of camper vans and wonder what sort of person would chose to spend a camping holiday in this searing heat and arid landscape, we discuss the days ahead. By tomorrow evening we should make Dakhla. The Challenge Disorganisers advise a rendezvous there with other teams to group for the desert stage. Convoys of four or five are the optimum, sufficiently small to be manageable, large enough to spread the support and sheer muscle necessary to nurse the larger vehicles over the sand. The search for a competent guide through the desert and minefield would also be carried out at Dakhla.

We encounter our first police check at Sidi Akhfennir on the 28th. parallel. We're ordered from the car and taken to a concrete block office in the middle of nowhere. Three polite khaki uniformed police interview us in the surprisingly cool interior. The senior officer asks for fiches, the information sheets prepared in the UK for such an occasion, as advised by the Disorganisers. They also check passports and ask the purpose of our journey. It'd been impressed on me not to admit we're on a challenge of any description, and never to utter the word "rally". So I explain, in the broken French that's still proving useful, that our purpose is "humanitaire, non-competitif". Although we're asked what, specifically, we're carrying as gifts for the poor of the Gambia, we're not being asked for baksheesh. They seem genuinely interested in our mission, and the largesse we intend to bestow. I tell them clothes, toys, guns, explosives, marijuana, cocaine and weapons of mass destruction. They seem quite happy with that. When asked what association we represent, I promptly point at Black Betty's impressive decals and lie, with conviction, "North Devon Animal Ambulance, Plymouth Town Hall, Plymouth, Devon, PL5 NTQ". Graham makes me write this down for future reference.

Clearly impressed with the worthiness of our cause, we're saluted and waved on to continue our quest.

Mid morning Black Betty traverses a deep but dry river estuary via a bridge. Ten minutes later we spot our first camels, a large herd, perhaps 200 strong, all one humped, and several tiny trainee humps suckling their mothers. Shortly afterwards we're stopped again by the police. This time they're content with the fiches. In the near distance, the posh cars of recreational fishermen. It seems that tourists do come all this way, just to fish. Two petrol stations loom up, one of them reputedly open 24/7, but with no sign of life. Also a couple of restaurants, one selling locally caught fish, otherwise nothing else, another one horse town.

We know we've reached the desert proper when the sand dunes become serious, rising to forty or fifty feet on both flanks, encroaching on the road in swirling eddies at first, later threatening to take over completely. The warm, dry harmattan blows constantly from our left towards the sea. Shifting sand makes the steering unpredictable. Graham moderates the speed to compensate, although traffic is sparse on this long, straight, boring road, between the majesty of the dunes.

At Tarfaya, a rough and confused fishing port, we spot our first shipwreck. An old fishing hulk, high and dry on the beach, the first of many. Tarfaya looks less than inviting, and with still no need for petrol, we speed by. A few minutes outside the port we come upon a broken down van, with two Arabs, apparently hitching a lift. Hurrying on, Graham figures we can't really help them, and this could be a disguised ambush. Armed bandits are known to skulk in the area, and staging a break down is a famous and well used ruse to entrap the unwary.

At noon we reach Tah, and the border of Western Sahara. There's no border control, and Tah itself will never exactly be world renowned as a vibrant, happening place. Nothing's happening at all. A couple of block buildings, which might be shops or houses, no signs of life or movement. We've entered another country, and nobody seems to care. The stink of rotting fish hangs limply on the air as we enter Dawra, with its one defunct petrol station and three pink domed houses.

Laâyoune, capital of Western Sahara, is reputedly Morocco's showpiece in the south. The approach is over a broad dry river estuary and long road bridge. Graham receives a message on his mobile phone and takes a wrong turn. But as the muezzin call the faithful to one o'clock prayer we pass through another police control and enter the main city.

Laâyoune has the air of being at the end of the universe. We drive a circuit through the main centre. Low, two storey buildings of the same concrete block, mostly painted with pink or yellow wash, dry dusty streets, almost deserted with the population either at prayer or asleep. No traffic control to notice, and indeed no traffic to speak of. It has a quaint, deserted, grey atmosphere, with no evidence of its former Spanish influence. Above all, it looks like it's been closed for years, the Miss Haversham of capital cities. There being nothing much to see, and the deserted chill of the place making it quite unattractive as a place to stay (though this was the advice in *The Lonely Planet*), we stop only for petrol. The sole petrol station has run dry, but the attendants, whom I catch devouring a lunch of vegetables and couscous, kindly invite me to share their meal in the gloom of the forecourt office. I'm touched and impressed with the kind offer but as the station has no "super sans plomb", I graciously decline. We push on a further fifteen miles to El Marsa.

El Marsa is completely surrounded by a defensive wall. The streets are even more desolate and unkempt than those of Laâyoune and it has the appearance of a little Beirut. Dust, litter and the waste and remains of years blows like tumbleweed through its deserted alleys. Here a burnt-out upturned lorry decorates a street corner. There, a dead dog, fly blown, gnawed at hungrily by two of the biggest rats I've ever seen. We pull up in a side road next to the one hotel called, appropriately, the Hotel El Marsa, being indeed the only hotel El Marsa boasts.

I wasn't hopeful, as we entered from the baking, dusty and deserted street. We stepped into a different world. The lobby was modern, clean, cool and tastefully tiled in blue mosaic. The manager was similar, apart from the tiles, immaculate in starched shirt, bow tie and silk waistcoat, in the manner of the European maitre d'. He bore a striking resemblance to the present King of Morocco, and I told him so, a complement he accepted graciously, with a smile. Applying the Marrakech Protocol once again, I asked to see the room before booking, and for clarity on what the fee would include. We needn't have worried on either count, for the room (and we were offered a choice) was both exceptionally well appointed and in pristine condition. Twin beds, fresh linen, an immaculate bathroom with European lavatory, gold fittings, hot and cold water. A television with remote control. The room was attractively furnished, crisply decorated and bright, with air conditioning and a balcony. We couldn't believe our intuition in carrying on beyond the not so promising Laâyoune to this war zone. And the tariff was posted on the inside of the door. There would be no surprises when it came to payment.

King Hussain, the regal and yet affable maitre d' spoke no English, and very little French, but was helpful and obliging. Black Betty could stay where she was, discretely parked in the alley, where we were assured she'd be perfectly safe. At least that's what I gathered to be the gist of his assurances.

Over the next couple of hours in our cool room Graham updated me on the complications of his conveyancing transactions back in the UK. They involved the sale of two houses and the purchase of another, and he'd come away on this adventure at precisely the wrong moment. Sally was holding the juggling balls, trying to keep it all together, but Graham had to share in the decision making. This was playing on his mind. We discussed strategy and tactics, in the face of offer and counter offer, employing some of the precepts of the Marrakech Protocol. A couple of horrifically expensive mobile phone calls to solicitor and estate agent later, the property issues were settled as best they could be. Graham felt easier, and we took a stroll around the war torn little Beirut, looking for post cards.

Perhaps unsurprisingly, we were unsuccessful in our search for anything that resembled a post card. Post cards of this forsaken country don't exist, and of course tourists seeking them are equally rare. However, sprinkled randomly about the dusty litter strewn and rat infested streets were lock up shops selling the bare essentials. Dark and cavernous, single storey, block built and half shuttered against the sun, they were just big enough to house their keeper. And perhaps a few dozen wares on sale; bread, groceries, dusty half hearted vegetables and fly blown meat. And jerricans, hundreds of them in all shapes and sizes and improbable colours. In these parts, jerricans are currency. We selected a five gallon example, in a pleasing shade of lilac, which would give us the comfort of, perhaps, an extra 100 miles range. I paid 30 dhiram, or £2 for this extra comfort. Morroco's national obsession with barter and bargain hasn't reached this far south. In El Marsa, goods have a price, and while this is never stated or clear, you have the feeling that traders aren't trying to rip you off as they constantly do in the tourist resorts. You're neither hassled to buy, nor obliged to barter.

Despite its bruised and torn appearance, El Marsa was friendly enough, and we felt safe. As we negotiated the paths and streets through upturned, burnt out lorries, scavenging packs of wandering dogs and the ubiquitous litter and detritus, we came across a bank, with a functioning ATM.

Back at the hotel, we sought to dine on something simple. It was six o'clock. Now for some reason hotels in places like El Marsa don't seem to have the concept of the evening meal. Even this up market establishment, with its perfectly satisfactory dining room and bar, couldn't cope with the suggestion that we might like something more substantial than the cake and mint tea that seemed to satisfy the local gentry. The saloon was soon full with djelaba clad men sitting in silence, drinking mint tea and coffee, watching different Moroccan soap operas on two televisions perched high on the wall. We ventured forth, in search of dinner.

We scoured dark alleys for anything that looked like an eating house, attracting the attention of a suspicious looking military policeman. Eventually, a couple of blocks from the hotel, we found a tajine shop. A small café with formica tables and plastic chairs and about a hundred tajines bubbling away over charcoal out front, on the sidewalk.

I pointed at the tajines and then at Graham. Graham held up two fingers as politely as possible, trying to convey the notion that we were two hungry travellers, at a tajine shop, clearly over stocked on the tajine front, and that we would like to buy two. Tajines, that is. From a tajine shop. To eat. The sign language got more animated and embarrassing as the scene unfolded, as if we were in that famous Monty Python cheese emporium. We are hungry, you have a tajine shop, and several tajines. We would like to buy two. Eventually the frantic gesticulations and vivid pictorial imagery seemed to bear fruit. We were instructed to select a dish of our choice. We hungrily grabbed a lamb tajine each, greasy, steaming and fragrant. Very tasty too, with a generous hunk of unleavened bread.

Within minutes the café was full of locals, following our lead. Elbow to elbow we sat with the heaving throng, eating tajine soaked Moroccan bread, exchanging political views, discussing the finer points of soap opera and drinking mint tea. Treated as equals in a foreign land. The tajines had set us back the princely sum of £3, and we were replete, satisfied and content to have taken part in another social convention in this West Saharan nosh shop, with the boys of down town El Marsa.

On the way back, we stocked up with dhiram from the ATM at the bank on the corner. Graham stood guard, while I conversed with the machine, and obtained £100 in locally acceptable cash. We'd be ready for another early start. We could also go clubbing it, Moroccan style, or at least sample the night life on offer in this West African dog hole. Back to the hotel we sped, eager to partake of the local night cap, coffee and mint tea, at a table with forty or fifty others doing likewise, glued stony faced to the television. An episode of The Phil Silvers Show was on, with Sergeant Bilko camping it up to Arab subtitles.

So we took to our room for another early night. Graham was soon fast asleep in his comfortable and commodious bed. I wrote up the travel log and then, before submitting to sleep, submitted to a rerun of *Chariots of Fire*, in English with Arabic subtitles.

DAY NINE
THE LONG AND NOT SO WINDING ROAD

We took an early morning walk around El Marsa. There were unfinished buildings with the jagged spikes of redundant scaffolding and shards of lethal corrugated iron, wrecked lorries and overturned burnt-out cars, the savage remains of civil war and insurrection. The redolence of rotting fish. A dog and a rat scavenged in a gutter, in competition for a morsel of indescribable filth. A lone road sweeper in faded blue fatigues shuffled by with barrow and shovel, clearing streets and pavements in perfunctory, languid motion. He was selective in his work, and we figured he's paid by individual frontagers to keep their stretch clear. We discussed the economics of this freelance operative. One dhiram per shop front per day would be the going rate. Amongst his litter, the skull of a sheep, the excrement of dogs and rats.

The Hotel El Marsa is an oasis within a dog hole, clean, tidy, modern, cool, immaculate and well managed, and at the modest fee of 300 dh (£20), for the two of us, we had been well served.

At eight o'clock we leave this shining metropolis and exit under the castellated plaster portico to the main road and Boujdour

People are walking to and from El Marsa, some dressed in elaborate silk robes, most in scruffy work fatigues and djelabas. Where are they coming from, and where are they going? What are they going to do when they reach El Marsa? I'm sure there's a local economy of sorts, but quite how it supports settlements like El Marsa remains a mystery. No evidence of work, apart from in the shops. We saw not one woman or child, only men, who spend the evening in groups drinking mint tea and watching television.

Our target today is Dakhla. *Lonely Planet (Morocco)* describes it as "a long lonely 520 km. drive through endless *hammada* and only worth the effort if you are making an attempt to get into Mauritania." *Lonely Planet* are not wrong. The road is unchanging, an everlasting ribbon of tarmac hardtop, unwinding in the already blinding light of the Sahara. The Atlantic Ocean on our right is never more than a couple of tantalising miles away and peeps through rocks to surprise us from the monotony of the road. Deep tyre tracks, left by vehicles larger than Black Betty, indicate soft sand and a need for caution. Pulling off the hard top at these points could prove disastrous, but with the juggernauts thundering from the opposite direction, and the road only just wide enough for two, there are a few anxious moments.

Lemsid, a tiny walled village with its own mosque and rhomboid houses, dents the monotony. Graham's driving is meticulous, even on this long and not so winding road, more from a wish to avoid attention from the police and a frivolous bribe than inherent respect for the law. Passing through villages such as Lemsid, he reduces speed to exactly the maximum permitted at the precise moment we reach the delimitation sign, even when no-one's looking. On the approach to the seemingly random police checks I stash the movie camera out of sight, as Muslim police and other officials don't like to be caught on frame. At the check at Boudjour we part with the usual two fiches, and continue on our way. Two camper vans, bearing the French tricoleur and painted sixties fashion, with psychedelic swirls, fare less well. The faintly suspicious looking occupants and their vehicles get a thorough going over by two outraged gendarmes. I wonder whether I should intervene with my schoolboy French and diplomatic skills, in the interests of entente cordiale. Graham persuades me that, on this occasion, the police seem to know their business, and it might be better to maintain a low profile. We leave the French hippies to their destiny.

Perhaps our minds have started to wander, but you can tell what a boring road this is. We begin to amuse ourselves with pointless calculations, estimating that the increase in fuel economy as a result of the better weight distribution of the inboard petrol will probably save us approximately one inch per mile. Every ten minutes or so I take a couple of minutes footage just to thrill my friends in the UK with the excitement of the rugged terrain and the incredible diversity of its wildlife. At 10.10 we share a cherry and currant bun. Purchased in Plymouth, it's been in the glove compartment and survived well in its cellophane bag. We begin to reminisce.

"The tajines were good last night, eh Graham?"
"Hmmm. Yeah, they were OK. Meat looked a bit sus though."
"I think it was lamb. Or goat. Tasty, I thought."
"I could really go a big juicy steak, me."
"Have you seen one then?"
"How d'ya mean?"
"Well, be honest, have you seen anything, in this country, on four legs, worth eating?"
"No, now you say, I haven't."
"Unless you'd like to chew on a donkey. Or a camel hump."
"I had a cow once. Well it was more a calf really."
"Yeah?"

"Yeah. Pretty little thing. But it wouldn't stand still. And a bugger to catch. I had to wrestle it to the ground, just like you see on them cowboy films."

"Really?"

"Yeah. It would *not* come in one day. So I chased it all over the meadow. Finally cornered it, did a flying tackle, grabbed it round the neck, pulled it to the ground on top of me."

"Bet that was heavy."

"It was. A bit. So there I am, lying in this puddle. Slurry it was. Cow piss. I'm lying in this puddle of cow piss and slurry, with this calf on top of me. I've got it round the neck, like, and it decides to lay on me chest. It's looking right at me. We have eye contact."

"So you were building rapport then. Communicating with the animal kingdom?"

"Yeah, and then it sneezed. You ever see a calf sneeze?"

"No."

"A couple of gallons of calf snot shot straight up me nose and lodged in the back of me throat."

"Oh, sweet Jesus! What did you do?"

"All I could do. A drawback. Sniffed it all up, juggled it about on me tonsils and gave a mighty gob. Gobbed the lot out. The calf weren't too impressed. He got up and ran off."

"I should've thought that'd put you off beef for good."

"Put me off salt for a while. That's all I could taste, for weeks."

"Anyway, I'll do you one in Dakhla."

"One what?"

"A nice juicy steak. If we can find any meat worth eating in Dakhla Station. We'll break out the camping stove and I'll do you steak au poivre. Or steak tartare."

"Oh, ta!"

At Boujdour the police station is under construction and closed for business. A lone flock of unattended sheep and a driverless donkey cart wander the deserted road. The next police checkpoint comes as a surprise, and jolts us out of the trance this monotonous road has begun to induce. The Gendarmerie Royaume de Maroc epaulets and cap badges betray Morocco's intentions with regard to the disputed territory of Western Sahara. To be frank, if a little uncharitable, I for one can see nothing of note to dispute, and if blood really has been shed over this territory in the recent past, then in my opinion it was wasted. But the police here are friendly, if noticeably disenchanted with their lot. Satisfied, officially, with a couple of fiches, they make the first request we have experienced, since the horrors of Tangier, for "cadeaux". I give them a couple of cheap ball points (one for the senior officer, one for his minion). Is this where corruption begins? A harmless little gift. Will we be so fortunate further down the coast?

There's a desolate but functioning petrol station in Boudjour, and we take the opportunity to replenish the tank, and the lilac jerrican. As the attendant squeezes the last drops of "sans plomb" into Black Betty and I part with another ball point, Team Old Gits pull onto the forecourt in their canary yellow Volkswagen Scirocco.

Graham Old Git, semi-professional rally driver, is running to a tight schedule. They're heading for Dakhla, with a preference for hotel accommodation. We discuss briefly the possibility of travelling onwards from Dakhla in convoy, but make no commitment. All parties will be considering options at Dakhla, including whether to travel through the desert and along the beach in Mauritania, or whether to stick to what we're now beginning to believe is a freshly metalled road. The Old Gits have booked a flight home on 20th. February (only flexible to the 21st.). Ours is scheduled for a few days later, so we're not in the same hurry. Whilst the Old Gits are travelling at speed and likely to reach Dakhla before us, we're progressing at a sedate, economical pace. We agree to continue the negotiations later in the day.

Out of sight, but still in Boujdour, we stop to secure the lilac jerrican, and are immediately swarmed by children. About fifty kids come from nowhere, climbing on Black Betty, poking about in the rear, threatening our precious stash of cadeaux. We jam the petrol in place, retreat quickly back into the car, lock all doors and windows, and flee, showering our invaders with dozens of pens and pencils as we make off in a cloud of dust. Another lesson well learnt—do not open the tailgate except in polite company, and keep your hand on your ball point. I have literally hundreds in the back of Black Betty and can well afford to be more lavish with presents, but I don't know how many police checks there'll be, or precisely how many children there are in the Gambia. I shall exercise caution and parsimony.

The constant dry warm wind blows offshore, nudging Black Betty from the left. The powerful heat beats down on the bleak fishermens' dwellings sprinkled on the beach, before the Atlantic rollers. We pass the first sign "To the Gambia", painted crudely in stove black on an old car tyre (a remnant from a previous year's Challenge?) Sand begins to drift, sometimes obliterating the road, making it hard to see and harder to steer. Sandstorms can kick up very quickly and without notice, so we pray we'll make Dakhla before conditions get too bad. In the midst of a sand storm there's nothing you can do but hunker down, don goggles and face mask, drink mint tea and stay put until it passes. I hope this'll not be necessary.

By lunch time we reach the Café Tazerin, half way to Dakhla. Not exactly a select establishment, it's noted for its characteristic aroma, predominantly rotting fish. There's no star rating, so we give the place a miss and munch on the remains of the All Butter Shortbread Selection and coca cola. Black Betty trundles through the sand, which swirls like a thin mist across the road in front.

In the afternoon we find ourselves in stonescape. Now if that's a non-existent word and I've just coined the expression, please excuse me. It's the only way I can satisfactorily describe the millions of piles of stones and boulders, pyramidal structures built by human hand, maybe thousands of years ago, maybe last week, that randomly decorate the dry hammada. They do'nt seem to mark anything in particular, nor are they arranged in any sequence, order or pattern. What connotation they have, scattered along the roadside and in the hills, what religious or pastoral significance, I cannot say, but they're startling in their sheer numbers and variety. Graham suggests there might be a recreational purpose. Perhaps your average Moroccan drives out here on a Sunday afternoon with his family to picnic, and build the odd cairn or two.

At Echtoucan, cave formations and a fork left to Timbuctou, 52 days away into the deep interior of the Sahara.

Fifty miles before Dakhla a white Peugeot 205 races by, klaxons blaring. The passenger is hanging precariously out of the window, filming as they pass. The driver clutches a mobile to his ear. Smoke billows from the interior. The distinctive PB07 Challenge sign on the rear window gives them away. We exchange waves, and will catch them in Dakhla.

Minutes later we come across the last petrol before Dahkla, and top up again. The attendants are becoming more demanding. One wants to buy whisky and my clothes. I give him a pair of shoes, and have visions of driving into Dakhla rich but naked.

The last 25 miles is on a peninsula, with the Atlantic on both sides of a narrow sliver of sand. It's a lunar landscape, with massive dunes and a mythic vastness of beach, an island in a lagoon, and the liquid sun glinting off the sea. We're riding in the centre of an awesome and mysterious grandeur in a convoy of camper vans and coaches. We experience our first mirages, of water on the road ahead, then a figure, a man with a carrier bag, but seen from a couple of miles away he appears at least forty feet tall. This is due, I am told by the engineer in the driving seat, to the coefficient of linear expansion.

Just before Dahkla Station we pull into "Camping Moussafir", the next Challenge rendezvous. The camp site is predictably spartan, a walled enclosure, with the bit of desert inside about as welcoming as the three hundred and fourteen miles we've just driven. We leave Black Betty and inspect the premises to ensure they come up to our exacting standards, before committing ourselves to two or even three nights stay. They don't. Come up to our exacting standards, that is. A breeze block office houses the manager, a charming cove who alternately smokes, spits and scowls from his mouthful of broken teeth. Beyond the office are unmarked gravel hard standings, to differentiate them from the rest of the world right here, which is one very large hard standing, without the comforting gravel. No services to plug into, no electricity or water. It's adequate, in a masochistic sort of way, for those with camper vans, but for the majority with tents, camping will be a hardship not worth the endurance. A few tents have been pitched, heroically I think, by securing guy ropes to the bumpers of vehicles, walls and the sharp ends of steel reinforcing that protrude threateningly out of the hard baked hammada. There are some twenty concrete boxes for those who prefer not to brave the hard ground and constant wind which is going to make camping a less than thrilling experience. They're windowless, fly blown hovels, furnished with two wooden benches, stained and dog eared mattresses, and a shelf for your camping stove. Each has its own concrete sun terrace, where, if you can bear it, you can relax in the searing heat, shelter from wind blast, and idly watch other campers as they pass to and from the stinking communal ablution block. I quite expect to find a sign announcing "Arbeit Macht Frei".

Shortly after arrival at this haven of peace and plenty we met Team Dumb and Dumber, Andy Morgan and Dave Barrow, who overtook us in the Peugeot. Andy and Dave, social workers from Beccles, had bagged one of the concrete hovels. Graham and I thought we'd try our luck in Dakhla town. We'd return in the morning to meet Dumb and Dumber, who seemed two likely lads, chaps we could consider teaming up with for adventures further south. The Peugeot (affectionately "Pug") had issues to address with its suspension, lower than ideal for the expected road conditions through the desert and beyond. She was fine on good town roads, but sat too low on her haunches, even unladen, to be healthy for the sump and exhaust. She could easily bottom out in a rut, and we expected there to be plenty from here on. Graham offered to lend his engineering skills to a little inventive skulduggery with the Pug's suspension on the morrow.

So we'd make for Dakhla town, find a hotel for perhaps two nights. Tomorrow would be for discussion and negotiation with comrade teams, and available guides. Graham could lend a hand with the Pug, Black Betty would have a well earned rest.

Graham had voiced concern with the leaded fuel and low octane ratings of the Western Sahara and Mauritania. As Black Betty was used to unleaded fuel and had been built with a catalytic converter, she might clog with the contamination. The question was, how much longer will the engine hold out, and whom to consult?

As we left "Camping Moussafir", and two more Challenge Teams pulled into the site, it was time to call home.

"Dearest, when you did your motor mechanic's course, did you, by any chance, cover catalytic converters?"

"Of course. What's the problem?"

"Graham's worried about driving on leaded fuel. The stuff down here is filthy, and there's no unleaded from here on."

"Oh, you'll be OK, for about 25,000 miles. If it does clog up, just knock a big hole in it. Must go. There's a tree down in the wood. Got to sharpen the chainsaw before I log it."

"Thankyou, dearest."

"Tit!"

In Dakhla, we quickly found the Hotel Doumss, and Team Old Gits, who'd already booked in. Operating our by now tried and tested Marrakech Protocol, we were duly offered a choice of rooms and elected for one in the front with better views and some sunshine. With its balcony, ensuite and only slightly suspect plumbing, it was a vast improvement on "Camping Moussafir". But, once more, no provision for evening meal.

We scoured the streets for something to eat. Dakhla Station is a UN base and the presence is evident everywhere, with military uniforms of the armed forces, military police, and a plethora of government buildings. There's an airport, tarmac streets and tidy pavements. Wide tree-lined boulevards service impressive rows of hotels and newly constructed flats. There's an atmosphere of people with a purpose. Straying briefly out of the main streets, we lost our bearings for a while, but were put back on track by two very large, very black, very friendly but very armed, American MPs, outside the military hospital. As we retreated towards the lively centre, we peered inside open doors, and noticed all sorts of activities going on after dark.

The search for victuals was abortive, so we returned to the hotel and Graham dug out the gas camping stove from the bowels of Black Betty. I returned to the dark streets of Dakhla in search of his juicy steak. Predictably, I suppose, the best I could manage was two bread rolls, purchased from a grinning Muslim pâtissier.

Back in the room I swiftly took the stove from its neat plastic suitcase and proudly erected it on the table. I'd selected a few tins from our reserves, bought in Agadir, and would attempt to impress Graham with my famous sausage cassoulet, a side serving of bread and frankfurters, and a rice soup starter (optional). The delicate preamble of food prep having been placed in my capable hands, I put the saucepan containing all above ingredients on the gas ring and twisted the ignition knob. Nothing happened. Nothing, that is, but the dull and barely audible electronic click and a blue spark. I tried again. Nothing. A third tentative twist on the ignition was equally disappointing.

"You have tested this equipment, haven't you?" quizzed Graham.

"Well, not as such," I countered, remembering vividly and with painful embarrassment the affair of the undersize tent in Meknes. "I'll try a match."

The special damp proof camping matches had also not been tested, as such, but they did the trick. They ignited the gas ring in a flash, quite literally. They also ignited the ball of butane gas that had by now leaked from the defective stove, which in turn ignited our eyebrows, most of the remaining hair on Graham's head, the little hairs up my nose, and our T shirts, and left telltale scorch residue on the curtains. When the fire ball had completed its obligatory three circuits of the room, consuming any other hairs and inflammables on its way, and finally subsided, we took stock. Graham blinked the soot from his eyes, and commented that the gas stove evidently needed some attention. It did. And this is where his engineering expertise again proved itself. In no time he had dismantled the stove, into its many component parts, deftly replaced the feed pipe from the gas cylinder to the burner element where it should always have been, and we were, quite literally, cooking on gas.

"Have you a tin opener?" chanced Graham, noticing that the meal's ingredients largely, if not entirely, depended on one.

"Why, of course," I rejoined, proudly presenting the tin opener I'd purloined not a few weeks previously from the Tyrrel charity shop in Ilfracombe's High Street, an establishment noted for its superior merchandise and above average customer relations.

"And have you tested this equipment?" posed the ever vigilant Graham.

"Well, not as such," I responded nervously, hoping that the damn thing would at least open tins. After all, I'd paid 5p for it, in good faith, and believed it must come with at least the guarantee that it would perform its essential function.

Of course, and rather unsurprisingly by now, it wouldn't. The Swiss Army Knife came into its own here, for cunningly concealed between the thing for getting stones out of horses hooves and the all weather cricket pitch, I found a selection of the most vicious implements and pointy things known to mankind. With a little stabbing and hammering, and only minor blood loss, the tins were duly opened.

A repast of the most splendid proportions and culinary excellence followed. Graham, who was to endure, or rather enjoy, my gourmet offerings several times on this our amazing adventure, was gracious in his appreciation.

But we'd still not solved the enigma of when and where do the people of Morocco and Western Sahara eat, as opposed to sit with their friends, watch TV and drink mint tea?

I left that thought hanging and planted the Western Saharan wishbone in what passed for the front garden (actually a pile of sand and a weed) in the dead of night.

DAY TEN
CLOSE ENCOUNTERS OF A DIFFERENT KIND

The sun's already high and the day hot and dry when we rise on Sunday morning. There's no particular deadline, no urgency to get on the road. This is Graham's first rest from driving since Long Lane.

We skip breakfast, mainly because we can't find any, and are soon off back to the camp site a couple of miles away to look at Dumb and Dumber's car and its suspect suspension. Driving on this dry, dusty, almost deserted road out of Dakhla, we notice women in dark blue saris with bright yellow patterns, men in flowing white robes. The dress is more colourful in these remote parts, women much more in evidence too. There's almost a gaiety in the air, a more carefree attitude to life than was evident in the overstretched, overpopulated cities of the north.

Back at camp we find Dumb and Dumber with the Pug. They spent a fly blown night, camped in their concrete cell with tents erected on top of the filthy mattresses and rickety benches. Dave counted, and filmed for posterity, at least thirty uninvited insects that shared their cell, despite a vigorous bombardment with citronella, fly spray and heavy duty chemicals which would strip the skin from a human body, but only seems to encourage a gentle and temporary nap in the average Western Saharan boot camp fly. Dave and Andy availed themselves, *in extremis*, of the filthy and even more fly blown crouch style lavatories, but have brought with them a clever portable shower device and are waiting for the water to warm in the heat of the sun before luxuriating in its tepid dampness.

Team Dumb and Dumber seem like two lads we're going to get along with. Now might be the time to forge a partnership. Dave's 35, married with a twelve year old son. He's tall, well built, muscular, ex army. Cool and laconic, he gives the impression of solid respectability with a slightly dissipated past. He loves to play with the two or more mobile phones he carries. Andy's in his early fifties. Married with two sons, he's shorter than Dave, and bears the marks of approval that life's bestowed upon him. With a wry sense of humour, a casual, even ethnic dress sense, Andy negotiates his way through the world with style, a knowing grin and a silly hat. His skill with French, even more schoolboyish than my own, may help in the negotiations to come, where he and I should make an entertaining double act. Sort of Two Ronnies do the Desert Dance.

By nine the Pug is jacked up. Andy and Graham are inspecting the workshop manual and the under side of the car's suspension. Graham looks both intellectual, in his wrap around shades, as he contemplates the finer points of the exploded drawings in the Haynes manual, and professional, in the one size fits all overalls Andy's provided to protect his modesty, if not his street cred. The legs and arms of the overalls are about fifteen feet long, so copious folds of material impede his otherwise lithe and graceful form as he grovels in the dirt of the car park. Andy, on his back close to Graham, nods sagely at the diagnosis, and passes him a perfunctory spanner.

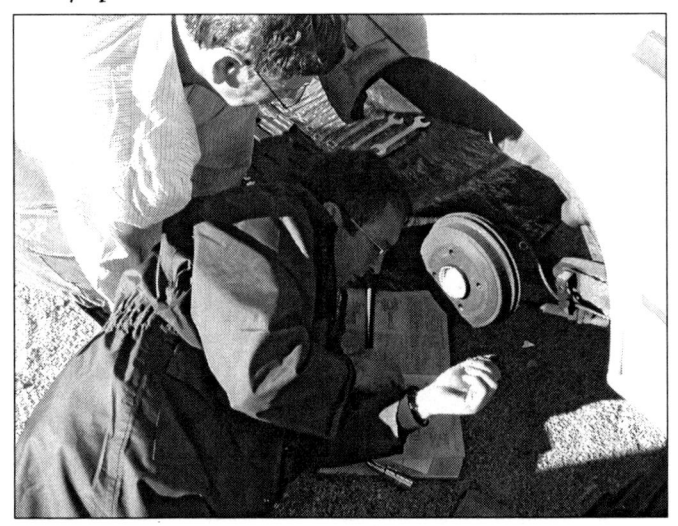

I am delegated to repack Black Betty again, after the ravages of the last couple of days. So while the Pug's wheel is removed, the brakes dismantled and the trailing arm detached, I prance about like a demented Alan Whicker, snapping photographs for the album.

I'm approached by a man in the car park. He's slight, black, bearded with smiling eyes and a kindly face. His dress is smart but casual European; dark trousers, pale blue cotton shirt and body warmer. He introduces himself as Mohammed Abdullah, late of the Mauritanian police, now operating as a guide in this area. I'm aware that guides will be looking for prospective clients, so I'm pleased to at least interview this likely looking and self effacing individual. I'm still wary of such approaches, not in a position to commit the others without consultation. We converse in French, mine stumbling his competent, and quickly establish rapport and an understanding. He produces copious good to glowing testimonials, in English, by past Plymouth-Banjul Challengers on the back of their fiches. They are credible, if dog-eared and sand blown. Mohammed looks the good side of forty, with an indefinable quality of agelessness. He has a wife (just the one) and young family in his home town of Nouâdhibou, Mauritania, our next port of call. With his background in the Mauritanian police, I figure he may prove an asset otherwise than for his purely navigational skills through desert and minefield. He's also an accredited guide through the Parc National du banc d'Arguin louîk, through which we may have to pass, an experienced driver and competent mechanic. I take to Mohammed. He's mild mannered, even tempered, not pushy. I explain I like the cut of his jib, but am not in a position to exchange contracts with early completion, as we've not yet established the route south. I truly believe Mohammed would be a good choice of guide, but have no idea of his rates.

Back at the Pug, it appears she really needs special Peugeot tools and parts to do a proper job, so this has to be a classic Challenge bodge. A wooden wedge, carefully fashioned to the appropriate dimensions, could be jammed between the trailing suspension arm and the rubber bump stop, secured in place with nylon cable ties. This device, if applied to both sides, will raise the rear suspension by two to three inches. Several sets will be necessary to replace those that break with fatigue or simply drop out. Graham and Andy make a template. Andy will go into production on the special "Pug Suspension Adaptor".

On this long day we meet a real character in the eccentric Ivan Beaman. Ivan is 75, rugged, bearded like Santa Claus, and a seasoned traveller, knees gnarled, bronzed and hairy poking out of his khaki shorts. He's gruff of voice and yet kindly. There's a twinkle in his eye that speaks a lifetime of experience. Disabled, he walks with a stout cane and a pronounced limp. He shuffles over from his palatial and well equipped motor home. We never see his wife, though she is within. Ivan tells us she doesn't want to be here on account of the heat, the flies and the terrain. He's returning from Senegal, having travelled to hell and back through the border crossing at Rosso, without a guide or any other visible support, and with one elderly complaining wife on board.

He recounts the horror stories of the Rosso crossing, where one is at the mercy of beggars and vagabonds who constantly want to rip you off, sell you something, hold you to ransom or sting you for a bribe. Ivan also warns us of the six mile nightmare called no-man's-land, the mine field at the Mauritanian frontier. We can expect rocks, bumps, ruts the size of bath tubs, potholes and unmarked land mines. This is encouraging, as I figure we ought to achieve the same in Black Betty, especially with a half decent guide. The Pug may have a little more trouble with its ultra low suspension, but we've resolved to see this through as a team.

THE IVAN BEAMAN GUIDE TO CROSSING MAURITANIA

- Change your money in the camp site in Nouadhibou for a better exchange rate than at the border.
- The road from Nouadhibou to Nouakchott poses no real problem. Travel through the desert sands is no longer necessary, since last year.
- Nouakchott to Rosso is tarmac, but full of potholes and badly maintained. Take care and factor in delays.
- 50 litres of petrol will cost about 13,000 Mauritanian Ouguiya. 20,000 Ouguiya will see you through the country, if you're not prodigal.
- In Nouakchott there's a hippy hotel called the Auberge Sahara, which is quite decent. You can cook your own food.
- For Nouakchott take either the second or the third island (there's a garage on the corner and a sign which says "Hospital straight ahead, Left for the International Stadium". Go straight on to the next dual carriageway. At the big island on the dual carriageway turn right into Rosso.
- To get through Rosso, the best tactic is to stand up to fake officials, bandits and hustlers. Eventually they just back off.
- On no account take your wife.

I take a note of Ivan's helpful guide through Mauritania, but have nothing to offer in exchange. He's desperate for reading matter, and has read everything in his camper at least twice. I have only our copies of *The Lonely Planet* and figure he could've written them himself. So we thank him, wish him a safe journey, and leave him to Mrs. Beaman.

Dave brews up on the primus, while Andy smears factor 112 on my face, which is beginning to tingle from the fierce rays. I fear the factor 112 may have been a mistake, and spend the rest of the day sporting a ghostly pallor.

There now follows a period of discussion, debate, and negotiation with other guides who've turned up to ply their trade. Mohammed Bomba claims to be chief guide and has the bearing to fit the role. Resplendent in brilliant white and purple, a tall negro prince of the desert, with confidence and machismo to match his stately majesty. I introduce Graham, Andy and Dave to Mohammed Abdullah, the guide already interviewed and a likely candidate.

In the concrete front yard of Dumb and Dumber's hovel, an understanding between the teams is reached that will see us through to Senegal. None of us hankers for the desert if that route's no longer essential, and we have it on good authority that the road from Nouadhibou to Nouakchott is now complete. We shall travel in convoy to Nouakchott with any other teams that arrive in the meantime and prefer tarmac to sand. From there the choice is either onwards to Rosso, and suffer the thieves, scoundrels, ripoffs, corruption and unknown hassle crossing the frontier into Senegal, or take the quieter but infinitely more hazardous route down the Diama Road. We're unanimous in our choice of the Diama Road, favouring ruts over rats, and Graham clinches our partnership with Dumb and Dumber by stating his mission, "to boldly get us all, and both cars, to the Gambia".

It's agreed we'll need a guide to lead us through the minefield into Mauritania, and from Nouakchott to Diama, avoiding Rosso.

Mohammed Abdullah agrees to meet us in the morning and guide us to the Auberge Sahara in Nouakchott (where we shall be enjoying mint tea, petits fours and idle conversation, while the other teams are getting lost in the desert) and then help us to Diama. His unwritten agenda is to deal with all the administrative kerfuffle through customs and police controls. The cost will be a minimum of 250 Euros (£175), so if we can attract other teams to our convoy the cost will be further divided. We agree to make some attempt to negotiate with those who have no desire to wreck their cars or lose themselves in the desert or the waves at high tide. Team Old Gits, in the yellow Scirocco, with their shorter time constraints, might be likely candidates.

We've clarified our intentions, and our partnership, but it's at least to a degree dependant on getting two or three other teams on board and signed up. Our guide is provisionally booked.

It's back to Dakhla town at lunch time, leaving Dumb and Dumber with the primus in their hovel. We've learnt some useful tactics in the morning's negotiations; listen, hover about like an expectant fly, absorb information gradually, state what you want and then reach a consensus. Once again, Graham and I, with our complementary skills, worked very well.

Graham washes his smalls in the early afternoon and hangs them out to dry on the tow rope he's rigged on the balcony. I prefer to throw away my discarded underwear and socks, saving me the bother. I walk into Dakhla town instead to buy bread. The short walk to the pâtisserie brings me out in a sweat, and as I glance down the long straight dusty road towards the camp site the haze plays tricks with my eyes. I see mirages of mid desert lagoons. It's well into the nineties Fahrenheit by now. I buy two round flat breads, coated in poppy seeds, from an open fronted fly blown garage. Three dhiram, or about 18 pence for the two.

As the muezzin calls the one o'clock faithful to prayer, Graham and I sit on the beds in our penthouse suite eating a concoction of sauerkraut, sausage, ham and potato out of tins warmed on the now fully functional stove. For dessert, a cornucopia of fresh (well tinned actually) fruit salad. I am careful to place a third portion in the bedroom wardrobe, as is the west African tradition.

We spend the afternoon in siesta. It's too hot and fly blown to do anything else.

Much later we return to the campsite, where several more Challenge Teams have arrived. Team Crazy Larry's, from Chelsea, the Costa Blanca Dons, Team Turbo Tortoises, Lord of the Sands and Norfolk 'n Chance. The Welsh lads we met in Gibraltar, and a Citroen 2CV sail jauntily into the campsite as we arrive. Team Clic Sargents and Harry and Tony of Team Hugh Jarse, with whom we dined in Meknes, are setting up the caravan they've towed thus far without a hitch. Just before five, the Reservoir Frogs crawl in, followed by Rattle 'n Hum in a battered Granada Estate and Team Flapjack in their tiny Lancia. These teams hurriedly erect tents and trailers on the unforgiving hammada of the car park, lashing guy ropes to vehicles and to each other against the gusting desert winds.

Negotiations and much beer swilling ensue. I don't feel comfortable in the bear pit, where we size each other up. We're not exactly competitors. This is not a race, like big brother Paris-Dakar. It's more like captains choosing teams at school sports. No-one wants to be the last selected. Some alliances have already been made. There's no order in the selection process, and the criteria are unclear. To be stuck with an insufferable Wally, or an incompetent Hooray Henry, could be disastrous. On the other hand, should I not put preference behind me and just support my comrades in adversity? In the event, choices are made by circumstance. It seems there aren't many teams prepared to travel otherwise than through the desert, despite the existence of the new and perfectly adequate road. Everyone else wants to generally arse around in the desert and on the beach.

We need to firm up matters with our chosen guide, Mohammed Abdullah. Andy and I, in our school French, get the crux of our decisions across to Mohammed. The Life Mechanics and Dumb and Dumber will travel as two teams in convoy. Mohammed can travel in Black Betty. We leave Dakhla early tomorrow and head down the coast, through the minefield into Mauritania and on to Nouadhibou. Then we travel onwards to Nouakchott and the hippy hotel on the new road. Mohammed will take us to the Senegal frontier on the Diama route, avoiding Rosso. The charge is 350 Euros, including an allowance for his camping and accommodation. Andy gives Mohammed a 50 Euro deposit to clinch the deal. In return, and as a gesture of good faith, Mohammed leaves his passport with me, an act of faith which I find astonishing and quite touching. Apparently, in the early days of the Challenge, guides would often negotiate deals like this and then disappear, never to be seen again, with the deposit, sometimes with full payment. Mohammed is clearly a man of different mettle. The deal is expensive for us, as the guide's fee is only to be split two ways (as opposed to the usual four or five). However, and whilst it's handsome for Mohammed, representing a couple of months pay for four days work, I consider the money well spent. We'll avoid all the hazards of the desert and the nonsense of Rosso, and leave early in the morning rather than hang about in the vain hope of meeting other teams willing to forego the pleasures of the desert and beach.

Graham reorganises Black Betty's rear seat and shifts the treasured tajine and sewing machine yet again. We store the petrol in the right foot well, to accommodate Mohammed in his comfortable, if not spacious, quarters. A guide, you would think, should perhaps occupy a front seat. However, I'm more interested in filming our demise in the minefield than in avoiding it in the back seat, so Mohammed will have to endure the privations of life behind Graham for a few days. There's no room in the Pug.

We leave the campsite, having struck a most satisfactory deal, and agree to meet Mohammed tomorrow for another dawn departure.

Back in Dakhla town Ian and Dan of Team 2 in a 4 have booked into our hotel. They have major problems with tyres on the Renault. The front of the car's slightly out of alignment with the rear. It's crabbing and tyres wearing out at an alarming rate. They've spent hours changing and repairing endless tyres as they progressed through the Rif Mountains and down this punishing road. They also lost an alternator and replaced it at a breakers yard yesterday.

This evening we search harder for a decent meal. Our interest in the remaining cans, and our spirit of adventure with the camping stove has waned. Scouring the tawdry back streets in the darkness we eventually discover the Hotel Restaurant Bahia, which seems to be serving something hot and European. Team Hugh Jarse have beaten us to it and are already seated on the front terrace with another team, travelling in a Volkswagen Beetle. The tables are quickly filled with Challengers, including Ian and Dan, and the contents of a 2 CV. Despite the European menu, I plump for the traditional tajine, which is hot, spicy and very tasty.

As we eat, we talk, as a bunch of men in the desert are wont, of our heroic endeavours, our disasters and acts of derring do. We talk of mountains traversed, streams forded, eyebrows burnt and miles gained. Team 2 in 4 are still up for the desert experience in the ailing Renault. Other teams are "doing the desert" alone, and without a guide. One team, driving a tiny Trabant, only made it as far as southern France after three engine rebuilds and a clapped out wiper motor. It's still there, just outside Cognac. Another, in a San Francisco Police Department patrol car, missed Dover completely and were last seen in Snowdonia.

Having finally exhausted ourselves and our companions with our tales, all, I believe, ever so slightly exaggerated, Graham and I leave the party to their reminiscences and their beer (still illegal technically, but nobody really cares in Dakhla) and make for our beds. We have another early start, another long day on the road.

DAY ELEVEN
MOHAMMED ABDULLAH, PRINCE AMONG THIEVES

"Fuck! Shit! Bollocks!" The pain is instant, searing, electric.
"What's up?"
"Stubbed me fuckin' toe on a rock. God it hurts. Oh, bugger!" Hopping on my left, clutching the big toe in both hands, the hammada in the dark is full of surprises. The left is now impaled on a neolithic axe head.
"What was that metallic sound?"
"It was me 'ead having an argument with the gate. Put the lights on Gray, for chrissake. Can't see a bleedin' thing. Think I've broke me dose."
"Haven't you got the torch?"
"Jus' put the fuckin' lights on willya?"

I'm fumbling in the intense dark on all fours, groping blindly for the torch, my specs and my pride. Silhouetted in the blaze of Black Betty's headlights, I cast an eerie shadow, as of some ghostly quadruped caught in a crossfire. The nose throbs, and the pain from both feet subsides to a dull ache as I nurse them in the dirt.

"Can you get Dumb and Dumber on the walkie talkie?," I struggle through my frustration, "I gave the other hand set to Andy last night. He may have thought to switch it on."

He had. As the radio crackled into life and Andy's distant voice came over the airwaves, we'd made contact. Andy quickly made his way to the gate, startled the keeper out of his customary slumber and prevailed on him to open the gates by candle light. Graham carried me over the threshold. Black Betty wasn't permitted into the enclosure at this hour without further, and probably expensive, formality.

Andy and Dave were ready, packed, and anxious to leave for Mauritania, but we had to wait for the tardy Mohammed, who didn't appear to keep our early hours, or have our sense of urgency and impending doom. We passed the time in pointless speculation, kicking our heels.

As day began to dawn, it was beginning to dawn on us that Mohammed might not appear at all, but rather make off and spend our deposit in the hot spots of Dakhla town on wine, women and incantation. It was only the thoughts that Dakhla town really doesn't boast a Pleasure Dome, that family man Mohammed didn't seem by nature the sort to avail himself of one had it existed, and the fact that I held his passport which must surely be worth more than the 50 Euros we'd entrusted him with, that made Mohammed's gentle unconcerned appearance at seven o'clock unsurprising.

The goal today was Nouadhibou in Mauritania, and our immediate aim to leave Dakhla as early as possible. It was vital we reach the notorious, and jealously guarded, frontier between Western Sahara and Mauritania before noon. The frontier closes for a leisurely lunch at 12.00 prompt, and may not re-open for three or four hours, or until the next day, or the next bank holiday, or a month with an "R" in it. It was important to start early and motor on, if we didn't want to spend days in tents on the open hammada in the company of other illegal immigrants.

Mohammed settled into the rear seat behind Graham. I nursed my aching and broken body, and the cameras. In the pellucid blue and gold of another perfect dawn, we left Camping Moussafir for the last time, with the Pug in not too close pursuit. For the next 25 miles we drove back through the lunar landscape we encountered two days ago. In stark white daylight the peninsula had possessed a kind of golden vastness, empty and solitary, and yet breathtaking. In the transient prussian blue and purple of dawn, it had an eerie secretive beauty, and a quiet coyness as haunting as it was mysterious. On either side, the Atlantic Ocean lapped noiselessly on the vast and sandy shore.

"'Ere, you're not waxing lyrical again are you?"
"No, this is more yer inspired prosaic. Got to catch it for posterity though, 'aven't I?"
"Yes, yes, very good." (from the back seat).

With the odd incongruity of camper vans silhouetted against the dawn light, we reach the main road to Mauritania, Nouadhibou and beyond.

Mohammed sits quietly in the back seat, cuddling the globe I bought at the recycling centre to guide us on this epic adventure and hand over to some deserving Gambian. I feel peaceful, secure and in high spirits. We're just north of the Tropic of Cancer, on a decent road in perfect weather.

The lights of Dakhla town twinkle in the distance to our right as we travel further south, and reach Argoub, on the Tropic, at five to eight.

The day ahead's going to be a long one, and I take the opportunity of getting to know our guide a little better. Mohammed has his full Mauritanian quota of one wife, and two young daughters. He has one hundred camels and some goats. Wealth is measured principally in camels, and with one hundred Mohammed could be described as "comfortable". He lives in Nouadhibou. His English is limited to "Yes, very good", slightly more extensive than my Arabic.

The road's endless tarmac and stony hummock, with long flat plains between plateaux of hammada and sand. The landscape alters by the day, often by the hour, encouraged by the constant wind. There's a total absence of meaningful signs, no hump backed bridges, pedestrian crossings or major roads ahead. The only signs are for bends, and after the first few of these Graham's used to the very gentle curves they portend. We figure the signs were erected more to alleviate boredom than to warn of hazards. Every now and then Atlantic rollers peep through the wall of sand. Mohammed's explanation for the thousands of pyramidal stone structures seen yesterday, and again today, that they represent the sites of removed mines, I find fanciful and far fetched, probably suggested to add drama to our day.

For the first time I can't get a signal on my mobile phone, purchased specifically for this hazardous journey into the remote. I knew there'd be a time when, due to lack of radio masts south of Morocco, we'd run out of signal and be ex communicado. That time has come earlier than expected, and it does focus the mind on how very alone we are. Still in radio and visual contact with the Pug, Dave confirms he lost signal half an hour ago. We're alone, except for each other and the reassuring presence of Mohammed Abdullah in the back seat. I console myself with my now well established roving reporter routine, sustaining us both with swigs of warm water and hot coke, and entertaining the troops with an endless stream of jolly banter and repartee. Graham drives on autopilot, along the longest, straightest and most boring road in the modern world. Probably. Mohammed alternately snoozes and cuddles the globe. If he partakes at the relevant hour of the necessary devotions to the Islamic creed, I'm not aware. I don't catch him facing east.

130 miles outside Dakhla we come upon a surfer's paradise, completely deserted. Miles of beach and Atlantic rollers, and not a soul to be seen. In the midst of this astonishing desolation, the road to Bir Gandouz forkes off to the left. We've travelled in the heat of the day now for several days, the windows open to admit fresh air, sand, dust and the roar of the passing desert. At this turning in our lives, well at this turning to Bir Gandouz, Graham switches on the air conditioning, to find it works! Blessed cool air and an equable, pleasant temperature waft deliciously through the interior, and Graham, Mohammed and I bask

in it for a few minutes, until Graham finds he might need his cardigan, Mohammed zips up his body warmer and I set to chipping ice from the windscreen in my fingerless gloves. Seriously, the air conditioning makes life in Black Betty much more comfortable, although we shall be conservative in its use while petrol's at a premium.

At Bir Gandouz we make a petrol stop, and use most of the remaining dhiram. Outside Western Sahara, we've been advised, dhiram are useless, and they can't be redeemed in the UK. Mohammed tells us they can be exchanged in Mauritania, if you know where to go, and he does.

As we leave the petrol station, an unladen lorry appears from the opposite direction. It's been delivering sand to another part of the desert, one of the principal occupations of the desert people. Sand is shovelled by hand and sand plough, from locations where it's found in unacceptable abundance, and transported to other desert locations where it's more sparse. At least that's what appears to be happening.

Eighty miles before Nouadhibou, the sight of rollers crashing along the endless desert shore inspire me to call Gilly. There's signal on the mobile, but she's not at home. Probably spinning in Berrynarbour at this crucial moment on Tuesday morning as I try to report progress down the West African coast. This is to prove the last call I can make on the mobile to my beloved until back on British soil.

The sand's become serious. Mountainous dunes, some three hundred feet high, shield our view from the more distant desert and dwarf us, as we charge, awestruck, down the valley.

About thirty miles short of the Mauritanian frontier I become a tad anxious at the closeness to the noon deadline. I don't relish an afternoon in the heat of the sun, less still a night under the stars, while we wait for the frontier to reopen. We reach the border at 11.30 a.m.

The exit from Western Sahara was predictably nightmarish. The road had been remarkably lonely for the last couple of hundred miles, yet here at the border throngs of desperate and dusty looking characters milled around, arguing and swearing with a purpose that eluded us. Some, wearing hopeless resigned expressions, sat in the dirt and drank mint tea. We joined the crowd nearest to the door of a concrete and tarpaulin "office" we supposed housed border officials.

There was nothing resembling an orderly queue, no instructions as to what to do or what was expected of us. We debated whether to emulate the locals and start waving our arms about, shouting and screaming incoherently, or to pick a fight with the nearest border official and demand our human rights, when gentle Mohammed sidled up, smiled and asked for our passports. Soon he was elbowing his way through the crowds to the passport hut where we saw him pass them to an anonymous hand protruding from the almost closed door. He smiled and appeared to pass the time of day with those inside, invisible to us, and then retreated to the outside of the crowd where he was soon deep in conversation with another local.

We waited for what seemed an age in the ill organised chaos, blinded by white sand, deafened by the clamour, hoping against hope that the border would not suddenly and unpredictably close leaving us to blister in the afternoon sun. From time to time a mysterious robed official appeared at the door and called out a name, to be answered by someone on the outskirts of the crowd who then fought his way through the heaving mass to the front, grasped his passport and made off. We strained to hear something, anything that might approach "Morgan", "Barrow", "Pugsley" or "De Meur" in a West Saharan accent. "Barrow" is a surprisingly common name in the Gambia, but here, just north of Mauritania, it's unknown. "Pugsley" isn't known outside of North Devon. It was "De Meur", heavily accented with its French influence, that was the easiest for the tongues of border officials to handle. On hearing his name, Graham surged excitedly forward into the melée, encouraged and manhandled by the rest of us, as we saw our chances of beating the noon deadline dwindle. We pushed, barged and bundled Graham into the crowd, and like some conquering hero held aloft by three crazed and triumphant revolutionaries, he seized the handful of passports brandished by the same anonymous hand that had taken them from Mohammed. We retreated, bruised and bloody, but more or less intact from the passport scuffle, congratulating ourselves that we were one step further to entering Mauritania. Then we put Graham down and attended to the issue of customs.

An imposing figure in pale blue uniform, gold braided epaulettes and flamboyant white officer's hat approached. He checked the cars with a cursory glance, but was intrigued to see under the bonnet of each, so we obliged by popping the hoods and pointing out all the hiding places for drugs, contraband and illegal tender. We were asked whether we had anything to declare and I resisted my natural temptation to respond with "Nothing but the crack in my bottom and an undying love for my wife". Something within the demeanour of the customs official, or perhaps his unholstered gun, guided my instincts. This was not a chap to be trifled with. He took the motor vehicle visa issued on the dock in Tangier, which had languished unnoticed in the document portfolio. I realised for the first time the importance of this humble docket. Had we been stopped by officialdom throughout the entire length of Morocco or Western Sahara and not been able to produce it, we could've been required to surrender Black Betty as an illegal immigrant.

The third set of officials mingling with the crowd, dressed in khaki, represented immigration. Again, our passports were demanded and studied, and we were asked the purpose of our visit. The stock reply "Humanitaire, non competitif" seemed to suffice, and we suddenly found we'd left Western Sahara, but lost Mohammed in the excitement of the moment.

In hindsight, our passage thus far had been eased by the presence of our excellent and self-effacing guide. He appeared to know or at least be acquainted with the entire population of Morocco and Western Sahara. As a native of Mauritania, our passage into and through that remote land seemed assured. We were anxious to leave this beleaguered place as soon as possible, and on the stroke of noon, as the border guards were shutting up shop for the siesta, Mohammed reappeared through a back door, in No-man's-land. He'd been chatting to old colleagues and generally oiling the wheels (and no doubt greasing some palms) to get us over the frontier in time. He resumed his seat in the back, we drove through the concrete gateway that delineates the border and about fifty yards into what we thought to be Mauritania, when we were stopped by two gendarmes, and asked for two fiches. A further fifty yards through the sand we were stopped again, by two police who required our passports for a third time, and another two fiches. I was of course happy to oblige, in the knowledge that, by now, surely the whole of the northern hemisphere must be aware of our departure from Western Sahara.

But we're not in Mauritania yet. At the furthest southern point of Western Sahara the road just stops. Black shiny tarmac hardtop ceases as abruptly as a tap being turned off. Just as abruptly, the rutted and pockmarked dirt and scree of the desert takes over. Mauritania doesn't begin for another 6 kilometres. Someone's had the foresight to insert a helpful minefield as a buffer between the two countries, known affectionately as No-man's land. There's not one track, but many through it. The tyres of countless vehicles snake away into the heat haze, punctuated by ruts the size of bath tubs, potholes the size of your granny's best jam saucepan and craters the size of, well, craters. Mohammed had demonstrated this in his drawing in the sand at the Dakhla camp site.

Anticipating I might not find a more suitable location, and figuring we could do with the good fortune, I plant the Mauritanian wishbone in a hollow in the sand and cover it with a couple of rocks. It'll probably stay undisturbed for centuries.

There's been an official ceasefire at the frontier of Mauritania since 1991, and you get the impression that nobody cares you've crossed into one god forsaken piece of worthless desert from another. However, this place once bristled with barbed wire and land mines, and whilst some of them have no doubt been removed, and others detonated taking life limb and mechanical bits to decorate the stratosphere, many remain.

We enter the minefield at a respectful snail's pace, keeping to the tracks of vehicles that have gone before, steering judiciously around the more dramatic craters and suspicious projections. Mohammed knows the route well, and is aware of those tracks that are contraindicated. He directs operations from the back seat, while Graham juggles with the obstacles and I film the experience, keeping one eye on the Pug following in our tracks ten metres behind. Every now and then Mohammed and I step gingerly out of Black Betty and walk ahead, keeping strictly to the tyre tracks, scanning with the right foot for rogue mines. I take readily to this mine inspection duty, fingers firmly jammed into my ears in the hope that, should something go bang, my ear drums will at least survive. It's a bit disconcerting to see Mohammed follow my lead.

The Road To Banjul

The piste (the more polite term for this track) is littered with the bones and innards of vehicles less fortunate. Cars and trucks, upturned, blown up or expired, mostly unidentifiable as to make and model, lie in heaps, a tangled, burnt out mess of wrecks.

We pick our way through the oily boneyard of death and recent destruction. Half way through we come across an enclave of the living, some twenty cars circled about two elderly caravans minus chassis and wheels. People drinking coffee and mint tea. A greasy spoon at the end of the universe, where you celebrate success in arriving thus far unscathed. This is where you swap stories of heroic deeds or what's just happened in the soap opera, and then, like ships in the night, press on. That's what it looks like anyway. We never do find out their business in the minefield. Are they tourists? Holiday makers? Perhaps they're illegal immigrants to Mauritania, awaiting the opportunity for a dash over the border.

Pleased we've chosen the inestimable Mohammed to see us through the minefield, my thoughts are with Ivan Beaman, he who passed this way, and back, unaided, disabled and with an aged grumbling wife.

Suddenly desert man emerges, tall and black, robed in purple and white, from Mauritania. We've reached the frontier.

Three ramshackle tin and sawdust sheds. We joined the queue of traffic and soon found ourselves at shed number one, passport control. Whether it was because we had Mohammed with us on his own home soil I don't know, but the entry into Mauritania was trouble free, if flyblown.

Now, if you've been paying attention, you'll recall our visas for Mauritania were valid for a period of three months from 15 February 2007. Today's date was 12 February. Would we be allowed in? Would a modest bribe assist? Would we have to separate from the comradeship of Dumb and Dumber and spend two nights and days in the middle of the minefield, with the other hopefuls, waiting to become legal? Would we simply have to purchase new visas at the border and write the trip to London off to experience? My breath was duly baited as we waited in the stifling heat of Mauritania (well, almost). To my surprise we were simply waved through passport control without a murmur. Graham and I were illegal immigrants, in a new and distant land. It felt ever so slightly naughty!

There was a woman's touch to shed number two, the gendarmerie. It'd been domesticised with chintzed curtains and the corrugated iron tastefully wallpapered in pink gingham. The large and very black lady constable enquired as to the reason for our visit. She lent heavily on the green chenille and looked searchingly into my eyes as I pleaded feebly with the usual "Humanitaire, non competitive". It's clear Mauritania doesn't get many casual tourists, not entering via this route anyway.

Shed number three was lined with cardboard and tomato boxes and dealt with car registration. Another large, black and very kind policeman helped me complete the necessary "engagement sur honneur". I was on my honour, it seemed, to drive safely and responsibly in Mauritania. As Graham had not signed, he could of course continue to drive with his usual reckless and irresponsible disregard. A fee of 10 Euros changed hands and the document was duly stamped about fourteen times. All in all, the border crossing had been more efficient, organised and pleasant, if quaint and dusty, than on the Western Sahara side. There was no hustle for bribes, gifts or payola. Of course, this might have been the result of Mohammed's presence, but I like to think the country is just more honest and responsible. After all, it produced Mohammed Abdullah.

We emerged into The Islamic Republic of Mauritania. Now, not many people have even heard of this vast country, less still know where it is. I hadn't, when I found it in an ancient encyclopaedia, which gave this passing tribute over forty years ago:

"*Mauritania, Islamic Republic of, independent state in west Africa and linked with the French Community (q.v.), which it joined after a plebiscite taken in 1958 at the inauguration of the French fifth republic. Independence followed in 1960. Mauritania has an area of 416,216 sq. miles, mainly desert, except in oases and along the Senegal river, which forms its southern frontier. The population is Arab with Berber and Fulani admixture. Livestock, gum, salt and fish are the chief products. The principal towns are Kaédi and Atar; its capital, Nouakchott, lies 220 miles north of the Senegal's mouth. Pop.c.730,000*"[3]

---
[3] Newnes Popular Encyclopaedia (An authoritative survey of universal knowledge) volume 6, page 2006. Published by George Newnes Ltd., 1963.

I suspect little has happened in Mauritania over the intervening forty years. Nouadhibou, our destination today, has become the second city perhaps, and would deserve more of a mention than Kaédi, which I had trouble locating on the map.

Mauritanians are blacker and more negroid than further north. This is the beginning of black Africa. There's slightly more evidence of a female presence too. For here, in the dust, sat women, immaculately dressed in flowing white and purple, sipping mint tea, something not seen in the north.

The road reappears after six kilometres of nonsense. Drifting sand's a reminder that we're still essentially Saharan, and care is needed, yet the going is reasonable. We're on the main road to Nouadhibou in the early afternoon, with not far to go to the day's destination.

The railway line to Choum, in the heart of the Sahara, carries the longest train in the world. Transporting ore and minerals to the coast, it's two miles long and featured in Michael Palin's *"Sahara"*. It's on the left. On our right, bedouin encampments, their huge and stately tents, the large Mercedes, pack donkeys, and a few camels just yards from the railway and the road.

We soon reach Nouadhibou. Nobody tells us of course. There's no sign at the city limits which declares "Welcome to Nouadhibou, gateway to the Islamic Republic of Mauritania. Twinned with Kamchatka and Slough. Population 13". In fact there's no sign at the city limits or anywhere else in Nouadhibou that says anything. You just sense you're in Nouadhibou when you find yourself amidst the donkey carts, the wandering goats, the dust, dead dogs and rats. It has all the charm and abandon of an eighteenth century Dodge City. Animals wander amongst piles of refuse, scavenging for edible morsels. Ancient and battered cars in a multitude of improbable colours limp on broken springs, belching exhaust fumes and marijuana. Large, menacing drug barons, with their henchmen, cruise the streets in hideously ostentatious Mercedes with cracked windscreens, the few existing lights broken and hanging off. Mopeds, held together with string and a prayer, buzz erratically about, putter to a stop and are pushed out of the way of the slightly more reliable rickshaws. The streets are rows of single storey concrete shuttered units, piles of sand and gravel, cars in various states of disrepair jacked up on the verge, some just expired and left to rot. No sign of police or law enforcement. No sign of authority of any kind. And not a sign of a sign. Anywhere.

And yet we felt safe here, unaccountably. Beautiful women in brightly coloured dress and headwear adorned the hellish streets, with statuesque splendour. Young children, immaculately turned out, picked their laughing way through the dust and rubbish. It's a slum of inexplicable extremes. Nobody seemed to be in charge, or to care that nobody was in charge. It's a wonder this town's inhabitants can exist in the abject squalor and yet appear so neat and tidy.

We'd no idea where to put up for the night in this lawless wild west town. All the indications were that accommodation, if it could be found, would be basic, verging on sordid. Campsites are a rarity, as road borne holidaymakers are not expected to venture this far south. Hotels, where they exist, are often thinly disguised brothels. Mauritania still has an estimated 100,000 black slaves, and many of the females, it is said, service the Arab ruling class. Standards of hygiene would be minimal, and we four feared for our virginity in a Nouadhibou hotel.

Mohammed came to our rescue again. Our well respected guide took us directly to his own house in the heart of Nouadhibou, where, he explained, we could stay for the night. Graham was told to pull in to the left and we found ourselves staring at a blank concrete wall with a single iron gate. The Pug pulled up next to us. Dumb and Dumber were as surprised and relieved as us to hear we had reached our billet for the night.

Mohammed's house was the next surprise. Through the iron gate we climbed, over a pile of builders sand and gravel in the tiny front yard, through a front door and storm porch (storm porch? Do they have storms in Mauritania?) and into Mohammed's spacious home. A long entrance hall, tiled and brightly lit, if blandly decorated, with five doors leading off in all directions. One of these must have been Mohammed's kitchen, which we never saw. One, a shower room and toilet. The other three were generic, with no furniture whatsoever, unless you count the small television and stand in what seemed to be his living room at the back of the house. We were led there, with our hand luggage. Furnished with rugs, throws and an abundance of colourful floor cushions, we lounged as politely as we could on the floor and talked, as embarrassed Brits abroad will, of the weather. Mohammed's young and ample wife sat in one corner, nursing the youngest child and gazing at the television. Occasionally she'd look around, nod and smile, surprisingly incurious and unperturbed to be invaded by this motley crew of improbably dressed and, to her, unintelligible foreigners. Then she'd turn back to her child, ensure she was plugged on to her voluminous breast, and continue with the soap opera.

Mohammed plied us with cool soft drinks, coke, lemonade and bottled water. We helped ourselves greedily. As we sat and took in this unexpected hospitality, we were joined by his friend, a tall, mustachioed gentleman, elegant in white and purple. He introduced himself as a journalist on the Nouadhibou Gazette. We convershed at length in faltering French, and learned much about the economy and political situation.

Meanwhile, Mohammed disappeared and we relaxed, grateful for the luxury and safety of his house, conversing with his friend, served mint tea by his wife in yet another portrayal of the curious ceremony (see DAY SIX for instructions), and catching glimpses of the news.

Mohammed reappeared hours later, bearing an enormous tajine, a metre in diameter. In it bubbled a fragrant concoction of fatty meat (goat, lamb or camel, probably all three), and vegetables, highly spiced and appetizing. He placed the brew on the floor before us, and ripped the large chunks of meat into smaller pieces. Six men in a circle, each armed with a French stick and our right hand, tucked in with a vengeance. Careful not to use the left hand (which in Muslim tradition is used for something quite different) we attacked the tajine hungrily, gnawing at the generous hunks of meat and slurping gravy laden bread. Mrs. Mohammed sat in the corner, feeding the baby and watching her soap. The scene was bizarre, and yet gracious and sociable in the extreme. And Mohammed went up a few further notches in our estimation, for he'd cooked the finest food we'd experienced since Meknes and the Royal Palace. He left the room with the remains and I presumed he was going to do the washing up.

But he returned, moments later, bearing this time a silver bucket and kettle. He proceeded to pour hot water over each of our hands in turn, allowing us to soap up with the tablet provided, and rinse with water from the kettle, drying them on a towel. I thought this the most touching and practical personal service I'd encountered, and an exceedingly civilised custom from a town that, on the exterior, looked about as rough and ready as they come.

After dinner, Andy asked Mohammed about changing the remaining dhiram and some euros into Oguiyas. We'd need money for petrol and a couple of days stay in Mauritania, and you can't take the currency out of the country. Mohammed instantly changed hats and became our banker and insurance agent. He disappeared with a quantity of euros and our passports and returned in minutes with handfuls of Ouguiyas, sufficient to see us through Mauritania. We'd need car insurance before leaving Nouadhibou, but the general consensus was that Mohammed would sort something out. He hadn't let us down yet, and we'd known him barely twenty four hours. We wondered again at the many and varied talents of our chosen guide, who'd become a sort of corporate Passepartout.

There was yet another dimension to his hospitality. As the evening wore on and an early bed beckoned, he expressed concern for the security of Black Betty and the Pug. Both were stacked with tempting gifts and goodies, vulnerable over night in the unlit lawless streets of Nouadhibou. He had the solution yet again, and our cars were moved to the other side of the road and parked right outside the dingy and anonymous gendarmerie that happened, by chance, to be located opposite. There, under the watchful, if reluctant, eye of his former colleagues, they'd be safe. And at no cost. It seemed that when we hired Mohammed, we'd taken a comprehensive package.

The vehicles' safely catered for, Mohammed took his leave with wife and young children, to stay at his brother's house for the night. This trusting man literally left his house and belongings in our foreign hands until early the next day, when he promised to return and take us further into Mauritania.

Graham and I slept in our sleeping bags on cushions in Mohammed's living room. Andy and Dave took an adjoining, and similarly "furnished", room as their billet. We slept fitfully and restlessly on the hard, overstuffed cushions, 3080 miles away from Long Lane Farm.

DAY TWELVE
THE HIPPY HOTEL

I stood and dully contemplated the medieval contraption before me. My feelings a mixture of consternation, anxiety, self sacrifice and pure disbelief, I had no idea how to tackle the logistics. The practicalities were overwhelming. For seven and a half days I'd travelled down this remote coastline with my doughty and resourceful colleagues, confronting and even overcoming with aplomb all hazards, enemies and distractions. We had boldly gone where no man had gone before. Et cetera.

But here in Mohammed's house, enjoying his hospitality, I would have to succumb for the first time to the uncertainties of the west African lavatory.

In anticipation of my plight, I'd taken instruction and one-to-one tuition from Andy and Dave, who, though not exactly aficionados of crouch and aim, had at least experienced the less salubrious facilities of Camping Moussafir. They could be said to have their "O"Level. We'd conducted heated debate. Andy had delivered a full seminar type presentation assisted by some rather interesting flip charts. The more worldly and practical Dave had drawn line diagrams and flow charts, which had appealed particularly to the engineer in Graham. But now the time had come to put all I had learned to use. I stood before the ceramic hole in the shower room floor and studied Dave's line drawings. It was immediately apparent I was facing the wrong direction. So I turned around and, facing the door, considered which of the three preferred positions, as described in Andy Morgan's useful volume on the topic, I should adopt; the classic Eton Crouch, the Andy Morgan squat thrust or the Dave Barrow Straddle and Follow Through, in the piked position. Remembering first to protect my trousers (and being ultra cautious I took them off) I chose the classic pose for this delicate operation, easier on the elbows and slightly kinder to the knees than Andy's experimental posture or Dave's revolutionary acrobatics. It worked first time. I even remembered the cardinal rule, which applies all down the west African coast, if not the hinterland. Take your loo roll with you. Supplies are rarely to hand, let alone within reach, in strange lavatories.

Pleased with my first and only attempt, the evidence was duly flushed away with bucket and water from the tap provided on the wall. The ancient cistern had clearly given up the ghost.

I must confess Graham and I were at a loss to understand why the resourceful and apparently affluent Mohammed, family man with lovely wife and two growing children, would put up with the privations of traditional Mauritanian plumbing. We'd seen European pedestal lavatories in abundance on sale in the plumbers' merchants in Morocco, and as far south as Tiznit.

I finished my haphazard ablutions in cold water discomfort and the smell of stale urine. (There are no U bends in Mauritania and the hole in the floor described above falls, I suspect, directly into the public sewer).

Graham followed my use of the shower room, and confirmed it's not a place to read the paper, contemplate in any depth or indulge in transcendental meditation. It's about as functional, or perhaps dysfunctional, as it gets.

The mournful bray of a donkey heralded the dawn, reminding me of home at Long Lane, where it's the donkeys, rather than the strident crow of Ashleigh Fuckwit our only cockerel, that calls us to breakfast. 3080 miles from home I felt slightly homesick and sorry for myself. Gilly had been contending with the first snows of winter, and the mud that goes with it. A brief telephone call on Andy's satellite phone had brought home to me the long, dark days of February, and, strangely, part of me longed for cold damp Devon.

Mohammed returned from his brother's, and we retrieved the cars from the reluctant police chief. Soon we were weaving our uncertain way through the busy early morning traffic of Nouadhibou, searching for motor insurance.

The offices of Mauritanien d'Assurances et de Reassurances, one of those faceless concrete and glass monoliths, were closed for business. Another of Mohammed's many skills came to the fore. He calmly walked to a half open window, put his arm through up to his narrow shoulder, slipped the catch on the office door and we were in!

I, for one, felt nervous and vulnerable at this point. Already an illegal immigrant, I was now party to breaking and entry, unlawful trespass in a foreign land and driving without valid motor insurance. My CV wasn't looking so good, and I anticipated the feeling of my collar at any moment, with the immortal words "Awl right my son, you're bleedin' nicked!". But Mohammed seemed unconcerned as we sat in the interview seats, awaiting the arrival of the authorities, who would surely have us hauled away to certain incarceration in some Mauritanian slammer.

Minutes passed. A middle aged man in trainers and bomber jacket, carrying a briefcase, entered from the street. Without a vestige of surprise at our presence, he placed the briefcase on the desk and gestured towards a table where rested all the paraphernalia for mint tea. Another invitation. (Return to DAY SIX for instructions). Soon he was brewing up, and Mohammed left us to conduct our business.

In due course the agent poured us a respectable twelve incher, and Dave and I were in the middle of our third silent glass of the treacly stuff by the time the subject of car insurance was broached. Communicating entirely by sign language, as the agent had even less French than us, we explained we were after the minimum three day insurance, and were successful in extracting a quote for ten. I produced one of the copy log books, and the international log book, which translated the vehicle details into Arabic. And on payment of about £10 I became the proud possessor of ten days insurance on Mauritanian roads for a Nissan Bluebird with unidentifiable United States registration. Of course, I queried the apparent anomaly, and was treated to a shrug and a wink from the agent, and another glass of steaming mint tea. Mauritanien d'Assurances et de Reassurances can only cope with the concept of the Nissan Bluebird, so all motor insurance in Mauritania is for that particular marque. Dave's insurance was marginally cheaper, presumably because his Bluebird was smaller.

Pleased to be at least apparently legal on the highways and byways, we left, both proudly clutching our Nissan Bluebird insurance certification and replete with mint tea.

Back in the cars, we awaited Mohammed, who had gone walkabout again. We soon discovered him, however, sitting comfortably and almost expectantly a few yards away in the back of a Nissan Bluebird, apparently waiting for us. I wondered for a moment at the powers of suggestion of the insurance agent, but then Mohammed realised his mistake and rejoined us in Black Betty.

Down town Nouadhibou. Goats and donkeys, healthier looking than their colleagues in Morocco, free range everywhere, scavenge on discarded cabbage leaves and refuse like some wandering unclaimed larder. Women, black and beautiful, children clinging hungrily to them. Men robed in blue and white, orange braided. Sand, dust, concrete shacks, tin roofed. And junk, vast quantities of broken metal objects, old tin cupboards, wrecked cars, litter the roads. One large compound entirely made of disused washing machines and tumble dryers could be mistaken for an al fresco laundry, except none of them are plumbed or plugged in. An optician on the right. A petrol station on the left. Battered cars pull into the traffic in front without indication, in fact without indicators, and then pull off again, without warning. Some of the cars have no doors. Two pretty girls are walking on the dust verge, when a large man in an even larger Mercedes behind takes us on the inside. The girls leap out of the way, screaming and gesticulating, but kind of accepting the situation. No traffic lights, no roundabouts, no signs.

On the outskirts the traffic becomes calmer, more sane, and there's one sign: *"To the airport"*. Yes, Nouadhibou boasts an airport, or at least a signpost to one.

One enterprising soul has utilised an old caravan, taken from its chassis and wheels, as a makeshift tea shop, and the compressed bodies of the clientèle can be seen through the murky steam. The odd minaret lends variety to the otherwise monotonous street frontage. Tiny lock up shops, little more than sheds, shuttered and barred by night, these businesses purvey everything from bread to bicycles. The shopkeeper stands inside, head and lower face swathed in protective robes, a suspicious sentry.

We stop for Mohammed to buy his breakfast of unleavened bread. Graham and I have already eaten the remains of the All Butter Shortbread Selection and last night's French sticks.

We pass another police check without event or comment. No exchange of fiches. Mohammed's unassuming presence in the back seat is our passport.

The road we are travelling is the only coast road from Nouadhibou to Nouakchott, the capital. It doesn't appear on my 2003 Michelin map. Constructed over the last couple of years and only open for use since the 2006 Challenge, we're among the first to travel it, and very possibly the only Challengers, with Team Dumb and Dumber, to use it at all. This part of the journey is where the Challenge pioneers were constrained to choose either the open desert or the beach at low tide.

The Desert Route

PB Challengers of yesteryear recount horror stories of those who took the desert route, risking life and limb, dehydration and banditry. There are endless excavations of vehicles stuck in sand drifts and depressions. Tempers are fractious, relationships strained to the limit. Breakdown, mental, nervous and mechanical, is frequent, often terminal. Everything, including death and dishonour.

The Beach Route

Teams that took the beach option will tell tales of dicing with death amongst the Atlantic rollers, the crash of sea against superstructure, the cry of the seagull, the joy of swimming with dolphins and the exhilaration of surfing in a clapped out Ford Cortina.

All of which I'm sure are true. But the point is there's now a perfectly good two lane hard top all the way, and with crisp black tarmac under your tyres, a tank of fuel and a following wind you can pretty well guarantee

The Road To Banjul

getting to Nouakchott in a few hours with car and contents intact. So we decided in Dakhla to take the safer, if infinitely more boring, route along the new road if it existed, as had Ivan Beaman. And the road is indeed every bit as boring as we were promised it would be.

Sand dunes, more sand dunes, and some quite spectacular sand dunes separate us from the narrow beach and the sea. The road, hot, lonely, and flat as a pancake, a never ending blue black ribbon across the dry hammada. The sand encroaches, making the going unpredictable, but hardly more fascinating. Here a stunted bush, there another pile of yesterday's enigmatic stones. Bedouin encampments, more common than further north, and camels drift through the scene, nonchalantly cross the road ahead or scratch necks on the rare and treasured road signs.

We find ourselves in the Parc National du Banc d'Argouin Louik, which the Mauritanians exploit by charging a toll, disguised as an entry fee to a paradise of natural beauty. We're financially embarrassed, having spent our last Oguiyas on petrol. Once again, Mohammed comes to our rescue and stumps up the necessary.

"Is no problem," he smiles, "you are my brothers."

In fact, although the monotony of the sand and hammada are marginally softened by the impression of passing through a national park, the countryside is unchanged. A few indifferent stunted bushes poke their less than inspirational way through the otherwise unremitting desert floor. Here, for the most part surrounded by sand, rock, and scree, with heat haze in the mid distance and the unmistakeable mirage of water shimmering on the road ahead, Graham receives a call from his solicitors in Stow in the Wold. Sue, the practice secretary, informs him contracts for the sale of his cottage are exchanged, with a completion date set for 23 February, the date of our return to the UK. Looking about us for a moment in the searing sub tropical heat and the endless dunes, like erupting pimples on a sunburnt chest, it seems we're as far as we could possibly be from Stow in the Wold.

At noon, we pull up for our only informal petrol stop. We've been lugging the fourteen gallons of spare fuel in the jerricans, delicately balanced for weight distribution about Black Betty, since Agadir. Mohammed tells me that, in Mauritania, petrol is easily available, if contaminated. The consensus is we can afford to empty the bulk of our reserve fuel into the petrol tanks where it belongs. Black Betty will be lighter, more economical and more comfortable for Mohammed. Dave holds the filtered funnel in place in the filler tube, while Graham pours the precious petrol. I kneel behind him grasping a plastic carrier to his ankles and around his trousers to protect them from spillage and splash. We empty three of the four jerricans into the tanks and both vehicles are again replete. We're about to abandon the empty cans, but Mohammed has a better idea, and advises we hang on to them for a few miles more.

An hour later Mohammed directs us to pull up at what appears a derelict and much patched plywood shed, with a tin roof. The only sign of life an empty and unattended donkey cart with a brace of the disconsolate creatures between the shafts, wandering in 110° Farenheit. But behind the shed is a multicoloured mountain of plastic jerricans. We've reached Jerricans-R-Us, Mauritanian branch.

Mohammed pads across the desert floor and deposits the empties. I wonder how he's aware of this jerrican cache forty five miles distant from where we refuelled, literally in the middle of nowhere. And who's responsible for the abandoned donkey cart? The clues within this desolate and windswept scene are a discarded rear axle, half buried in the sand, and the sun bleached skull of an unfortunate bovine. It's as if some unlikely Agatha Christie mystery, perhaps *Murder in Mauritania*, unfolds before our eyes.

Mohammed beckons us to follow him into the shady interior of the shack. Suddenly the mystery's solved. This is an abandoned shack with a difference. In fact it's the well stocked grocery emporium of his nephew. Shelves groaning with tins, jars and bottles. Fruit, vegetables, meats, water and soft drinks, cigarettes and chocolate. A desert Arkwrights, par excellence. Granville sits on the dirt floor behind the counter, completely invisible to the casual caller. He brews the mandatory mint tea (see DAY SIX for instructions) as we inspect his wares and replenish our stocks.

Business done, we're invited to partake of the mint tea. Now Andy and I are into this sweet refreshing pastime. Dave and Graham prefer their regular injection of caffeine, but tactfully join in. For the second time in less than two days six adult men sit on a floor, this time in the bizarre location of a fly blown tin shack, behind a counter where only the tops of the heads of the taller of us are visible. We swill mint tea, a professional eighteen incher, washed down with water chasers. Whether it's my advanced years, or my distinguished dress sense and manners, I'm regarded as the elder statesman, deserving preferential treatment. I'm served first, and dutifully savour the proffered mouthful, and several others besides, before I'm permitted to take some interesting photographs of the wandering donkey cart, the rear axle, the bovine skull and jerrican pile.

Stepping back into Black Betty is like stepping into a furnace. At 83°F in the shade, Graham observes it's quite warm for February, and the car has become infested with flies. We make a hasty departure with all windows open to wrest control from them.

Sand dunes, more sand dunes, and some quite spectacular sand dunes again. Plastic fencing has been erected in an attempt to hold the sand from the road, but it's not too successful. Sand dunes, again. Et cetera.

Lemcid, a tiny village on the beach and one of the few on the map. A heavily laden twin axled lorry balances on rocks on a bend, its driver lies underneath. He's changing one patched tyre for another. The odd expired car, victim of a head on collision (with what?), on its side, stripped of its essentials.

Twenty miles short of Nouakchott a customs official in military uniform pulls us over and requests a couple of fiches and the "Declaration d'honneur"

The closer we get to the city, the more frequent are these tedious routine checks. We're stopped by the gendarmerie twice more before Nouakchott half an hour later. Each time, I experience the anxiety of the illegal immigrant. Each time I have to be reminded to stash the movie camera. But the officials are polite enough, demanding, each time, only fiches and the purpose of our visit. We are troubled more by the bothersome flies infiltrating the car as soon as it slows down. And we soon discover the reason.

Nouakchott is the biggest city in Mauritania. I'm sure it has a rudimentary sewerage system, and its streets are at least illuminated in part. Broad sandy verge passes for what in any other city in the world would be sidewalk. But its method of dealing with city refuse is unsophisticated. It's taken to the outskirts and spread liberally about the thousands of square miles that surround the city centre. Nouakchott sits at the epicentre of its own dung heap. And amidst the stink and squalor of the city waste, a thriving industry of amateur recycling takes place. People of all ages, notably women and young children, root amongst the filth and trash and make a kind of living. As do the flies, when they're not, out of pure curiosity, invading the privacy of visitors passing through.

First impressions of Nouakchott, apart from its refuse system, are however slightly more favourable than the lawless Nouadhibou. Here on the outskirts are plush residences, double and treble fronted, hacienda style. There's a sprinkling of modern provision merchants, self service in the making. A couple of nights here will be a welcome break to prepare us for what might be a difficult entry into Senegal.

We pulled up to the Hotel Auberge Sahara on the main drag into the centre of Nouakchott. It's a kind of hippy hotel where people of all nationalities put up for a short stay on their way south. Architecturally, it's relaxed cosmopolitan drop out. There are two rooms, one for six, the other for eight to ten, simply furnished with cots, mattresses and mosquito nets. The kitchen and showers are communal, toilets and washing facilities basic and functional. You can book a bed, or camp in the front garden or on the roof. In the front yard is a full sized Bedouin tent, used as overflow accommodation by those not too fussy about mosquitoes and marauding street goats. It has a gated parking compound, which, if cramped and dusty, is at least secure against marauding street humans. Above all, it's cheap and has a friendly ambiance, rather like a '60s youth hostel. Dave, Andy, Graham and I took the smaller of the two rooms, which would accommodate the four of us, plus Mohammed. In fact Mohammed chose to stay elsewhere, probably at the house of one of his countless cousins or nephews. He never seemed to run out of brothers. We decided to stay two nights, and sample the high life and night spots of a bustling capital city. Probably.

Technophiles Dave and Andy made their way to the internet café spotted on the way in to Nouakchott, to post updates on their website. Graham selected a cot for his afternoon siesta. I, rather more prosaically, took to my cot and my journal.

It was a lively evening for Dumb and Dumber and the Life Mechanics, with me on cook house duty. To the strains of mandolin and guitar in the Hippy Hotel, I presented my usual cordon bleu masterpiece from the tins and packets of our pooled resources. We dined on frankfurters and couscous, rice soup, noodles and bread, heated on the suit case camping stove in our room. Dave was char wallah.

Later, snug in our cots, swathed in mosquito netting and Deet, the room was faintly reminiscent of the boys dorm at some long forgotten minor public school in the home counties. We're four men, away from home. Under the humour lurks the apprehension of the days ahead.

(Andy)	"What are you reading Keith?"
(Me)	"It's an autobiography of Bette Davis. Found it in the bookshelf out there. Only thing I could find in English, apart from *Billy Bunter of Greyfriars School*."
(Andy)	"Any good?"
(Me)	"Bloody awful. What a self centred cow she was. And she can't write for toffee."
(Graham)	"Who launched the air biscuit?"
(Dave)	"Sorry. But it was me ring tone, not me arse."
(Andy)	"Anyone remember Billy Bunter on the telly? Hundreds of years ago. Who was it played Billy?"
(Me)	"Yeah, I can just remember him. Cor lummy. Yaroo! Don't be so beastly. Et cetera."
(Graham)	Snores.
(Andy)	"Yeah, and midnight feasts, and tuck shops, and Mr. Quelch with his cane. I don't recall a love interest though, or any sex."
(Me)	"That's because they only had Bette Davis back then."
(Dave)	Another air biscuit.
(Andy)	"Please sir, Pugsley is reading by torch light."
(Me)	"I give up on this bollocks." I douse the torch, drop Bette Davis in the trash, prepare for sleep.
(Graham)	"Gerald Campion."
(Dave)	"Who?"
(Graham)	"The bloke who played Billy Bunter. Gerald Campion. Think he gave it up and became a butcher."
(Andy)	Grunts.
(Dave)	Another air biscuit.
(Graham)	Snores.

DAY THIRTEEN
A CULTURAL INTERLUDE

I'm sitting in the back seat, pretty and demure in a full length wedding frock, a fussy voluptuousness of white lace and chiffon. Mohammed is beside me, distinguished in blue body warmer and top hat, his moustache closely clipped and waxed above a beaming smile. Facing us from the bench seat are Dave and Andy, rouged and beribboned, fetchingly got up in pink and lilac bridesmaids gowns, simpering in the sunlight as the desert rushes by. Graham at the wheel doggedly manoeuvres through goats, donkeys and ostriches, a chauffeur's hat perched jauntily atop his shiny brow. And in the front passenger seat, where I should be, lounges an ageing Bette Davis in black net pill box hat. A thin plume of smoke drifts from the long gold cigarette holder she grips between scarlet lips and scowling teeth.

We hit a rut. Six heads simultaneously hit the roof of this extended Black Betty and we all turn on Graham, spitting invective. Suddenly we're all fighting each other, struggling to gain control of the steering wheel from the puzzled Graham. I'm tangled in the many folds and pleats of my wedding gown. As I try to clamber into the front seat (Bette has left, where did she go?) my arms and legs are ensnared in chiffon and lace. I can't move. I feel the panic rise and begin to tear at the dress with teeth and nails. I kick. I lash out. Graham's cooing, asking me to keep still. *Keep still. Keep still....*

The Road To Banjul

I awoke in a cold sweat, still struggling with the chiffon and lace. The voluminous mosquito net that hung from its frame above my cot was inextricably entangled about my face and body.

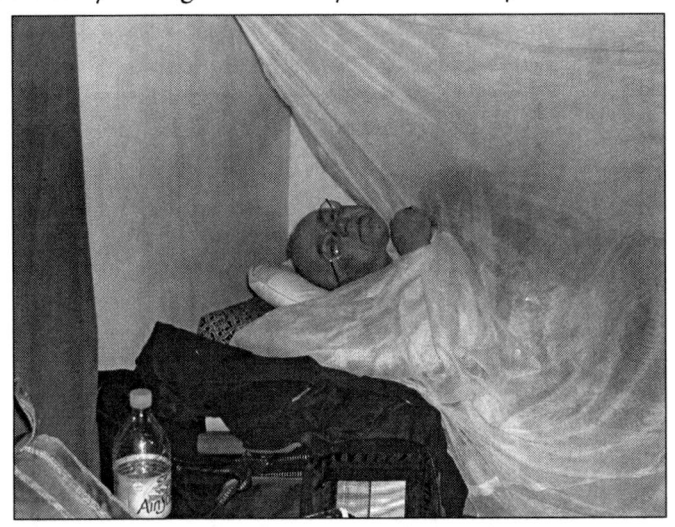

It was dawn on St.Valentine's Day, in the hippy hotel, on the fringe of Nouakchott city, and we'd all sent greetings to our loved ones. Graham had been scraping the residue of melted chocolate hearts from his socks and Y-fronts, savouring all that remained of the treats randomly scattered in his luggage by an adoring Sally and first discovered in Biarritrz. Now he disentangled me from the netting, and I set to, in my Superman pyjamas, boiling a kettle for coffee and the full mint tea ceremony. (See DAY SIX for instructions.). I poured a steaming eight incher into plastic picnic mugs to the accompanying cheers of Dave and the others. Soon we happy band were making a hearty breakfast of fruit cocktail, eaten out of tins, sitting on our cots in our underwear, with delicate British refinement.

The routine at the Auberge Sahara was as relaxed as the ambiance promised. Our first night under mosquito nets had been unbearably hot and sweaty with no air conditioning to speak of, but not a mosquito had been heard. It seemed the nets were more cosmetic than practical.

A queue for the shower relaxed patiently on a throw covered sofa in the vestibule, chatted sociably. The cleaning lady, a beautiful statuesque Creole, pushed a lazy broom about the floor, returning the night's incursion of sand to the outdoors. The strains of guitar mingled insistently with the gentle cries and gurgles of hidden children. A cat padded across the floor, the first pet since Spain. Residents at the time of our visit included a motley crew of Dutch adventurers, three Scandinavian ethnics, a couple of French hippies and we, four blithe Brits on a mission.

While I waited my turn for one of the only two showers, I changed the unreadable Bette Davis autobiography for a plodding but reliable Clive Dexter *Morse* novel, which I thought might see me through to Gambia.

Today would be a day of rest and recuperation in readiness for the push south into Senegal. Andy fancied taking in a little culture, so we asked Mohammed to give us a guided tour of the principal monuments, places of interest, cultural centres and the like. Perhaps we should have taken his quizzical look as a hint that collections historical and artistic are thin on the ground in Mauritania.

Finding a taxi into the city centre was no problem. The Auberge Sahara is on the main drag into town and although there's a sort of rudimentary bus service, you take your life and your faith in your hands to use it. As a prospective passenger, you have to jump on to the moving vehicle through the hole in the side, and just hope it's travelling in approximately the right direction. There are no signs indicating destination. This is left to the discretion of the driver who takes a sort of Mauri poll, and then drives roughly in the direction of the consensus.

So taxis are the preferred means of transport, and they're plentiful. Usually they're beaten up ancient Mercedes (easily confused with the cruising drug barons, who've also adopted them). Customarily they're piloted by huge sweating bearded black men.

Mohammed flagged one down and we all piled in. Being the smallest, I was crammed in last, after Andy, Dave and Graham had spilled across the entire pockmarked and stained back seat. I found myself perched half on Graham's left knee, half on Dave's right, my face contorted into a gargoyle as it wedged tightly against the window. The massive driver gunned the engine, slipped the clutch, and we lurched forward into Nouakchott. Mohammed sat, wisely, next to our driver, pointing out the many sights of scenic splendour and historic interest as we sped past the brick factory.

The Mercedes raced along in the busy traffic, overtaking, undertaking, mounting the sandy sidewalk. A strange brew of cars, carts and pedestrians stirred briskly, without the slightest seasoning of order. No traffic regulation at all. No signs, no rules or restrictions, and yet police everywhere, directing the traffic at random, often against the instructions of their colleagues. One such waved our driver down and we supposed he was in for a roasting. But Mohammed smiled sweetly, chatted amiably for a few minutes and, with a brotherly handshake, we were off again.

Mauritania, where Arab meets black Africa and we were in the capital, soaking up the curious culture of this vast anonymous country. The Arabs are the supervisory and managerial class. Black Africans do the hard work. I wondered whether we were witnessing some of Mauritania's slaves at work; shovelling sand, making concrete building blocks in wooden moulds, driving donkey carts laden with water. We passed one cart with a child lying in the back, howling at the traffic, presumably on its way to nursery. A plumbers' merchant, displaying modern European sanitary ware, confirmed arrangements need not, indeed, be as primitive as at Mohammed's house.

The taxi dropped us at the *Bibliotèque Nationale*, an imposing brick and glass monolith with a doorman. My faded French reminded me this was a library, and one of the few cultural centres worthy of note to a passing traveller. But I was now armed with my trusty Clive Dexter and none of us were interested in delving too deeply into the undoubtedly sophisticated research facilities, so we passed on, to the *Musée Nationale* around the corner.

Culture at last. And from its modest beginnings as the country's capital city in 1957, an impressive collection of well presented artefacts had been established under glass. There was something for everyone. Examples of ancient ceramics, stone and bronze age axe and arrow heads, pipes, jewellery and statuettes with religious significance, glass exhibits, bobbins and a set of travelling scales (discovered in 1973 but dated 1119).

Dave took a particular interest in the sculpted bone fragments, an accurate scale model of the mosque at Koumbi Saleh and a coat of chain mail found in the mosque. Calabashes for grinding grain and other cooking purposes, pestles and mortar in pottery and stone, a 1940 manuscript of the Koran, a canon from an 1816 wreck.

Particularly fascinating for me were the photographs of the 15th. August 1932 floods ("l'inondation") when the Senegal river burst its banks and Lieutenant Garbit had been at the scene to record Nouakchott under water. Some examples of rural board games, played with sand, stones and sticks, and a pottery doll's house, with fittings and furniture made for the children of Ovalata. A display of rifles and bullets, drinking bowls, halter and saddle for camels bore witness to Mauritania's hostile past. Displays of medicinal herbs, hoes, mattocks, stones for grinding couscous, fishing spears, hooks and nets paid tribute to it's more peaceful and prosperous present.

Andy went for the drums and stringed instruments, the leatherware. Graham favoured the forge and metalwork equipment such as bellows, anvil and hammers, evidence of an industrial history.

The exhibits and the care with which they'd been assembled and displayed were impressive indeed, but a security guard promptly reminded me that Mauritania wishes to keep its splendid past a secret. No photographs were allowed (except this one of Graham standing in front of the turtle shell, which I took surreptitiously and at great personal risk to my liberty, when nobody but Graham, and perhaps the turtle, was looking).

We left the *Musée Nationale* refreshed and invigorated at the knowledge that this country did indeed have a past and a culture of which it could be proud. But what of its present? For that we looked to Mohammed to lead us to the hot spots of down town Nouakchott.

What we found was a market, a heaving mass of open air stalls selling all manner of dry goods. Leather, metal work, jewellery and trinkets, but predominantly fabrics, literally thousands of bolts of highly coloured cotton prints, curtains, sheets and bed linen. The central market is on three floors of a multi storey building, the more professional stalls occupying small shop frontages, the less prosperous taking to the corridors and balconies between. And everywhere bolts of cloth, interspersed with sewing machines, treddle and hand crank, operated by sweating care worn women and men as they laboured to make a few ouguiyas from the passing trade. Customers were in shorter supply, and we had no trouble picking our cautious way through the disorganised mélange. Where the market was for this vast supply of cotton print I couldn't begin to imagine, but I saw no money change hands during our wanderings through Nouakchott market. Although we were frequently importuned to buy something or to partake of some curious service or other, by and large the tradesmen here seemed to understand a firm and gentle refusal, much more readily than their Moroccan counterparts. We soon learnt that to touch an object on offer is to evince an interest in it. A great deal of time and embarrassment can be saved by the simple expedient of saying "no, thank you", and sticking to that position.

The overriding impression of the market, and indeed of Nouakchott city was of unimaginable filth. The detritus of the market littered the acrid streets. Here a young man sat in the dust and skinned the head of a goat. There a child rummaged through discarded vegetable leaves in the gutter, sharing them with goats and dogs. The men mostly sat, little troubled by the flies, in the shade of sparse sub-saharan trees, drinking mint tea (see DAY SIX).

Mohammed brought us to a street café where we shared ice cold coca cola with the indigenous fly population. We'd played the tourist role for a few hours, and agreed that, for all of its faults, we'd felt strangely safe and welcome in Mauritania, and would be sad to leave it tomorrow.

Another bent and knackered cab set us down outside the Auberge Sahara. The hippy hotel was in full swing. The Scandinavians were doing their best to wash their smalls under the single cold water tap in the front yard. The French contingent lounged in the lobby, lazily strumming guitar and mandolin, humming folk music. Some Germans marched by to attention, on their way to the cold afternoon showers. We took to our cots and spent the afternoon snoozing, reading and drinking mint tea. (See DAY SIX).

ooOoo

"What was the highlight of your day, Andy?" I'm in roving reporter mode, lying in the cot, clutching the Clive Dexter.

"The museum, I think. And the taxi ride. You know, this country might be disorganised, a bit basic. But it's so much freer here. Not nearly so much regulation and restriction as we have. I like it, me."

"How about you, Gray?"

"Did you see that horse outside the grocer's? In the shed? It was going mad with boredom. And the leather water bottles in the tree? You'd think they'd stick 'em in the fridge. Have you Deeted Keith?"

"Yes, duly Deeted, thanks. What about you Dave? What was your highlight?"

"Your duck cassoulet, without a doubt, mate. Very tasty. Where did you get the duck?"

"The Frenchman in the kitchen. He cooked too much. That was his contribution to entente cordiale. Nice tea, by the way Dave."

"Good wasn't it. Sorry I could only manage a three incher."

"It all comes with practice. Have you read DAY SIX?"

"No, must do that. What was the highlight for you, Keith?"

"Oh, the taxi ride, undoubtedly. I still have the scars. And I think I'm pregnant."

"Well, goodnight John Boy."

"Goodnight Gran'pa."

"Goodnight Ma. Goodnight Pa."

"Goodnight Mary Ellen."

"Goodnight Jim Bob."

"Goodnight."

DAY FOURTEEN
RUNNING THE GAUNTLET

"It's the fifteenth of February Gray. We're legal."

"Thank God for that."

"No longer shall we fear the ominous trudge of the jack boot, the clatter of rifle butt on door."

"The wail of police siren in the lonely night."

"And we won't have to hide you buggers in the wardrobe, with the fruit salad," Dave chips in. We were free and legal in Mauritania for the first time, on the day we were to leave it, for Senegal.

We'd never revealed our illegal status to Mohammed, more from a wish to draw attention away from ourselves than a desire to protect him, an ex police officer, from the embarrassment of harbouring enemy aliens. And though I nursed a sneaking suspicion that our trespass might be regarded as illegal *ab initio* and not legitimated by the mere passage of time, the border officials were unlikely to include an academic lawyer of any standing. Speculation on the precise legal situation could probably be overcome by the offer of a modest "cadeau".

The euphoria over our new legal status having subsided, we showered, dressed, packed and were ready to leave. It was a cool, clear morning at the hippy hotel, with the promise of another hot dry day ahead.

In the car compound I met Paul, a tall, bronzed and muscular Frenchman. The sun glinted on his gold tooth as he proudly demonstrated his mobile living quarters. An ancient red Renault, it had begun its long life as a fire service ambulance in Amiens. As he showed me around the cramped but well appointed quarters, he told me he'd retired from the fire service ten years previously. The Renault retired with him when he saved it from the scrap heap. He'd been travelling the lesser known routes of the African continent ever since.

Paul was typical of the free spirits encountered in the hippy hotel, with more taste for adventure than money. Not much clue of where they're headed, so long as they have a good and mainly musical time along the way.

For breakfast we followed Mohammed's lead and visited the "Épicerie Sahara", a lock up outside the grounds, for bread and water.

Promptly at eight, the convoy of two pulled out of the compound into the heavy early traffic. Graham pointed Black Betty in the general direction of the outskirts and put his foot down in the west African way.

Box vans, posing as buses, weave in and out of donkey carts and stray goats. Would be passengers run alongside until there's room for one more in the seething mass. As the opportunity presents, the runner dives into the moving vehicle, struggling legs akimbo to gain purchase, often assisted by those on board. On the other side of the bus some unfortunate, displaced by the new arrival and the operation of Archimedes' Principle, tumbles bewildered but resigned, to the road. I wonder whether there's a practical or statutory limit to how many may ride on a bus in Mauritania, and conclude that the maximum is determined by the number of handles, rods, bumpers and pieces of string attached to the bus, from which a prospective passenger might cling. But then travel on these buses seems free. There's no sign of the smartly dressed and equipped conductor of my youth.

Just before leaving civilisation we stop for petrol and replenish the tanks with the cheap, villainous low octane rubbish which is to see us to the frontier with Senegal. We're left with a few paltry Ouguiyas.

On the outskirts of Nouakchott are goat and camel markets. I estimate five hundred fat, well tended beasts in each. Just past the brick factory the main road's closed. The President's due to pass through with his entourage. Mohammed, in the back feasting on dry bread and coca cola, directs Graham to a subsidiary road.

The Road To Banjul

We're heading for the Diama Road. From there, Mohammed will guide us to the border with Senegal and leave us to make for today's destination, Zebrabar, the last mustering point before Banjul. The first police check just outside Nouakchott poses no problems. We hand over two fiches, and boast our passports, which for the first time reveal our legal status in Mauritania.

The road gradually deteriorates on the way out of Nouakchott, where the pretence at civilisation can perhaps be relaxed. The return to breeze block tenement and shed is sudden. Goats and donkeys roam the main road south through encroaching sand. Bedouin encampments, interspersed with herds of inscrutable camel, are dotted randomly about the suburbs, starting where the refuse tips leave off. It's a dull but mercifully cool start to the day, though Graham's prediction that the sky looks full of snow is, I think, fanciful.

Now sub Saharan, the next one hundred miles are more populated than we've been used to for days, but otherwise unsurprising, even banal. Concrete houses, set in compounds of more yellow concrete. Inside wander goats and scrawny cattle. At Tiguent, half way to the infamous Rosso, we're overtaken at speed by a Renault. I count nine passengers, all smartly dressed as if for a wedding, crouched perched and crammed into the improbable conveyance. A camel herd, helps his animals to water from a drinker.

We trundle carefully down the sandy tree lined avenue, respectful of free range livestock. Respectful too, of the many human inhabitants, attractive dusky people for the most part, casually going about their business. Women in brightly coloured gowns and robes cluster around rough wooden stalls, converse with the men in the deep orange sand, drink mint tea in the shade and tussock grass. This seems, for women, a much freer, more liberal society than the towns of the north. The houses, tin shacks with cloth roofs, are testimony to the indigenous poverty, and yet the place swarms with healthy, happy children. To my right, a football game in full swing, barefoot men and boys kick about a loose bundle of clothing. Somebody's shoes are the goalposts. There are no spectators, and the teams are of indeterminate size. Anyone who wishes may, apparently, join the team of his choice.

Butchers' shops are booming in southern Mauritania. Every couple of miles, in the middle of nowhere, a rough hewn bench on rustic posts, cloth canopy for a roof, a small set of beam scales and a scraggy bit of fly blown offal, the Dewhursts of the desert. The traditional straw boater, striped apron and meaty moustachioed face have been replaced by some indifferent and hungry looking ten year old, or one of the more intelligent of the donkeys tethered nearby.

Ten miles before the Diama Road we stop twice in quick succession for police checks. Nobody takes issue with the telling dates on our visas. Parting with a couple of fiches and the merest suggestion that we're diplomatic envoys, we're politely waved on. A donkey rolls languorously in the sand. A long eared Nubian goat takes a nonchalant pee.

Nothing could've quite prepared us for the Road to Diama. On our map it barely merits a mention, appearing as a narrow line next to a row of crosses, which marks the frontier with Senegal. On the ground the road's even less well marked. Just before entering the hell hole of Rosso, Mohammed instructs Graham to turn right, between a roofless shed and a burnt out Citroen. We enter a cross between a refugee camp and a breakers' yard. The track of sand and dirt threads its way through some of the most desperate poverty we've encountered. Rough, shabby corrugated iron dwellings line one side of this road that seems to lead nowhere. Broken fences and an attempt at animal enclosures line the other. As Graham manoeuvres Black Betty around and over the deeply rutted apology for a road, we're stalked by hoards of children, bare foot, ragged-arsed, almost naked. Soon we're carrying a payload of five or six kids on each running board, all hustling to guide us through the difficult route ahead, or at least for the next hundred yards or so. I pay them off with a handful of ballpoint pens thrown from the window. Looking for the Pug in the rear view mirror I see them scrabble frenziedly in the dirt for a trophy.

This is, according to Mohammed, the better road to Diama. We bump and bounce gingerly along it for a couple of miles, through the outskirts of the refugee camp, fearing in particular for the Pug's suspension. A tiny sliver of doubt begins to wedge itself into the armour of confidence forged since Mohammed has been on board. Can this really be the *best* road to anywhere? Sixty miles of dirt track with muddy savannah to the left and crocodile infested mangrove swamp to the right. There has to be a better way.

Then we reach the dam.

It's a sort of concrete raft at rightangles to the dubious track we've begun to get used to, thinking, well, this isn't too bad really. When Mohammed blithely instructs Graham to drive off the end of the raft and onto the peak of the dirt ridge beyond, the bowels that have sustained me thus far, despite a diet of All Butter Shortbread Selection and mint tea, turn to water.

"What? Down there? Oh fuck!" I exclaim. (I know they were my words because they're captured on the video camera I was nursing at the time). And this is the point in my travels where my trust in Graham's driving is put to its most serious test. I really cannot see, from any perspective, how this can be done, without Graham, Black Betty, Mohammed, tajine, All Butter Shortbread Selection, sewing machine *et al*, sliding inexorably down the bank and into the mangrove swamp below.

"I'll straddle it," remarks Graham coolly from the driving seat. He edges Black Betty gently but firmly forward, launches her front end into the unknown. I'm astonished, exhilarated, and deeply gratified to feel the bump of wheels on the ridge, followed seconds later by the rear wheels. We've landed safely. One small step for Black Betty. One giant step for me. We disembark, and as I wipe the sweat from my brow and check the availability of fresh underwear, Mohammed helps prepare the Pug for his encounter with raft and ridge.

A worried Dave is at the wheel.

"The man's a numpty. He cannot be serious. This can't be the right way."
"Come on Dave, I'm sure it'll be OK. He seems to know what he's doing."
"No way. Pug won't do it."
"Left hand down a bit."
"Yes, yes. Very good."
"No, right hand down. Gently, gently."
"Yes, yes. Very good."

Andy and Mohammed on the ridge gesticulate and shout largely contradictory instructions. Graham and I stand on the sidelines, witnessing and recording the event objectively as the Pug pulls forward. The town car has minimal ground clearance with its sporty low suspension, and the wooden spacer pegs fashioned at the campsite in Dakhla have worn away long ago, somewhere on the road to Nouakchott. So when Dave hits the throttle, I think it's on purpose. Pug shoots forward, wheels spinning, and turtles across the edge of the concrete raft onto the ridge in a flurry of sparks and grinding steel. Remarkably, though the bottomed Pug has scraped both sump and floor pan on the vicious unyielding concrete, the only damage sustained is to the front number plate. Andy quickly reattaches it with a bent wire coat hanger and some nails.

Now we really are on the "best road to Diama". It's been an act of faith with Mohammed from the start, and we just have to believe he knows the way out of here. There's certainly no going back, and the way ahead's far from clear. Black Betty travels at a maximum 18 m.p.h.,

The Road To Banjul

slowing down for ruts the size of the Khyber pass. In radio contact with the Pug, I can give Dave notice of the more major obstacles. With sixty miles of this craziness to endure, none of us fancy coping with a busted spring, a holed sump or even a shot wheel. It's unlikely the R.A.C. will be close at hand at this southern extremity, where mangrove swamp meets paddy field.

Despite the horrific conditions, there's something inexplicably engaging about the Road to Diama, and the population it conceals. Signs of civilisation are more frequent than in the dead deserts to the north, but it's a strange kind of life. Goatherds guide their charges along the narrow road margin, where they graze on the few stunted bushes that have survived recent bush fires. Bullocks graze in the tangled mangrove swamp, up to their knees in water and silt. Half-hearted tents and reed shacks, canoes and settlements of fisher folk, eking a poor existence out of the swamp. A ruin of concrete and steel looms up like a ghostly Atlantis. On the ridge walks desert man again, an apparition in white, blue and gold, with a plastic carrier. Five young boys appear from within a reed hut, naked but for loin cloths, each bearing a strange cooking implement and between them a vast cauldron. An elderly man sits outside a battered reed hut working mangrove into yarn. A pterodactylian heron flies by, a large and resigned looking fish hanging from its beak. A herd of long horned white cattle emerge from the mangrove and wander across the road in front. Graham pulls up and kills the engine while they disappear into the thick undergrowth. With the engines dead, only bird song disturbs the profound silence.

There's a tin shack police station about forty miles down the Road to Diama. The adjoining reed shack and tumble down wooden shelter is reserved, Mohammed explains, for the C.I.D. All are lined up against a rough hedge, which serves as the ablutions, amidst all the refuse that two rural policemen can create. But the police are friendly and pleasant and, of course, know Mohammed. After the usual formalities they wish us a pleasant journey with a reminder that we're still in the Parc National. Naturally a 5 Euro fee applies. Each.

A couple of miles further on we chance upon an ancient bicycle, propped carefully on its stand, as if awaiting the return of its owner from the post office. But neither post office nor owner are to be seen. Is this, perhaps, an example of Mauritanian surreal art?

The last ten miles of the Road to Diama is like riding on 50p pieces. The road is ridged and scarred from erosion and decay. Both cars and crews rattle violently. By the time we reach the frontier our teeth ache, our buttocks are sore and our nerves frazzled from the constant staccato road noise. We're glad to step out, even though this means parting company with Mohammed, and taking our chances with Senegalese customs without his famous support.

Mohammed had proved a prince among men, and as a guide, an absolute star. I wrote as much on the glowing testimonial I was deputed to give on the back of a fiche. He'd guided us down the loneliest parts of the Sahara coast, and the entire length of Mauritania. He'd hosted us at his home, and vacated it so that we four might take advantage of it for the night. We'd been shown the better side of Nouakchott, guided through a perilous minefield and down the hazardous and, by anyone's judgement, ridiculous Road to Diama. Now he saw us through customs and the final police control, as we exited Mauritania, free, safe and financially viable. We paid him his dues at the frontier and invited him to choose the customary gift from the many still on board. Andy fixed him up with a "new" mobile phone, such being almost currency in these parts.

Now Mohammed had sat for several hundred miles in the back seat of Black Betty, clearly admiring her elaborate and expensive looking radio cassette, perhaps wondering why we preferred to travel in silence between bouts of sparkling repartee and humorous observation, rather than be entertained by Sounds of the Sixties, Mauritanian style. The fact of the matter is the radio wasn't connected. To anything. I had, as you will recall, simply shoved a spare car radio into the conveniently radio-shaped hole in the dash months before, to tidy up the interior. Connecting it to anything sensible was quite beyond me, and the expense prohibitive. So the radio had sat silent for over three thousand miles. And when Mohammed pointed to it and asked whether I had another such for him, I promptly snatched the machine out of its resting place, wires flapping, and thrust it at him gratefully. My gesture was obviously deeply appreciated by all present, particularly Mohammed and his police comrades, who regarded me with awe and inspiration. Probably.

Anyway, we took group photographs with Mohammed. We'd become brothers during our brief association and there was a bond of respect and affection between us. We bade him farewell. He took his overnight bag and a carrier of gifts, and disappeared back over the border.

I doubt I shall ever see him again, but I feel I have a friend and a guardian in Mauritania.

Romantic though it might sound as a concept, there is no place called Diama. It's just a bridge. Or at least a concrete raft thirty yards long by about ten wide, which crosses something which you have to consult a map to discover is in fact the Senegal River. There's no sign, no tourist information office, no duty free shop. There's not even a display cabinet, no museum with interesting artefacts marked "a present from Diama", not so much as a hint that the featureless raft of concrete we'd just crossed had brought us, technically, into Senegal.

At the far end of the bridge a shadowy figure emerges from the bushes. Wearing jacket, chinos, sandals and a shifty smile, he walks to the centre of the road and gestures we should stop.

"I am Ali," he says, leering at Graham.

Well, there's a surprise, I think. Half the population of west Africa share that name. The other half are Mohammed. Even the women.

"Welcome to Senegal. Crossing this bridge is 10 Euros."

I reach for the wallet.

"Each," he adds.

My face must betray my surprise at such a demand, unprefaced as it is by any suggestion that a toll might be levied for crossing this choice piece of elaborate Senegalese architecture.

"You are in west Africa now my friend. It's pay, pay, pay all the way," he chortles gaily.

He smirks as he pockets the 40 Euros. I want to hit him. I sense Graham too is a touch peeved at having been stung in the first few metres of Senegal. He guns Black Betty in the general direction of border control. Ali clings to the door pillar, balancing on the running board, determined not to lose his meal ticket. We hurtle through dust and rut but are unsuccessful in shaking off our unwelcome passenger. Ali has usurped Mohammed's place in our affections and adopted the position of our guide through the difficult entry into Senegal, whether we like it or not. I can only hope and trust he will prove useful, as he will certainly be demanding payment for his dubious services.

And indeed Ali does contrive to make our entry into and first experiences of Senegal memorable. Frustrating, aggravating, infuriating, hot, difficult and expensive. But memorable for sure. What I'm about to recount is embellished in no way. The facts have not been changed to make it more interesting or protect the innocent. This is exactly what happened next to Graham, Dave, Andy and me.

Ali directed us to a pockmarked breeze block building. He tentatively opened the door and the Famous Four peered inside. A large wooden desk in the middle of the small room was littered with papers and magazines. A set of cheap plastic pens stood to attention in an elaborate desk tidy-cum-ink well. All the paraphernalia of the reluctant bureaucrat. Behind and to the right of the desk stood a large threadbare sofa in brown moquette. And on the sofa, a sleeping policeman. No, a real policeman, short and very black, in khaki drills, sam browne belt and holstered pistol. Asleep. The reluctant bureaucrat, I thought, as we regarded the recumbent figure, facing away and snoring gently into the moquette. It was after four on a hot and drowsy afternoon in this lonely fly blown place, and I suppose I should've expected slipshod behaviour. But when he rolled over, half opened one sleepy eye and muttered "Go away. I am tired. Come back later," I must confess my sympathy for the overworked, overstressed and underpaid police force of north western Senegal paled a little. Before I had the chance to remonstrate with this arrogant little shit, Ali hustled us from the room suggesting we leave the fellow to his slumbers and return when he might be suitably refreshed. This particular policeman was known, apparently, not to take too kindly to angry white males.

We were hurried over the yard to a tin shack. I assumed the next uniform to assail us would represent customs or passport control. We were indeed asked for our passports, and one driving licence per car. This second official was reasonably polite, if disinterested. There was even a token smile as he took us for 10 Euros. Each.

We'd need compulsory motor insurance to pass through Senegal, Ali rather unnecessarily explained, and, coincidentally, the man from the Pru could be found at this time of day in the very next shed. Sure enough, a man bearing a briefcase and a striking resemblance to the Mauritanian agent in Nouakchott rapidly fixed us up with minimum insurance for ten days, having been persuaded we were intent on leaving this expensive country at the earliest opportunity. Studying the policies later, I found that our Nissan Bluebirds (yes, the very same Nissan Bluebirds, of different sizes, that we'd been insured for whilst in Mauritania) were indeed covered by some sort of token gesture in both Senegal and the Gambia. Further encounters with rogue insurance salesmen wouldn't be necessary on this trip. We parted with a further 20 Euros. Each.

It was time to return to the Sleeping Policeman. Now suitably rested and relaxed, he might be in a position to grant us the privilege of the audience we so craved. When we presented ourselves at his couch he slowly opened the same eye, yawned extravagantly, and muttered something about we should have waited at the border until there were four or five cars, sufficient to justify waking him. He was still tired, but as he was now awake he would attend to the necessary formalities, in the fullness. We gathered expectantly around the desk, sitting patiently in this Holy of Holies on the chairs provided, while the Ayotollah studied the coffee time crossword puzzle. We waited patiently. But our patience in the heat and the sweat and the dust of the afternoon was growing thin, or at least mine was. He filled in a couple of the boxes in the crossword, yawned again, pulled a little pad of printed forms towards him and started to write laboriously, and in the best copperplate script of a five year old, with his cheap scratchy pen.

A face appeared at the door. Some friend or colleague perhaps, come to tell him news or simply to gossip. The social banter ensued for what seemed like hours, was probably only a few minutes. By this time I was steaming with anger and frustration at the power play. The friend left, and our genial host returned to his crossword, deep in thought. Another face at the door. This time a woman. His mother perhaps, come to bring him his dinner, or just popping in to see how her little boy was on this hot and unconditioned afternoon. The minutes ticked by. An argument. Raised voices. The Ayotollah's mum left in a fury of banging doors. Eventually, and when he had composed himself for the labours of the afternoon, he completed the docket, and handed it to Ali.

Meanwhile the Famous Four were in the dark, completely at a loss as to what was occurring in this hot and, by now, very tense office. To cross Senegal in an elderly car (i.e. one more than five years old) you must be escorted by a government official who ensures the vehicle's not sold or abandoned. You have to pay for the privilege. The slip of paper the Ayotollah had taken so long over and made so much about, was in fact our border pass. Without it, we'd not be allowed out of Senegal. If stopped on the highway we'd have to produce it, at pain of incarceration in some dreadful Senegalese prison and forfeiture of the car. The cost was 350 Euros (£245), but it covered both vehicles. We'd made a slight tactical error in crossing as a pair, as one pass would've covered up to ten. Our escort would be particularly expensive. However, the relief at being released from the concrete box and the Ayotollah, was palpable. He'll never know how close he came to being duffed up, such was my anger. It was the wise ministrations of Dave, Andy and Graham that calmed my fury from the white hot to the red, and probably saved me a short sentence in the slammer.

We climbed back into the cars and, with Ali now ensconced in what had been Mohammed's seat, made for Zebrabar. Ali, for whom I nurtured a profound distrust and dislike by this time, was apparently self appointed guide to the interior, a situation with which I was less than happy. Frankly, I blanched at the thought of travelling the entire length of Senegal in his company. My fevered imagination began to plot ways in which I could make his stay with us uncomfortable. I wasn't to know that Graham and my other travelling companions were thinking similar thoughts, as we approached the next police stop, half a kilometre later.

This time the local gendarmerie stood in the middle of the track, hand in the air with an unmistakeable suggestion that we should stop. Another demand for passports, fiches, driving licences (all four this time) and another 10 Euros. Each.

The road to St. Louis, perhaps twenty miles distant, was quite attractive in a rural unkempt sort of way. We were by now strictly sub-Saharan, and the Senegal River, which meanders towards the coast, was lined with mangrove and trees. A woman, tall, svelte and beautiful, stripped to the waist and bathed in the shallows. Children splashed and played. Cattle waded and drank of the murky waters. I missed some of these scenes, grumbling at my first and very poor impression of Senegal. I rounded on Ali in the back seat and vented my spleen, spitting insult and invective, swearing retribution. He smiled genially, and took it all in, rather too philosophically for my liking. I wanted him to be hurt and scandalised. He preferred the calm and stoic approach.

"Sto-o-o-o-o-p!" gestured the next uniform, this one heavy and very black, with epaulettes on his epaulettes, and a huge and vacuous smile. The Laughing Policeman. He demanded Graham's driving licence, and as I scrabbled frantically in my folder of paperwork, where I had "tidied it away", he also demanded sight of our fire extinguisher and the two yellow reflective jackets and red triangles that Senegal law, strict on all matters of health and safety, obliges the motorist to carry. At least the foreign motorist. Well the fire extinguisher was no problem, and although I'd not been advised of the legal requirement, Graham had the foresight to suggest we carry one in a readily accessible position. It'd travelled over three thousand miles in the front glove box. Our gloves were elsewhere. I grabbed the extinguisher and shoved it in the general direction of the Laughing Policeman. I'm not sure that he noticed the venom I spat after it. I was pretty cross by now.

Then I clambered out of Black Betty in search of the reflective jackets and red triangles. They'd been packed carefully away in the bowels of the luggage compartment and repacked several times. They'd take a deal of finding. I unpacked as methodically as I could, placing all our worldly goods, including our valuable gifts, in piles on the road. Predictably, the locals swarmed about me, hustling for "cadeaux". Very soon Graham had to join me to fend off the muggers, beggars and hustlers. The Laughing Policeman wasn't interested of course. He waited to inspect our reflective jackets and triangles.

I'd located both yellow jackets and one of the triangles and was steaming from the ears with the heat, the anger and the effort of this pointless exercise, when Ali arrived at the rear of Black Betty to tell me the Laughing Policeman was now satisfied we had the necessary, and we could move on. So I started to throw our goods and chattels back into Black Betty, a little relieved at the progress. The relief was short lived. As I shoved the last crate of mobile phones and the tool box in the back, the Laughing Policeman came to the rear of the car and wanted to see the second red triangle. I saw red triangles everywhere, in fact my whole vision misted up with furious red triangles, and if I'd discovered the second triangle at that precise moment I probably would've wrapped it around Ali's head.

I delved once more into Black Betty's rear, taking my time on this occasion, determined the policeman would indeed inspect the triangle. Behind us, the Pug had been similarly turned over, but Andy knew they only had one triangle. They copped for a 20 Euro fine. Each.

I was adamant I wouldn't fall for this ruse, and knew our second triangle was to be found somewhere. And find it I did, between the spare wheel and the bottle jack. I produced it with a triumphant swagger, and the disappointment of the Laughing Policeman was almost conspicuous.

Hastily repacking Black Betty for the second time I threw the yellow jackets and red triangles in the back with a gesture of disdain, clambered noisily and grumpily back into the front seat. We were ready for the off. But Black Betty wasn't. Whether the events of the last few minutes had seriously depressed her, or whether it was a show of protest at the excessive heat, lousy low octane Mauritanian fuel and stop start motoring, Black Betty simply refused to go any further. We'd broken down for the first time.

I popped the hood and gazed, amazed, at the huge lump of engine that lurked beneath. Graham, Andy, Dave and I, the Laughing Policeman, numerous passers by and most of the children of north west Senegal peered under the hood and offered suggestions as to what might coax Black Betty back to life. Graham's diagnosis, that she was simply hot, fed up and suffering a slight dose of fuel starvation in the unbearable heat was probably correct. She just needed to be left alone for a few minutes, to gather herself. But, not wishing to contravene any of Senegal's sophisticated traffic code, Graham felt the situation should be properly managed. So we retrieved the red triangles and yellow jackets once more from the luggage compartment, and, both fetchingly attired in canary yellow, Graham set off into the distance with one triangle for the rear. I set the other up a couple of hundred yards in front. And we took our time. When Graham was barely visible in the dust, heat haze and traffic several miles away, with a madly gesticulating Laughing Policeman between us, I felt we'd made the point.

The Laughing Policeman had stopped smiling by now, and was evidently losing his rag. He wanted Black Betty removed from his highway. Still she wouldn't start. I thought I'd try a trick Neil Caley showed me back in the UK, and prove to my colleagues to be the wizard mechanic they already suspected I was. As Neil had pointed out, if an engine is hot, it can become flooded with petrol if the fuel injectors build up pressure before the plugs kick in with a successful spark. The main injector pipe can be simply removed from the block and the pressure released.

Without any warning, I unclipped the hose from the block. A jet of petrol vapour shot from the hose and sprayed the red hot engine. Andy and Dave dived for cover. The Laughing Policeman leapt over the bonnet of his Mercedes. Half the population of St.Louis gasped in fear and astonishment. I quickly replaced the hose and the lethal petrol stream ceased. I had diced with death, or at least with cheap Mauritanian low octane fuel, and come through. I shut the hood, dusting my hands nonchalantly.

The Laughing Policeman was furious by this time. He brushed the mud from his epaulets and insisted we move Black Betty, or summons the assistance of a real mechanic. The implication behind his threatening

The Road To Banjul

demeanour was that failure to move her immediately would result in a fine for illegal parking. 20 Euros. Each.

The Pug came to the rescue. Dave hitched Black Betty to his tow ball and he manfully pulled us out of danger, that is to say away from the Laughing Policeman and his cronies. As a parting shot, the Laughing Policeman asked for one of our yellow jackets as a gift! Suspecting perhaps this was yet another ruse to render us susceptible to fines further down the road, I declined his suggestion. But I did give him a tip. I advised him not to lift his gladioli before the spring. He seemed pleased with my advice horticultural, and the vestige of a smile returned to his lips.

With a couple of miles of breeze under her bonnet Black Betty coughed into life and we were able to unhitch her from the uncomplaining Pug. The experience had been a demonstration that she didn't take well to stop start motoring, in the heat on crappy fuel. We'd need to keep going if we could.

We enter St. Louis to the strains of carnival. The women of Senegal are lithe, lissom, bright eyed and amongst the most beautiful in the world. They glide with grace through the streets of St. Louis, with its overcrowded buses, battered French cars, bicycles and colourful horse-drawn taxis. A symphony of colour and noise. The architecture faded French colonial, it's not as cosmopolitan as I'd imagined, but it has a distinct and unique charm. Bougainvillaea strewn shops and offices in the town centre vie with the Gendarmerie Nationale for attention, and the sounds of children, whistles and jazz thread the air.

Graham and I, self conscious in yellow, anxious to keep on trucking through the confusion, tuck in behind a horse and cart loaded to the heavens with unsecured mattresses. We cross a railway line, pass the tyre factors, creep through the labyrinthine market, and edge towards the outskirts of this busy town.

"Sto-o-o-o-o-p!" cries the next policeman, a shifty and unpleasant individual in blue trousers and shirt. He's a special, I think. He barks at Graham. The odious Ali translates.

"There is too much luggage on your rear seat. 20 Euros. Each."

I see those red triangles again. And I remember Ivan Beaman. I will stand my ground.

"I don't think so, Sunshine, (for some reason I suddenly adopt the vocabulary, accent and mannerisms of an Eastender). This is how it's going to work. You give me ticket now. When I return to the UK, I shall send you 20 Euros. Each."

"No. You give me 20 Euros now. Each. I send you receipt tomorrow."

"No. You're not listening. You give me ticket now. I send you 20 Euros from UK. Each."

Graham gets out his mobile phone and pretends to phone someone official. Ali and the special go into a huddle and appear to discuss the issue.

"He says he will settle for 10 Euros. Each."

"Oh, is that so? Great. Well now, this is how it works. You give me ticket for 10 Euros now, and I send you 10 Euros when I get back. Each."

Another swift huddled conversation between Odious Ali and the special.

"Okay. You can go."

Result. With this brief exchange I've broken through the web of corruption and collusion that's been taking place ever since we entered Senegal. I'm jubilant. But Black Betty's still depressed and refuses to start. Again, the Pug comes to our assistance and tows us out of immediate danger. Again, Black Betty soon bursts back into life and we carry on, into rural Senegal.

"Sto-o-o-o-o-p!" As we grind to a halt at the command of the next policeman, Ali's first out. He speaks to the police privately, out of earshot or understanding. I now realise he's almost certainly priming the police not to try the "too much luggage in the back seat" scam, as this wasn't successful. So "do him for not wearing a seatbelt, and I'll back you up," he says, Graham translating.

"He saw you not wearing your seat belt", Ali says to Graham, who sits, clamped tightly in the drivers seat by his belt. "20 Euros. Each."

Finally dispirited and broken, I pay up. 20 Euros. Each.

We finally dropped Odious Ali at the turning to Zebrabar, where he would catch a taxi back to the border. His fee for all the helpful advice and assistance - 20 Euros. Each. Well, that's what he asked for, but we had all had enough and he had to settle for 10 Euros between the four of us. Oh, and I did give him that rather helpful tip about gladioli. I hoped that was the last I'd see of him, but rather expected it wasn't.

The track to Zebrabar forks off the main road. As the light began to fade, we drove the last five miles through a complex of lakes, swamps and forest, and across a bridge, which has to be negotiated at low tide. We entered Zebrabar at dusk on a moonless starry night. It was like entering heaven after the mental hell of the day behind us. Graham and I won the toss for the last available luxury bungalow.

Zebrabar is an upmarket hippy commune. Set among tall palms on the sandy beaches of the Senegal river, it has a rustic barbecue restaurant, a bar with ice-cold beer and an honesty box. Cabins and luxury bungalows, sand-rendered and thatched, circular in the Senegalese style, are peppered about the complex. They have mosquito nets and all mod cons. Campers pitch tents where they will.

In the company of Challengers who had beaten us here, we consumed a meal of salad, pasta, yoghurt and four large beers. Each.

As the evening of gentle conviviality wore on, I found a hammock strung between two giant palms. I climbed into it and lay a while, gazing at the constellations of the tropics, listening to the distant strains of an ethnic combo in Zebrabar Village. My companions sat by the camp fire, mellow with beer, chatting to the strum of soft guitar. We'd travelled 220 miles this day, and several constellations.

DAY FIFTEEN
ZEBRABAR

When I awoke in our luxury bungalow, I knew it would serve us well over the next couple of days. Zebrabar was to be a haven of peace and recreation, somewhere to recuperate from the rigours of the road, and in particular the last twenty four hours. We'd lick our wounds, patch ourselves up and ready ourselves for the dash to the border and the Barra Ferry.

The beer last night had been nectar. Cool, limitless, apparently free and drawn from a bottomless chest freezer. The company'd been good too, and surprisingly comforting. The evening was our first encounter with alcohol and gently subdued laddish behaviour for what seemed an age. Tarifa, perhaps, in southern Spain, was our last social with some of the other Challenge Teams. As the beer quickly did its job and introduced its mellow buzz to the relaxing brain, Graham and I joined in the self congratulation. We'd travelled well over three thousand five hundred miles on some of the most awful roads in Christendom and Islam. We'd been imprisoned, ripped off, suffered the privations of the Mauritanian lavatory, and triumphed with the nonsense at the Senegalese border. Black Betty had crossed a minefield, scaled the ridge of the Diama Road and overcome depression and the ignominy of being towed by the plucky Pug. We'd be ready for anything after a couple of days here.

The route back to our luxury bungalow (swimming pool and room for a pony), much beer later and in profound darkness, had been somewhat confusing. But Graham's sense of direction hadn't failed us all the way down the coast of Africa, and didn't desert him now. So when we eventually stumbled blindly into the dark interior of the luxury bungalow (sauna and steam room on the mezzanine floor) and found the gas bottle empty, I quickly offered to return for a fresh supply. Meanwhile, Graham would attend to the minor plumbing works required to secure the promised hot water.

I staggered back towards the barbecue restaurant in a haze of mist and beer. When I chanced again on the hammock I swung clumsily into its enfolding warmth, the gas bottle taking a distant priority in my fuzzy reckoning. A beautiful starbright night, I could clearly make out Orion and The Plough, before I dropped into a deep and soundless sleep.

Several hours later I came across the luxury bungalow again, and fell into it. Graham slept peacefully on the shower room floor amidst a selection of spanners and a monkey wrench. I didn't disturb him.

This morning everything looked quite different. As the jack hammer in the skull eased, we decided to explore the place and enjoy a short holiday. Black Betty could be tidied and repacked. Perhaps she'd have a bath. The last of the reserve petrol could go in her tank. We could look for postcards, and recharge batteries-camera, mobile phone and emotional. We'd also plan the next stage.

A stroll around Zebrabar confirmed last evening's beery impressions. Stepping expectantly into the warm, blue light of day, a perfect idyll of palm and sand, against the clear rippling waters of the Senegal. The luxury bungalow was set among extravagant trees, infused with the colour and sound of exotic birds; parrot, cockatoo, red and green finches flitting in and out of the bush. Black Betty stood, calm and demure under a banyan tree, resting as we had after the horrendous entry into Senegal. The tranquility was intense, tangible, laced with the call of cicadas and the rainbow colours of dragonfly. I wished Gilly had been present to enjoy the magic and the romance with me. But I'd have to make do for the time being with the company of my good friend Graham. The magic wasn't lost, if the romance was diminished.

I climbed to the top of the scaffold and plank watchtower, which gave a birds eye view. Stepping carefully over the sleeping Welshman at the top, I took in the surroundings. In all directions a carpet of palm stretched as far as the eye could see, broken only by the fringes of the Senegal river, a sprinkling of thatched bungalows, cabins, a few tents and cars. Zebrabar is in the middle of a palm forest.

We breakfasted on boiled eggs, bread and butter soldiers, apricot conserve, tea and coffee. Our first English breakfast since the UK. Dave and Andy joined us, and the sleeping Welshman (now he was awake) whom I recognised from the post office in Gibraltar. He'd arrived last night, hot and annoyed from crossing the frontier, and soused the night away. Unable to locate his bungalow or team mate in the dark and stupefaction, he'd climbed to the top of the watchtower and spent his first night in Senegal under the stars.

Mellow now, in the morning sun, the remnants of thick heads fast dissipating, we each recounted some of our experiences since Gibraltar. The Welsh team had travelled through the desert without company or a guide, and with nothing more than a few minutes with a shovel to recount. The Costa Blanca Dons, in their Cherokee Jeep, had become separated from the group and guide when they stopped to photograph a baby camel. Nothing had been seen of them since. Team Rattle and Hum had all but destroyed the suspension on their ailing Granada, expecting too much of it on the rocks at low tide in Mauritania. Substantial welding, and some rubber bands, would now be required to hold her together.

Several of the teams would be resting up at Zebrabar to effect essential repairs after the debacle in the sand and on the beach, which we, with Dumb and Dumber, had avoided.

The conversation turned to home. Specifically, the conversation turned to those things that we would perhaps appreciate more about living in England, in light of our experiences as innocents abroad. I took the minutes of the meeting of the

PB07 Senegal Breakfast Club.

- ♥ Sanitary plumbing that works
- ♥ Bleach
- ♥ Lavatories you sit on
- ♥ Officials who aren't motivated by bribe
- ♥ 240 volt electricity
- ♥ meaningful traffic rules, properly enforced
- ♥ no driving on the pavement
- ♥ cars with brakes and steering
- ♥ insurance for anything other than a Nissan Bluebird
- ♥ water pressure
- ♥ potable drinking water from a tap
- ♥ lack of the all pervading stench of sewage
- ♥ clean streets

- ♥ no harmful mosquitoes
- ♥ flies you can swat
- ♥ lack of predatory snakes and insects
- ♥ food you can trust
- ♥ clean petrol
- ♥ quiet time
- ♥ care and respect for animals
- ♥ no begging, hassles or hustles
- ♥ beer
- ♥ freedom of movement and expression
- ♥ All Butter Shortbread Selection

Graham and I spent the rest of the day in idle relaxation. I buried the Senegalese wishbone in the sand at the base of the banyan tree, and retrieved the gas bottle, still swinging in the hammock. Graham repacked Black Betty for the umpteenth time, making the most of our space in anticipation of an early escape and dash for the frontier. The reflective yellow jackets, red triangles and fire extinguisher would be kept close at hand for the remainder of our time in Senegal. We emptied the last of the reserve petrol into the tanks of Black Betty and the Pug, minimising the need to stop before the border. The need for reserve fuel was behind us.

The currency in Senegal is CFA's (Communauté Financière Africaine) or "seefas". We'd need some for petrol, but not many, as the currency changes in the Gambia. We'd have to seek out a bank at some stage, or try to get by with Euros.

Repairing frazzled tempers and recharging emotional batteries was proceeding swiftly in this calm and wonderful place. Recharging the batteries in the cameras was not so simple in the remoter parts where there's no 240 volt electricity. Most of Zebrabar operates on 12 volts and battery power. However, I found the only mains socket with a multipoint adapter in the kitchen. A lone mobile phone was receiving its daily charge. I plugged in, found a chair and studied the route map on the wall, trying to appear studious and nonchalant. I lurked for two hours while the chargers did their work, to the gentle lilt of traditional music. Finding Martin, Zebrabar's genial host, I broached the question of currency. We could probably get by with Euros, although the exchange rate always involves a rip off. Alternatively, the nearest bank is in St.Louis.

As the afternoon wore on, further Challenge cars arrived. Team Old Gits, in the yellow Volkswagen, had chanced their arm in the desert and nearly got washed away on the beach. Team USIMW ("You stood in my wookie"), in a Ford Escort, had Trevor delusional on an overdose of malaria tablets. Rattle and Hum had commenced work on the Granada's ailing superstructure. We chatted about our various experiences, compared notes as if long lost comrades. I hadn't set eyes on some of these men since Dakhla, Tarifa, or even at the launch party long ago in that field outside Collumpton in Devon last June.

Dinner was an ethnic affair. A sumptuous barbecue of fish and steak, with generous salads of beetroot, aubergine, okra, mushrooms, cauliflower, carrot and potato. Followed by carrot cake with white and chocolate sauces.

I'm sitting in bed now. I've written in my journal and I'm reading the Colin Dexter "Morse" novel *"Last Seen Wearing"* borrowed from the hippy hotel. I find it gentle, English, comforting. Graham's becoming an expert on the history and geography of Senegambia, using the *Lonely Planet* as his text.

We're a fortnight out and missing home.

DAY SIXTEEN
ST. LOUIS

Founded on a strategically placed island in the Senegal River in 1659, St.Louis was the first French settlement in Africa. Until 1958 it was the capital of Senegal, and its administrative influence took in the whole of Mauritania. This ancient, in African terms, island of culture, is fabled for its creole food, beautiful women and jazz. St.Louis, Missouri, is named after it. It was less than an hour away by road. The consensus of the Breakfast Club was that it merited a visit. But not by car. Appetites were healthy for breakfast, but none of those present had the stomach to brave the chaos that re-entering St.Louis by road would entail. Few could afford the "fines". We'd need to share taxis or some other means of transport.

As the last mustering point before the ultimate Challenge destination, Zebrabar is where those taking a more leisurely approach catch up. Teams who've suffered mechanical or structural difficulties hunker down to essential repairs. Team 2 in a 4, the clock menders from High Wycombe first encountered on the ferry to Tangier, limped in on patched tyres. The Renault 4 had crabbed manfully through the desert, its front wheels out of alignment with rear. Probably the legacy of some homespun welding by a French farmer. Ian and Dan were travelling with a rear seat and luggage compartment full of tyres, begged, borrowed, but probably not stolen from the many breakers' yards and second hand tyre factors along the west African coast, where tyres are more plentiful than petrol.

What of our other rare and complex companions? It was at the Breakfast Club that Graham and I were to connect with some of the disparate teams that made up Group Four and discover the mix of personality that brings men (well, mainly men) of all ages to leave family and security behind and charge through Africa in search of adventure.

We'd already established a good, if transient, friendship with Team Dumb and Dumber. Dave Barrow's wicked sense of humour manifested itself in rare unexpected moments between playing with his several mobile phones. Dave was missing his wife and young son, and looking forward to a triumphant return. A college course and qualification as senior social worker awaited.

Andy Morgan, famous for his silly hats, ethnic dress sense, picturesque vocabulary and quietly cultured approach to life. More at home, I suspect, in an art gallery or museum than a west African bordello, he was missing the wife too. He had adult sons in his native Suffolk, and a sister in Berrynarbour, minutes away from Long Lane Farm. Calm, self assured, wryly humourous, he'd eased my passage into Senegal and earned my respect at a time when I'd felt I might explode with anger and frustration. Andy had been looking forward to Senegal's music and culture.

Trevor and Scott of Team USIMW ("You stood in my wookie") added a further dimension to our stay in Zebrabar. Trevor was a tube driver on the Metropolitan Line. Tall, rangey, and distinctly Essex, in his lucid moments he was an excellent underground raconteur and bon viveur. Much of Trevor's trip had been spent in a beer and malaria tablet induced coma. Scott, his travelling companion, was one for the ladies and had ventured into the hotspots of Marrakech and Casablanca on the prowl for a different sort of adventure. Today, his purpose in St.Louis would be to search for red triangles. The Team had been relying on home made articles, fashioned from bits of plywood painted with red gloss, and they'd not been well received by the border bureaucrats.

We'd encountered Team Old Gits briefly in Dakhla in their yellow VW. Graham, a professional rally driver, deeply bronzed, in shorts sandals and trendy wrap around sun specs, knew most things that needed to be known, including "how to deal with the locals". His companion Alan, a little more beige in coloration, was quietly supportive in the background.

These passing impressions barely scratch the surface of the personalities encountered on our passage through Africa. There wasn't time to build lasting friendships as we hurtled headlong down that coast. It was only during this brief semi-colon in the journey that an understanding would develop into a fleeting acquaintance. After all, one week from now and we'd probably never meet again.

News swiftly flew around the Breakfast Club of a fishing trawler leaving for St.Louis within the hour. I galloped back across the sand to Black Betty like a demented Man Friday, to find Graham at the wheel, engine running to charge his phone. He was in the middle of an important call to his solicitors in Moreton–in–the–Marsh. We grabbed the essentials and within moments were on the banks of the Senegal, wondering where the expected ocean going liner, the steam packet to St.Louis, would dock and disembark. No pier, no jetty, as such, could we see. Just a few posts driven haphazardly into the beach head, indifferent canoes beached and tied to them. Disinterested fishermen tinkered in the shallows. Graham joked that we'd probably wait at this municipal boat stop for some hours, and then two ships would turn up at the same instant.

Other Challengers appeared. We formed an orderly and very English queue on the beach and talked of the weather for the time of year, cricket scores, a parliamentary by-election. Each politely, but secretly, jostled for position, anxious there mightn't be room for all on the expected vessel, each determined to make it to St.Louis. Dave and Andy joined the queue. We synchronised watches. The boat was late.

Another example of west African inefficiency and sloppy attitude. I could sense the mood of this happy band growing ugly as we stood, gazing up river, shielding our eyes from nothing in particular, the way sailors do, trying to make out a hint of billowing smoke on the horizon.

A fisherman, tall, dusky and handsome, clambered lazily out of his canoe anchored in the shallows. Wearing nothing but a long grey smock and an ivory smile he waded to the shore with his catch, five or six fine looking denizens of the deep, sole I think, dangling at his knees from a chord clutched in his meaty left hand. He bade us good morning, and disappeared into the palms. Barbecued fresh fish for supper tonight, I mused, a veritable feast for these wandering heroes to return to, if we ever did leave this shore.

By 10.45 our hopes of a day in the fabled city were dwindling, when the fisherman suddenly returned. Still smiling, still dripping from the smock soaked to the waist in river water, he introduced himself. He was to be our captain, our pilot and our guide to St.Louis. And his little canoe, the *Ursula Samira* out of Zebrabar, was to be our means of transport.

Those of us wearing shorts and sandals skipped playfully into the water and headed for the canoe. The more stolid British amongst us removed our shoes and fair isle socks, rolled up the trousers we'd worn thus far to protect our nether regions from marauding mosquitoes, and waded into the murky water, valuables held aloft. Most made it into the canoe without too much difficulty. I hauled my short but perfectly formed body up and over the prow, and slithered clumsy and gasping, into a heap in the stinking bilge. Graham vaulted, rather more athletically, in beside me, grinned, and remarked "I keep thinking it's Tuesday!"

All aboard, our captain weighed anchor, pushed the canoe off the sand bar, and deftly leapt into the stern. We were en route for St.Louis. As the outboard coughed into life and chugged its merry way up stream, the PB07

Challengers performed a clever, almost balletic, balancing act. Passing cameras and other valuables up and down the boat, shifting position to achieve optimum weight distribution we took orders from one of our number, an airline pilot from Shepherds Bush, who'd pulled rank and assumed control. Our captain looked on in amusement. In truth, we were all troubled by the boat's jaunty and unpredictable progress through the water. But we maintained our ten upper lips stiff in the face of adversity, and were soon recounting past stories of adventure and derring do on the high seas. I very nearly broke into a sea shanty mid stream.

The *Ursula Samira* was basically a log, hollowed out and sharpened, about 30 feet long and maybe 3 feet wide amidships. I sat proudly at the pointy end, with only Scott between me and St.Louis. We two gave helpful guidance and navigational tips to the captain at the stern, but these may have lost something in the translation through a series of Chinese whispers. In any event, most of my directions ("left hand down a touch, hard-a-starboard, mind the horse", etc.) seem to have gone unheeded. Behind me, Trevor and Graham consulted a map of the London Underground and discussed the finer points of the Metropolitan Line. Dave Barrow played with his mobile phone. Andy Morgan, sitting amidships in the most comfortable section, compared the passing craft with pictures in his *Lonely Planet* and waxed technical as he declared "That's a pirogue, I think, sort of a skinny dugout with a sail!"

Keith Pugsley

Behind Andy perched Biggles from Shepherds Bush, and his team mate Algy. Both had removed their leather flying helmets and goggles and were busy baling out the bilge water, which had risen to an alarming level in the overloaded canoe. Team Old Gits at the stern, blissfully unaware of the midships leakage, helped the captain nurse the sputtering engine upstream.

It was thus employed that we, the doughty crew of the *Ursula Samira*, proceeded at unhurried pace towards St.Louis. The river was surprisingly busy. Busboats laden with black passengers chugged laboriously towards the villages downstream. Pirogues, their sails patched and tattered, scudded alongside, upstream. Canoes wove in and out, fishermen tending to their catches and nets. On the shore, horses, some riderless, from this distance apparently legless, drifted amongst the palm and savannah. Fishing settlements, tents and rough shelters. A lighthouse gave fair warning that the Atlantic Ocean is only a short distance at high tide. On this bright, sparkling and optimistic day we could've been taking part in the Henley Regatta, were it not for the baobab, the palm and the ever present thought that crocodiles have been known to reach this far up the Senegal. We were still shipping water. Biggles worked feverishly with his helmet. Trevor looked forward to the pint of Guiness and a decent curry that might be had in St.Louis, where the laws against alcohol are dramatically relaxed.

Our arrival in St.Louis was as low tech as the departure from Zebrabar. The boat bumped and ground over the rocks and gravel in the shallows. The captain was first out and he hoisted his drenched smock to relieve himself. Our disembarkation lacked the finesse I'd been quietly practising in the pointy end. We basically tumbled out of the *Ursula Samira* in a heap. Picking our way through the foot or so of rotting fish and crab, polluted with river slime and the captain's pee, we crossed the corporation refuse tip, clambered over some rocks and a wall, and found ourselves standing, dazed and blinking in the sunlight, on the dock at St.Louis. We were to enjoy three hours here, and to return on the outgoing tide.

St.Louis on a Saturday lunch time was not quite as we'd expected. I'd envisioned Rio at carnival, a riot of colour and noise with scantily clad, lithe bodied maidens strutting their samba stuff in the streets to the rhythm of drums and whistles. A flamboyance of ostrich feathers. Well, there was none of that. St.Louis wears a gently faded splendour. It's colourful, but jaded. The French colonial streets are washed in pale blues, canary yellows, ochre and madder, draped in bougainvillaea and clematis. Horse drawn taxis clatter up and down the cobbles. Beaten up cars and mopeds putter in and out of dusty alleyways. The by now characteristic odour of putrescent food and bad drains gives way eventually to a less intense assault upon the nostrils as you leave the port and enter the town. Lop-eared goats wander in packs of three or four at every corner, keeping a safe distance but indulging their curiosity staring at you in a haughty, incredulous manner.

We'd passed Gustav Eiffel's Pont Faidherbe, linking the island to the mainland, and although it's reputed to be "a grand piece of 19th.century engineering, originally built to cross the Danube, transferred here in 1897 and once rotating to allow ships to steam up the Senegal River", I confess I found his earlier efforts with Blackpool Tower infinitely more attractive.

We'd arrived at St.Louis paying no fines or bribes. There'd been no trouble from border bureaucrats and not even a speculative enquiry from the Gendarmerie, who were closed for lunch. But the hustlers were soon on the scene, with their cheap carved trinkets, jewellery, rugs and pots. We'd learnt that eye contact with hustlers must be avoided at all costs.

You must never express even the mildest passing interest in their wares, and on no account touch the goods. This may be taken as a contractual commitment to buy. The only viable strategy with the hustler is to completely ignore his existence. Blank him. Engage your colleague in earnest conversation about the weather, the football results or the price of chips, but on no account acknowledge the presence of the hustler on your shoulder. The four of us were chased, cajoled and herded around the streets of St.Louis until one of us, Andy I think, ducked through a door guarded by a policeman. We all followed.

We found ourselves in the smallest bureau de change in the world. Probably. This tiny chamber, no bigger than a telephone kiosk, was intended to accommodate one client at a time, ably guarded I'm sure from street hustlers by the policeman we'd trampled in our panic to escape the hordes. We four huddled cosily in the cramped quarters and awaited instructions. A tinny voice which appeared to emanate from Dave's navel announced the stern presence of the, as yet unseen, bank official. We all breathed in and, at the count of three, turned simultaneously, to stand back to back, Dave facing the counter. The official was remarkably efficient, in his bijou quarters, and Dave, speaking through the navel into his inclined ear quickly managed to exchange sufficient Euros for seefas. We rotated around the booth in unison, performing a sort of cramped square dance, until we'd all had enough of the experience and our wallets were replenished.

Back in the streets we wandered freely, but of course now loaded with local currency, were prey to the street corner pests. One such latched onto me, a boy of about 16, urging me to inspect his wares. He thrust into my chest a hideous African mask knocked out for the tourist trade. I'd learnt by now to reject these overtures, quite forcibly I think, until he mentioned the mask was in fact a gift.

Now, always prepared for a bargain and wishing to cement Anglo-Senegalese relations, I took the young man at his word and graciously accepted. But it seems in these parts the tradition is to expect a gift in return, and this young man wanted seefas as his reciprocal gift. A concept quite alien to me, I don't think it's recognised by British law. A sort of conditional gift, the condition precedent being that money or something of moneys worth is due in return. I engaged the young

African in legal debate as we roamed the streets of St.Louis, and felt the more incisive and logical my argument, the more he seemed to believe and take on board my point of view, which was naturally based in strict jurisprudence and legal theory. In any event, when I eventually rejected the kind but conditional gift, based, as it had been, on an honest misunderstanding of the conflict of laws between nations, he just as graciously accepted the position. Our contract was void *ab initio*, and we parted company, both wiser for the encounter, and Anglo-Senegalese relations undented.

Graham and I were, however, in the market for trinkets and presents for those back home. We had an interesting bargaining experience in one of the more respectable emporia in a side street, where I bought postcards and stamps and, for the bargained price of 12,000 CFA (£12), a beautifully carved Mancala game. The proprietor ("Le Patron"), a bulky but immaculate lady dressed in a canary yellow silken tent, had all the charm, charisma and business acumen that her colleagues on the streets so sadly lacked.

Early afternoon. The street vendors and hustlers are lying down, dozing on the sidewalks in the scarce shade. We step carefully over them and pass from the heat and torpor into the blessed cool interior of a street café. With a little help from my friends I make it to the summit of a bar stool, cross my short legs and strike as cool and seductive a pose as I can manage. I order four ice cold beers. The beers arrive in frosted glass with a backcloth. A Black Venus. I gaze into her smiling eyes and am in love.

Dave's engaged in heated negotiations with one of the hustlers. He spotted our nifty manoeuvre into this bar and, with his eye on a deal, has come to do business. Dave wants football strip for his young son, if possible from each footballing nation he passes through. Mr. Fixit thinks he can help. A deal is done. Mr. Fixit disappears into the underworld of St.Louis to fetch the goods.

Graham and Andy are deep in conversation, I suspect on the culture and politics of Senegal. A pair of Victor Meldrews in high spirits, they, like me, are enjoying the peaceful cool and temporary safety of this urban oasis.

Meanwhile, the alcohol hits the spot. I'm gently fuzzy at the edges as I take in the beer and the ambiance. The violent carnival rhythms have given way to something more vibrant and traditional. A white lady of indeterminate age sits in a corner at a lonely table for one, nibbles at a brioche, sips Pernod. She is faded, but not yet jaded, and I wonder what brings her here, what is her exotic past, her apparently purposeless presence.

Mr. Fixit returns triumphant, bearing football strip in all the colours, all the sizes and for every conceivable league team in Senegal. Dave settles for strip bearing the name of a player who, he tells me excitedly, also plays for Bolton Wanderers. I'm amused, mildly, but not excited. Football isn't my game. And I'm intrigued by Edith Piaf in the corner.

Graham and Andy have set the world to rights. Dave's business is done. Our fourth beers are finished. It's time to leave the bar. I tear my regretful heart from Black Venus, my eyes and thoughts from Edith Piaf in the corner. We leave the caged cockatoos and the cool air conditioning and re-enter the sun-bleached pink and beige of St.Louis.

Dave and Andy head for the Cyber Café. Graham and I, both internet dinosaurs, follow unenthusiastically. But this is another new experience for us. A traditional café it's not, and if we require further sustenance after those four beers we're going to be disappointed. But computers it does have, and in abundance. Thousands of them, and all in working order, or so it seems. Dave quickly accesses the Challenge Website for news of our colleagues. The Costa Blanca Dons are still missing, last seen in the desert in Mauritania. Andy accesses the Dumb and Dumber website and posts news of recent exploits. Graham and I get a mention, but to make sure we shall send more conventional postcards from here on the way back to port.

The return trip was uneventful. I waded through the rotting fish soup and the pelicans feasting on it and boarded the *Ursula Samira* with a flourish. Seasoned sailors now, but still British to the core, we adopted the same positions as on the outward voyage, as if these had been reserved in perpetuity. Biggles manned the pumps, but with less enthusiasm. We all seemed more relaxed, perhaps subdued from our experiences in the sleepy banana republic. The fact that we sat in several inches of water didn't seem to matter so much on the return. After all, the water was only in the bottom of the boat, and if we all leaned to the left, the leak seemed less severe. Oh, a life on the ocean wave.

Close to the left bank, the captain suddenly cut the engine. We drifted silently across his nets and came to a halt in the shallows with a gentle bump. Safely home from its epic voyage, the crew of the *Ursula Samira*, weary and salt stained from its exertions, made its way through the thousands of small land crabs that infest the beach at low tide, each scuttling to its own hole in the sand. Graham set me gently down, and I scuttled gratefully back to our luxury bungalow.

Dinner time. We're joined by Rattle and Hum, whose team name really suits their car, a venerable but battle-scarred Ford Granada fresh out of theatre after a day of major corrective surgery. The desert and road to Diama have taken their toll. The suspension, which has become largely independent of the chassis, is now parcelled together with girders and cross members. Access is via the windscreen.

More Challenge teams arrive. Team Hugh Jarse, last seen in Dakhla and now minus the touring caravan, abandoned in the deserts of Mauritania. The Reservoir Frogs, Team Flapjack and Beauty and the Beast all join us for beer and bonhomie around the barbecue.

As we share stories of horror and success in the desert, on the beach and particularly our inauspicious welcome into this corrupt country, a dilemma occurs. Graham and I want to leave at dawn, if we're to make it into the Gambia before dark. We know we must be escorted to the border. The authorities expect us to travel in convoys of at least ten cars, presumably because they don't employ an unlimited supply of escorts. So are there ten teams ready, willing and able to proceed at crack of sparrows? And where's the necessary paperwork, the exit visas for our cars paid for so dearly on our entry into Senegal two days ago? I can't find our visa. Andy can't find the visa for the Pug. Nobody can find their visa. It's inconceivable we've all lost these vital documents. It's widely believed our escort at the border, Odious Ali, retained them all. And how will Ali know we need to leave tomorrow? I'm really not prepared for this much uncertainty. A heated debate ensues.

We elect Graham of Team Old Gits, to take up our concerns with Martin, the host of our resort. But we're angry now, and the realisation that we've all been so monumentally ripped off fans the flames of discontent.

"I want to kill that smarmy little bastard Ali"
"We should do him some damage, like major damage, if we see him again"
"We could tie him between two of the cars and tear him up a bit"
"Better still, we tie him to a tree, pour petrol over him and have a bonfire"
"I'm not wasting petrol on him, I'd rather piss on him"
"What about we tie him to a tree. Put a sign around his neck saying "I take it up the arse for 20 Euros. Each?"

And in this way we mutter and plot riot and insurrection, torture and unutterable mayhem long into the night. I think we settle on nicking our exit visas, burying him up to the neck in a termite's nest, and racing for the border in different directions. But I'm too drunk to remember. It's time for my bed. Tomorrow's another day.

DAY SEVENTEEN
ANOTHER GAUNTLET

I awake at 2.00 a.m. with the horrors. The beer's worn off and I lie in a stupor of anxiety and guilt. Will I get out of this place today? Will I get out of this place at all? The escort's bound to arrive without our exit visa, because I've lost it, apparently. He probably won't arrive at all. We daren't leave Zebrabar without the visa. Black Betty might be confiscated. We're prisoners in this place. Trapped, and I got Graham into this. And Black Betty. This is a human rights issue. Gilly would get me out of this mess, if only I could contact her from this blessed country. I haven't heard her voice for days. The expensive mobile phone is useless. I'm useless. I feel lonely, inept, incompetent, vulnerable and guilty. I must see Martin at the earliest opportunity and insist he check on our team and registration number. It's vital we leave here today, and early. I don't want to be left behind. I want to go home.

Daylight now. If Graham's been suffering the same anxieties, he disguised them well. He's slept like the proverbial baby and is repacking Black Betty from scratch for the first time since Long Lane Farm, taking this opportunity to prepare for the dash to the border. As we have a spare seat in the back, vacated by the sorely missed Mohammed, I suspect we may be chosen to accommodate Odious Ali through Senegal. Graham sits in the front passenger seat, surveying our possessions, looking for inspiration. An aged sewing machine in its case, a large globe of the world, all that remains of a kitsch seventies table lamp, a tray of mobile phones, the tajine that's sat quietly on the rear seat covered in newspapers since Meknes. There's a contemplative but maniacal glint in Graham's eye.

"Pass us that lump of wood Keith, will you?" I pass the heavy baulk of timber purloined from Neil Caley's yard in Bugford to put under a jack in the desert. It's served no purpose so far. This is its debut appearance. Graham secretes it under a blanket on the rear seat.

"And the tool box." I hand over the dented blue cantilever tool chest that's held our motley selection of wrenches, spanners and duct tape since its only use in Okehampton. With a grunt he shoves this in the left side rear foot well, next to the lilac jerrican.

"Chuck us the jack handle, and the tyre lever." I comply. He wedges them between the jerricans and the transmission tunnel, and they project hideously into the limited rear seating area.

"What are you up to Graham", I chance, as he sprinkles the rear seat liberally with rusty nails, jubilee clips and bent wire.

"Well," he retorts with a grin, "just making the back seat comfortable for Ali."

I leave him checking the child locks.

I'm feeling more positive about our departure. Martin's unsympathetic to our plight. He dismisses my human rights protestations as an overreaction to what is, in his view, west African idiosyncratic behaviour. I'm angry. A bit. But I suppress the discomfort and accept assurances that the escort will arrive shortly and all will be well. And if it's not, a modest financial inducement will see us over the border. Probably.

Zebrabar's alive and wide awake. There's a will to leave and to move on, and a sense of urgency among the Challengers to commence the final leg. Each expresses his restlessness in a different way. Graham, apparently satisfied with the torture chamber he's created in Black Betty's rear seat, checks her lights and the fluid levels. I kick the tyres. I'm not sure why, but I kick them again, for luck.

Rattle and Hum are putting the last touches to their modified suspension. They've spliced together what's left of their tent pegs, and are hammering them into the Sierra's nether regions, desperate to reach the Gambia before it collapses completely. 2 in a 4 are sitting in the sand beside a mountain of tyres, busily mending and patching. They're not leaving today. Dumb and Dumber are staging an impromptu boot sale. While Andy tries to offload the spare radiator he's lugged from the UK expecting disaster in the desert, and a nifty patent fart detector, Dave's opened his own branch of Carphone Warehouse. He's doing a brisk trade. The local kids crowd around, with their chorus of "Cadeaux, cadeaux, cadeaux!"

At breakfast, discontent and revolution are on the brew, reaching boiling point. Trevor and Scott are for making off without the visa or the escort and taking their chances in south Senegal. We've been told the escort should be here by ten. Any minute beyond that'll be critical. We've about three hundred miles over rough unsigned roads to travel before the border with Gambia. The infamous Barra Ferry lies beyond. There's general consensus we must make the last daylight crossing. Time is tight. It's already 10.15.

The escort is rumoured to have arrived. I'm relishing the idea of bundling the little shit, Odious Ali, into the rear seat of Black Betty. There he will sit on a plank of wood and some rusty tacks, his knees touching his chin, in a locked enclosed rear seat for three hundred miles in the blinding sub-Saharan sun. However, my feelings change when I meet the escort some fifteen minutes later. I'm delighted, almost ecstatic, to find it's not Odious Ali, but a perfectly affable and pleasant Negro, as blue black as his baggy uniform, with a smile and a gold tooth that make him almost piratical. He pulls his dusty Mercedes into the sandy arena, and commands our instant attention. A small part of me's disappointed we shan't have Odious Ali in the torture seat, and I shan't have the pleasure of joining in his humiliation. But then that's my darker side.

Seven cars pull, scrape or are dragged into line, jostling for an ill-defined pole position. Nobody quite knows where in line it's best to be, but we seven are ready to go. There's a last call for border runners. The escort wants ten before he'll leave. Hot weather and mechanical breakdown have led to fractious behaviour between teams, and sometimes to badly disguised temper tantrums. Rattle 'n Hum scowl at each other. Neither accepts responsibility for the parlous state of the Sierrra.

Three further teams, two of which only arrived a few hours ago, have been persuaded to make up our complement. Now we are ten. The line snakes from the barbecue pit to the gate. Engines thrum. Exhausts hum. The convoy nestles in a haze of blue smoke.

"Looks like we're in a rally," comments the ever observant Graham.
"Either that, or there's something at the front of this queue worth waiting for."
"It'll be beer, I expect."
"That, or mint tea."

The formalities are finally over. Our escort communicates instructions in broken French and sign language to the assembled teams at a sort of briefing session. We are to stay in close formation and not drop behind. If one has to stop, we all stop. Radio contact will be intermittently maintained between those with radios. It's up to us to ensure we're strategically placed in the pecking order to achieve this. Old Git Graham has been appointed Trustee, holding all of the drivers' passports, so we'd better stick together or else.

At 10.45 the escort steps into his Mercedes, gestures to us to follow, and leads the motley convoy out of the resort. We're off! Ten cars plough through the soft sand and pine cones. Behind the escort, Hugh Jarse in the Iveco van bedecked with the flags of all nations leads the convoy. The flag of Senegal flaps in the breeze on the roof-mounted pole. The Old Gits follow closely in the canary yellow Scirocco, something vivid to concentrate the attention of the back runners. Biggles and Algy in their Volvo, Team Flapjack in a tiny Fiat, the Pug and Black Betty follow. Behind us, the Reservoir Frogs, and Beauty and the Beast bring up the rear. The raggedy arsed diplomatic mission crosses the sand spit causeway at low tide and heads for the road to St.Louis.

Travelling at about 20 m.p.h. to maintain grip on the still soft sand, the road's a confusion of dust and rubbish and the clamour of children begging for cadeaux. The gaps between cars are already opening, and Graham guns Black Betty a little harder. We don't want to lose sight of the lead car.

At the junction with the main road the convoy takes a right. St.Louis is where it should be now, behind us by my reckoning, and we head for Louga. Vultures circle ominously above. Boney cattle wander listlessly on the tarmac hardtop. We weave our way through the obligatory ruts, but are moving south again and making good time, despite the late start.

The landscape, once a novelty, has become boring. Sand, grassy tussocks, the odd habitation. We're motoring along the easy highway at 55 m.p.h., keeping in line, obeying orders, an eye or two on the Senegalese flag and the yellow blob in the distance.

At Ngaye Ngaye Graham wonders whether we'll make it to the Springtime Hotel (his name for the Safari Gardens), where the Challenge terminates, before dark. We pass a sign for "sheep crossing". A lone horse and cart trots in the opposite direction.

Our first petrol stop, just outside Rao. Petrol's pumped by hand in rural Senegal, but the process is surprisingly swift. The attendant, a fourteen year old in dashing yellow reflective jacket, talks interestedly as he draws on a cigarette and winds the ratchet handle back and forth in the dry heat. Black Betty's fourth in line for petrol and the storage tanks are emptied on her. We now have three quarters of a tank of low octane dregs, and can expect some trouble. But we're not grumbling. Those behind go without. The apologies are profuse, but petrol is not such a rarity here.

The attendants shut up shop for the afternoon and are soon seen kicking about the forecourt the football one of the Challengers has passed them as cadeaux. Rural Senegalese strike me as real people. Friendly, happy, undemanding and honest. Not wealthy, but not uncomfortable either. I prefer them to the frenetic Arabs of the north.

Fass. A tree-lined boulevard with most of its population sitting in the afternoon shade. The village houses are circular, mud constructions, thatched and windowless. We're not far from the capital, Dakar. My father was here as a petty officer on an aircraft carrier during the war, and wrote a coded message to my mother in Watford which passed the censors undetected. I'd like to visit Dakar, if only to discover the effect my father's message had on the outcome of the war. But it's not practicable. The challenge, in Senegal and in a car, is to get through it.

Paye. The escort arrests the convoy to check we're all in line. The local population is getting blacker, more negroid by the mile. Masses of children, well fed, and clothed, if barefoot. Long horned cattle, also healthy looking beasts, graze the sparse roadside verge. A lorry, balanced precariously on a bottle jack and a pile of bricks, waits for its wheel to be changed. No sign of the Health and Safety Executive.

We reach Louga at noon. The roads are kind to us, but on the map the distances are deceptive. Our target today, the Barra Ferry, Gambia and Challenge destination. They seem a long way off. We may yet be camping at Toubacouta, a few miles short of the Gambian border, if light fails. My arms sting from yesterday's sun in the boat to St.Louis. I still haven't broken out the sun cream. Saving it for best. Probably.

There's a dead steer in a field just outside Barale Ndiaye. Three men haggle over its destiny. A thriving community with overloaded buses— converted vans with no rear doors. Cattle range freely. Compounds of plaited reed fences enclose four or five bungalows in the Senegalese style. A dead horse, its outline barely visible through the carpet of munching flies.

Louga's a decent sized town, the first since St.Louis. Wrecked cars litter the main street, tyre factors and kerbside bicycle mechanics line them. We stop for petrol and squeeze in 9,000 CFA's worth. The pumps are electric this time. Women and children sell bananas from car to car, but they do take no for an answer. The bananas look great, but we've been warned not to accept fresh fruit from strange women.

A cow, long dead, is the focus for two mangy curs who argue and snarl as they snack at the empty hide. The population stand and stare, or some of them do, with a faintly expectant look. What can they be waiting for?

The convoy has stretched out now. Hugh Jarse has become tail end Charlie and the Senegalese flag flaps comfortably in the rear view mirror. The Pug's between us. A tall, black watermelon girl waves as we leave her village. Graham stabs the brakes as a large white longhorn steps out of the bush, hesitates, steps back again.

Kebemer. The reckless goats lie where they've been killed. Children wave, hold out their cadeaux hands, giggle, scavenge amidst the pitiful refuse at the town tip. Another headless animal, antelope or donkey, it's hard to tell, recumbent and fly blown. A horse-drawn cart carries a troupe of young girls with colourful headdresses. They're country folk, quite unlike the cosmopolitan chic of St.Louis. In the middle distance, a forest of baobab, the first we've seen, despite my insistence to Graham since Morocco that the whole of Africa's full of them.

1.40 p.m. Bargua. More goats and long horns with a death wish. Graham's getting concerned.

"For chrissake Andy. Get a move on. Keep up!"
"What's the problem, Gray?"
"Well, it's Andy. Lovely bloke an' all that, but too polite. You just can't let people in like that when you're in a convoy."
"We'll catch up."
"Yeah, but I hope it's before Barra!"

We do catch up, because the convoy has stopped for us and Hugh Jarse, still at the back. We're welcomed by children running along this dusty road with big waves, expansive smiles and gleaming white teeth. They seem happy and healthy, if dirt poor.

Another petrol stop, but Black Betty needs none right now. She just needs to keep rolling on. When called on to start again she refuses. She's hot, tired, and cheesed off with the filthy petrol she's been fed since Mauritania. The Old Gits return to help get her started. With cold water sprayed on her injectors, and a little patience, she struggles back into life. We must get out of this village and keep going. With the airflow over the engine she's just about happy.

We're in Thies at three o'clock, and most of the population are lying down in the dirt for their afternoon snooze. It's been a long and boring drive and I wish I could join them. Instead we turn right, carve up a horse and cart and take the B road, reputedly in better condition than the A Road we've been on. Soon through Thies, we're following the Old Gits now, immediately behind the escort. We've returned to pole position, on the road to Djourbel. Black Betty's running lumpy, but we have the escort in sight. I keep my eyes peeled for the Pug in the wing mirror.

Djourbel. The Wookies set down the two Canadian hitch-hikers they've carried from Zebrabar. They're heading for Dakar and the coast. They can catch a cab from here. Once again, Black Betty doesn't like stop start motoring, but we're helpfully given a bottle of octane booster by the Reservoir Frogs, and empty it promptly into the tank. The engine's still lumpy, but I think the booster helps.

Gossas at four o'clock. The same dog-eared shops, and rutted road, colourful people, tired animals. Here a group of ladies, in flowing gowns of yellow, pink, cerise, red and green, with matching turbans. Perhaps the Gossas and District WI, but I don't hear "Jerusalem", and see no mango jam.

Kaolack at five. The last three vehicles are missing. Black Betty's been holding fourth place since Djourbel and I pass the message forward on the walkie-talkie. The escort stops, turns and races back in search of the tail end. Kaolack's more of the same. Dumped cars, suicidal goats, bicycles, mopeds, horse carts, donkey carts, mechanics. Washing-lines laden with the multi-coloured day's wash straddle the main street. Most of these Senegalese towns and villages look like they're recovering from an earthquake. Slowly. Yet there's an undeniable charm about its tree-lined boulevards and sandy sidewalks. A bus overtakes, passengers clinging to the sides, blaring "La Cacaracha". The bus, that is, only some of the passengers.

Here's an opportunity to take stock and evaluate the position. Toubacouta's another two hours away, and it's unlikely we'll make the border, let alone the Barra ferry, before dark. By all accounts Barra's not a place to be trifled with, after nightfall. The advice in the Road Book is to camp before Barra if necessary, and catch an early ferry, rather than attempt a night crossing, or deal with the shady characters that abound just over the frontier. After a deal of soul-searching and some heated negotiations, it's agreed that five teams will overnight somewhere near Toubacouta. The others, perhaps braver, perhaps more foolhardy, are determined to make for the Barra Ferry tonight.

The escort returns with our last compatriots, Hugh Jarse, who had a problem switching over to reserve diesel in the Iveco, and Dumb and Dumber, who stayed with them in support. We share our plans with the escort who, obligingly, agrees to take the Toubacoutans to a hotel in the vicinity. He'll then lead the Barra Boys to the border so they may reach Banjul tonight. He'll return and stay with the Toubacoutans, and take us to the morning ferry. Our target's clear at last, perhaps for the first time today.

Once more we're off. The last bit of bad road has bounced Black Betty's rear fog light from its mountings, and it's hanging by its cable. Figuring fog won't be a meteorological issue for the Gambia, I've hacked it off and thrown it in the back seat. A hasty roadside repair carried out under the intense scrutiny of three hundred jostling children.

As we approach the southern extremities of Senegal, the houses have become tin shacks, villages of corrugated iron. A concert entertains the villagers sitting in deck chairs as if in a park in England on a Sunday afternoon forty years ago. A game of football, teams in full strip, blues versus yellows. Behind the goal, a dead cow is consumed by two slavering dogs.

Light begins to fail, and it's cooler. These roads and tracks must be really punishing for some of the cars, but Black Betty copes well, provided she isn't hot and bothered. The concentration required of Graham is intense, if we're to avoid the larger ruts and potholes, and yet maintain reasonable speed. Two wild boar saunter in front.

Street lamps are on now. Street vendors ply their trades in the gloom. Bananas, mangoes and matresses. Suddenly, we reach the Hotel Les Palentuviers, where we're to spend our last night in Senegal. Amidst the filth, the clamour, the open sewers and the poverty, we pass through a gate and enter an oasis.

The swimming pool's a showpiece, set central to a host of luxury Senegalese bungalows. Ours is air-conditioned.

Dinner was ample, if disappointingly British. Soup, chicken with rice, chocolate mousse.

(Me, in Alan Whicker mode, pointing the camera) "This is Dave Barrow, of Dumb and Dumber. And what do you think of it so far, Dave?"

Dave	"It's been awesome. It's been excellent. Roads lovely. All the police and customs we've met have been polite. Welcomed us on our way to Banjul."
Me	"Excellent!"
Dave	"It's been crap!"
Me	"Trevor, what would you like to say? How has it been for you, Trevor? Did the earth move? Clearly it did."
Trevor	"It's been educational and enlightening. And I want to go home."
Me	"And you Graham?"
Graham	"I'm tired and shagged out after a long squawk."
Dave	"Who with? Who was she then? Give me her number."
Graham	"There have been some hard days. Interesting days. I've seen some things I never thought I'd see. Did you see that cow on the side of the road, that was dead? And two dogs eating it?"
Trevor	"I saw a dog eating a donkey's bum. That was nice."
Graham	"Yeah." (yawns).
Me	"This is Andy of Dumb and Dumber. What would you like to say, Andy? What were the highlights of the tour for you?"
Andy	"Highlights of the trip? Blimey, that's springing one on me. Watching Dave drive through the minefield. Food round Mohammed's house. Watching the world go by the window, and enjoying the sights."
Me	"And would you do it again?"
Andy	"At the moment, no. But I don't regret coming. And in five years I might say yes again."
Trevor	"Madman!"
Andy	"But if I do, you can section me under the Mental Health Act."
Probably.	

DAY EIGHTEEN
THE BARRA BOYS

We hadn't been complacent about mosquito precautions. Since Tarifa in southern Spain we'd taken the Malarone tablets ritualistically, at the earliest opportunity each day. Applying Deet to legs, arms and faces had become a greasy but unmissable precursor to sleep since Dakhla. But we hadn't actually seen or heard a single example of the dreaded culicidae. So it was with a little surprise that, in the dark air-conditioned sanctuary of our bungalow in the Hotel Les Palétuviers, I felt the high pitched whine of something suspiciously recognisable whisper past my right ear.

"Was that you Keith?"
"No, I thought it was you. I think we've got company."
"What, at this time? Bit inconsiderate that."
"We'd better see him off the premises. I'll get the light."

I fumble in the midnight blackness for the fob switch of the table lamp that used to be by my head. Another whine, this time at the left ear, injects a sense of urgency. I find the switch under my pillow. The forty watts flood the room with an eerie incandescence.

"Bloody 'ell, there's 'undreds of 'em." I drag the bedsheet up and under my nose.
"And they're in here, with us".

Looking up into the vaulted top of the mosquito net I estimate at least a hundred of the spindle-legged little blighters clinging to the inside, glaring malevolently at us, waiting to pounce and suck the very lifeblood from our veins.

"Get the knock-down, I'll cover you from the rear," yells Graham as we fling back the sheets in unison and leap from the bed, Graham in his boxers, I in my Superman pyjamas with the tights still tucked into the trunks.

The knock-down spray is buried in my socks and underwear, deep in the recesses of my holdall. I skirt hurriedly around the perimeter of the room and rummage frantically for the aerosol, hurling clothes and contents about the room in wild abandon. Meanwhile, Graham grabs a rolled-up newspaper and leaps about the bed with a thrust and parry that would put Errol Flynn to shame, fencing off the larger of our intruders. He corners the hydra, a giant of an insect, with a vicious spiny proboscis and hatred in its beady deep-set eyes. With a lightning pass and a timely lunge, Graham thrashes the insect to a pulp on the otherwise unmarked yellow plaster.

"Gotcha. Quick, trap the little buggers in the net", yells Graham.

We circle the bed, each take hold of two corners and gather in the folds of the mosquito net. We have them trapped. I break open the tin of knock-down spray and with a firm grip and steely determination empty most of its contents into Graham's blinking and spluttering face.

But we've won in the mosquito wars, and each side retreats to attend to the wounded. With a pat on the back, Graham brings up the worst excesses of the DDT. As for the mosquitoes, those that aren't immolated or mashed to a sticky paste limp away under cover of a white flag. And as we retreat and redeet, battle-scarred and weary, under the war stained mosquito net, I'm already composing the above story for the Breakfast Club.

In daylight, Les Palétuviers (named after the species of lush vigorous water tree that surround and infiltrate its manicured gardens) was even more upmarket than I'd suspected. With its swimming pool, snooker hall, restaurant á la haute cuisine, a complex of superbly appointed and ethnically styled bungalows set in palm and baobab, it was a haven for road weary travellers. A haven too for the Walloon Belgian and Dutch who predominate among holidaymakers in Senegal. There was a fishing lake, terraced lawns, excursions for the more active, a laundry and a snack bar. A pity it was that time didn't permit a more leisurely stay.

The food had been anaesthetised and Europeanised but breakfast was both varied and sumptuous. A choice of juices, cereals, pumpernickel and croissants, jam (papaya, tangerine and blackberry) honey, gorgonzola and omelettes. Almost too much choice.

The target for today was Banjul, capital of the Gambia, and in particular the Safari Gardens (aka Springtime) Hotel, the finish line for the Plymouth-Banjul Challenge 2007. 3,838 miles behind and only fifty to go, but the Barra ferry lay between us and our goal. I'd read and heard stories about Barra in the Road Book and was't particularly relishing this last major hurdle.

The remaining Challengers gather at the base of the stupendous elephant tree that marks the reception at Les Palétuviers. At nine o'clock sharp we climb into our vehicles and make for the border. Seek (pronounced Sek), our escort, leads the Old Gits, Biggles and Algy, the Life Mechanics, Dumb and Dumber and the Wookies through the tall security gate, out of Les Palétuviers' pristine splendour and into the abject squalor beyond. We find ourselves immediately back in rural Senegal with its mud and reed huts, dead and scavenging goats, dirt roads and open sewers. The stark contrast between European luxury and Senegalese poverty is embarrassing. Although there are a few more substantial stuccoed haciendas, nestling within their own more prosperous compounds, the cool slightly overcast morning does little to disguise the desperate conditions.

Through Daga Babou, the centre of the reed harvesting industry. A greener and more pleasant land. Poor, but green and pleasant. Cattle wander through the wooden benches and thatched shelters of the market square. The road is still a decent, if neglected, hardtop, bordered by sand and termite hills, some of these five to six feet high.

Kerang's a busy border town reminiscent in its outward appearance of Nouadhibou. Decent tarmac hardtop peters out and gives way to the dusty cart tracks of rural Gambia. We're waved down by a tall black Mandinkan police officer who smiles, salutes and speaks in clipped precise well-rehearsed syllables.

"Good morning gentlemen. Welcome to the Gambia. May I see your passports, registration document and driving licence. Thank you."

After the most civilised police experience since leaving the UK, we're invited into the Amdullai customs post. This has all the ambience and presence of a rural police station in England. Sergeant Dixon at the desk waits to inspect passports, driving licences, log books. The station officer at Amdullai is a large black avuncular woman in her forties. She has charge of three other officers who are stamping passports, taking names, having a laugh and joke. She commands instant respect.

"Which car will you leave for my office as a gift?" she quips. I almost take her at her word. We're treated with respect, which is returned in kind, and leave her office with all formalities quickly and efficiently dealt with. As we pass the slammer, it's occupied by four youths. Graham asks Sergeant Dixon what they've done wrong.

"They have been bad boys," she replies with twinkling eyes. Old Git Graham feels the necessity to take a photograph. I think this bad form and a little insensitive. Sgt. Dixon seems to expect it.

We're in the Gambia. Yellow and green striped taxis and taxi-velos. Herds of moped, hordes of children playing, running, laughing and smiling in the streets of dust.

Black Betty's on the road again. Momentarily. Graham's seeking out the deepest ruts and obstacles to drive through and I amuse myself pointing out some he's missed.

"Don't worry, we'll get those on the way back."
"We're coming back then?"

"Well, I thought this was a trial run. I'm sure I can do better with practice." I think he's stir crazy, missing the desert.

We're bumping along a rutted dirt track and I'm throwing pens, pencils, minor items of jewellery out of the window to the Gambian kids who appear from the bush, smiling, laughing, hands held out. Some are only two or three years old. The shell of an ancient Austin A30 is dead ahead. Graham swerves off track, taking Black Betty on to what passes for a sidewalk. The soft dry sand's more appealing and kinder to our bottoms and her suspension. A store on our right boasts, enigmatically, "For all your needs - rice, sugar, onions, cement."

On our right, a sign for ferry tickets. A slight figure dashes from the office, gesticulating wildly, as if welcoming us to his country. Biggles and Algy in the Volvo and the Old Gits in the Scirocco ignore him and speed on, soon lost in a dust cloud. But Graham's not so rude, and much more observant. He pulls off the road into a large car park in the middle of which stands a tiny concrete box. The ferry ticket office.

Crammed into the minute kiosk, the port official who risked his life with the Scirocco, and his three clerks, argue over who should take the money and who have the honour of printing tickets. The Wookies were stiffed with "cheap" currency in Morocco and are still nursing over £80 of worthless dhiram. Here in the Barra ferry ticket office they're unlucky again. Their ticket has been printed in Euros, and once printed, cannot be "unprinted". Scott's still grumbling at the fistful of seefas which will now prove, as the dhiram, useless outside their native country. Inexplicably, most of my remaining seefas are unloaded on to the port official and gratefully accepted in payment for our ticket. It can only be my superior charm. Probably.

As we leave the port office and return to our cars, and I'm still wondering obliquely whether we too have been stiffed, or whether the tickets will indeed get at us on the ferry, the canary yellow Scirocco screams full-throttle back across the dust. The Old Git at the controls is looking fixedly ahead and steaming at the gills as the sump hits a rock, his head hits the roof, he wrestles with the controls and grinds to a halt in the car park. Apparently Graham's intuitive stop at the ticket office was a good call. Deep joy!

The Barra ferry is a progressive form of torture. It comes in three stages.

The Barra Ferry, in three stages

Stage 1: We try to infiltrate the endless line of traffic, cars, push carts, mopeds and cycles, dust covered and broken, that border the track leading to the dock. Yesterday was Gambia's Independence Day, and today a public holiday for schools, so countless street urchins mingle with the shady hustlers, freeloaders, bumpsters and "lazy boys". We're approached every other second by a water seller, a fruit vendor, a trinket salesman. It's already hot and dry, but we'd rather fry in Black Betty than venture outside.

Graham's slightly safer from incursion than I, in the nearside seat. I sit in the middle of it all, jostled and cajoled by the crowds, trying to maintain an aloof but respectful demeanour. I don't want to be drawn into any sales or other negotiations, but nor do I wish to appear distant. I've been wearing the fishing waistcoat Gilly bought me for the warmer climes. It's lavishly provided with pockets for my camera, wallet, tape-recorder and hankie. But stepping out of Black Betty in this crowd will mean I have to protect all my possessions in their various pockets at the same time. When I do this I look like a vestal virgin guarding her honour. Only not so pretty.

"Window Gray."
"Sorry!" Graham operates the electric windows to let some air into Black Betty. He also lets in a bumster.
"You want the Barra ferry?" he enquires, innocently enough. But since this road is at the extremities of human endurance and only leads to the Barra ferry, I figure he already knows this.
"Yes, thank you. It's just over there", I indicate, so that he realises I'm in the know.
"I make sure you get on next ferry. You pay 20 Euros."
"I think I'll wait and see thank you."
"No, I make sure you get on next ferry. Is no problem. 20 Euros please."
"But there are five of us, and we all want to get on together."
"Is no problem. I get you all on for 20 Euros. I have friends."
"What do you think, Gray?"
"Might be worth a punt. What do the others think?"
"I'll have a word. Let me out."

Graham flips the central locking and I climb out of the relative safety of Black Betty and into the chaos last described by John Milton in Paradise Lost. Clutching my valuables about me in the pockets of my now famous fishing waistcoat I wade through the hordes, brushing aside the more aggressive hustlers, politely dealing with their kind offers of help, cold drinks (€5), warm pond water (€1), and trinkets of inestimable value. Dumb and Dumber are easy to find. Andy Morgan's silly hat stands out in the middle of a crowd of bumsters. He and Dave are up for the deal. We should have a whip-round. The airline pilots in the Volvo, Biggles and Algy, have been similarly approached with the €20 executive treatment. A deal is done. For the €20, which I have now parted with, this kind but unofficial looking young man will ensure our safe passage on to the next ferry out of here. I'm not sure which young man approached me in the first place, but I've given the cash to Del Boy.

I climb back into Black Betty's comforting security. Graham flicks the switch and I'm locked in, safe from the madding crowd.

There's a tap at the window.
"Window Gray."
"Sorry." He flips the switch and the window slides open again.
"You are wanting the Barra ferry?" I have a feeling of déja vu.
"Yes, thank you. It's just there".
"I make sure you get on next ferry. €20."
"I'm OK thanks. All my needs have been duly attended to."
"I get you on next ferry for €20. Is no problem."
"No thanks. I've just said, I'm sorted. I have done a deal with Del Boy."
"Well fuck you."
"Thanks."
"You are racist. No good mother fucking bloody racist!"
"Yes, thanks awfully."
"Racist!"
"OK. Window Gray."
"Sorry."

Eventually we're in a sort of queue. More a melée really. I can't be sure who's in front, but the large metal portals to what I assume is the Barra ferry are opened and foot passengers are crowding on. They're pushing carts, herding goats, carrying babies on their backs. Many carry chickens under their arm, their heads drooping with thirst and exhaustion. I wonder where these desperate birds are bound. Are they pets perhaps, being taken on an outing to Banjul, or is their destiny of a more sinister nature? Women carry bundles of clothes, baskets, huge earthenware jars. They all crowd in no particular order onto the ferry. I begin to wonder whether we shall get aboard. Will there be room?

Finally, the attendants gesture for the cars to drive aboard. Graham's trying to obey the gestures of four or five different attendants, some apparently official, others not, each wanting him to move Black Betty in a subtly different direction. Each contradicts the others. The Volvo's immediately in front. Algy's obviously wrestling both with the steering wheel and his own better judgment. The Volvo hits Black Betty a glancing blow. It pulls forward, reverses, hits us again, gouging an ugly gash in its own rear quarter, leaving Black Betty insulted but unharmed. A third strike seems to satisfy the Volvo, and she edges her way through the portals. The officials are gesticulating wildly, swearing, shouting, incoherent.

Stage 2: We're actually only on the slipway, waiting for the incoming ferry. We're in a concrete roasting dish, about a hundred yards long and fifty feet wide, with walls twenty feet high on both sides and the tall steel portals at each end. Black Betty's in a queue of cars hugging the left wall and making the most of the modest shade cast at mid-morning. We're in the middle of the queue, hemmed in by a small truck in front and the Pug behind. Foot passengers mill aimlessly about us, carrying bundles, baggage, and the odd chicken sitting dull and listless in the crook of an owner's arm, some hanging by the feet from their owner's hand. We're not safe from the hustlers even here, in fact we're locked in with them, prisoners to their endless unremitting prattle.

"I give you good price."
"No thank you."
"Is no problem. You give me €5."
"No thank you." "
"OK, how much you give me?"
"Look, fuck off will you. Be told."
"Cadeau! Cadeau!"
"You are racist. You are no good racist."

Graham's trying to snooze, seeking oblivion from this endless, pointless harangue. I'm trying to keep my temper. It's too hot in here to lose it. I try to make friends with the locals, who're fine. The children are particularly engaging. One little girl who can be no more than five, wanders by in a yellow floral dress, a tea tray perched on her head carrying plastic bags of water. I buy one for cash and throw in a pen. The beaming smile on her face nearly brings a tear to my eye, but it's important here to maintain the old upper lip as stiff as poss. A young lad of 14 steps up to the window. He speaks exceptionally good English. He's at school, he says, and I take an interest in his conversation. At least it's a diversion from the bumsters.

On the other side of the roasting dish the lorries bake in a line. They're chained together, as only the leading lorry has an operational battery and starter motor. It's towed all the others on to the slipway in a heaving, clanking snake formation. The foot passengers are crowding on. Some have four feet. A large, entire white longhorn bull, dragged on the end of a rope by his bearded and grubby owner. The whites of the longhorn's nervous eyes dance madly in their sockets. He's clearly very hot and either frightened or angry. Probably both. He's tied to the bumper of the rusting hulk opposite Black Betty and stands, glaring at us from his bondage, twin beads of spittle drooping from his foamy mouth. The same characters walk endlessly up and down the queue of cars, hustling, begging "cadeaux", selling water, fruit, coconuts, fizzy drinks.

The young lad's returned to Black Betty's open window. He's Ali Jarreh, nineteen, a student at college in Banjul. He makes this trip every day to carry out his studies, he says. He wants to be an accountant and shows me his school work, an exercise in elementary chemistry if I'm not mistaken. I give him a mobile phone and an inflatable globe which I've carried from the UK, a present from Gilly to emulate the inflatable globe carried by Michael Palin in *Around the World in 80 Days*. I inflate the globe with some difficulty, and point at Plymouth, where we've come from. Ali has a keen interest and no idea whatsoever where on the planet he features. He gives me his sister's telephone number, hoping I'll contact him from the UK and invite him to stay. I know this is unlikely, but I humour him.

The incoming ferry has docked. Foot passengers are crowding off, pushing their way through the bumsters and hustlers. Many of them carry dying chickens, perhaps on their way back from an exhausting day in the City. We're frying now, in the early afternoon. Dark sweat shadows under my arms and the salt tide marks on my fishing waistcoat give away my obsessive need to protect my valuables in their allotted pockets.

The bull's on the loose, running, stumbling, fearful, angry. The owner seems to think it's a great joke, and he laughs aloud as he skis past us at rope's end, the heels on his slippers grappling for purchase in the dust. I dive back inside Black Betty and cower on Graham's lap. I'm closely followed by two of the foot passengers who've taken the opportunity of temporary safety. Two more are perched on the bonnet, and I think there are some more opportunists on the roof. Black Betty's become the unwitting port in the storm created by the rampaging bull. Now he heads back again into the crowd of disembarking foot passengers. People leap out of the way as the bull, his head low, skewers the less fortunate and tosses them high in the air. The farmer skis past once more. Now his eyes are wide with fright and mania.

One more pass and the bull's composed himself. The mayhem he's caused is replaced by the sheer chaos of loading the Gambian ferry. It's a free-for-all. Cars and lorries are still coming off the ferry as the cars in front are mounting the ramp to board it. Foot passengers, some driving goats, dodge indiscriminately between. We're beckoned by four different men frantically waving at us in very different and conflicting directions. Only two look vaguely official, so Graham opts, quite reasonably I think, to cut an average and steer Black Betty between them. Algy's opted to follow contrary directions, and the Volvo bounces off the Escort and strikes us a glancing blow. Some more bits of metal and plastic fall from her ruined rear quarter.

The bull makes a dramatic entrance without assistance or directions and his surprised owner follows him sheepishly on to the gangplank. The cars in our queue have started to move forward. We should be next, but the foot passengers hurrying on at the same time make chaos out of a confusion. The ferry is apparently full. The slipway doors are closed.

I catch Del Boy by the arm as he scuttles by Black Betty.

"You said we'd be on the next ferry Del Boy."
"Yes, certainly. Is next ferry. You will be on next ferry."
"But that's the next ferry. We're not on it!"
I think Del Boy can sense that I'm not a happy man.
"Yes, next ferry. Ten minutes. You will be on next ferry."
"C*nt!"

The ten minutes become another ninety. In all we are locked in that concrete sweatbox with all the thieves, vagabonds, hustlers and bumsters for three and a half hours in the growing heat of the day, with nothing but suspicious pond water in plastic bags to drink.

Stage 3: The real treat is yet to come. The Barra ferry boat's not very big. And since its twin, the other Barra ferry boat, sank with all hands and all cars a year ago, it's had to cope alone with all traffic and foot passengers who want to cross the River Gambia in either direction. Perhaps this accounts for its haphazard and unwritten safety policy, which is basically to load on as much as possible. Never mind the quality, feel the width. Black Betty's parked amidships. On all four sides she touches other vehicles. On the left, the Pug. Graham cosies up to Andy Morgan, their faces a few inches apart. On my right, the Wookies. I spray warm water in Scott's face to keep him cool. In front, a small white truck carrying a workforce of labourers to Banjul. They chat to the farmers' market that's established itself on Black Betty's bonnet. Behind me, the two escapees from the bull sit quietly studying the tray of mobile phones.

And here we shall sit, until Banjul. Stepping out to stretch our legs is simply not an option. We're prisoners in our own vehicle. Escape impossible. For two further hours in the baking sun we amuse ourselves contemplating the escape route in the event of catastrophe. Ali Jarreh consoles us at the window with tales of disaster at sea. The "other Barra ferry boat" was much older, much less seaworthy. Unconvinced, I look for instruments to cut a hole in the roof. Perhaps the tin opener will redeem itself.

It's obvious we've finally arrived when the ferry hits the dock with a resounding thwack. It tries again. Another alarming, grinding thwack. Third time does it. The vibrations settle. The ferry doors open. Foot passengers are the first off, and I'm fascinated, if alarmed, to note that the tradition of women and children first applies even here. Except that disembarkation is not the orderly affair that must have attended the evacuation of the Titanic. There's no evidence of prizes for this, but every foot passenger seems intent on being first off. Women, children, men and goats, in that order, clamber over the cars, the lorries and each other, carrying sacks of meal and their dead and dying chickens. Meanwhile, a Land Rover mounts the ramp, apparently to hold it down for the cars to disembark.

One of our bonnet passengers squeals as he extracts his foot from between Black Betty's bumper and the truck ahead. The foot passengers leave en masse. The bull glares at its owner and steps warily across the precarious ramp.

We're next in line. Graham guns the engine and slips her into drive. She bucks like a stallion and hurtles down the ramp, jumps the gap and we're on shore.

We've entered the quaint traffic and the seamier side of Banjul. Dirt roads, ladies of the night, scavenging dogs. Banjul is yellow and brown. In front of us a green and yellow taxi stops. Its passenger opens the boot and out jump three goats. Animal transport in the Gambia is not, apparently, regulated by Defra's stringent requirements.

We've lost sight of all Challengers except Dumb and Dumber, following at a safe distance. I'm navigating with the help of a schematic map found on the back of a leaflet in the travel agents in Barnstaple. We're looking for Fajara, a suburb of Banjul, and specifically for the Safari Gardens (Springtime) Hotel, where the Challenge is to end. We're travelling the Atlantic Highway, the wind blowing through what little hair I have left after the Barra experience. Black Betty's made it to Banjul, we're all but there and I experience a feeling of triumph. Graham, cabin crazy from the last five hours, is cranking up the speed, giving her the last decent run she'll get with him at the wheel.

We stop for directions from two policemen who look the worse for wear and ganja. We must go straight on until we see a hospital on the right, turn left at the pregnant goat, right at the Breast Milk Clinic. At least that's what I made of the directions. Graham has his doubts. We take another right, ask another policeman, consult with Dumb and Dumber.

The main roads in Banjul are broad, straight hard top with lane markings, the best since France. We find ourselves racing in convoy towards the famed Triumphal Arch, only opened for special occasions.

I look at Graham. He grins back.
"It's got to be done, hasn't it?"
"What, the Triumphal Arch?"
"Why not? It's our triumph isn't it?"

The Triumphal Arch in Banjul serves much the same purpose as our Marble Arch or Paris's Arc de Triomphe, though it has to be said it lacks the ornate splendour and gothic proportions of either. It's a concrete and adobe structure with faintly modernist pretensions, painted pink. It's only supposed to be used on state occasions and then only for the personal passage of the President and select members of his family. Well, in the few moments it takes to drive at speed down Banjul's equivalent of the Elysian Fields, there seems no reason to counsel Graham against this foolhardy breach of international protocol. We charge towards the central arch. Brief moments before our reckless triumphal passage, I notice, before Graham I think, the essential difference between Banjul's arch and its counterparts in London and Paris. It's the cunningly disguised and nearly invisible padlock and chain that spans the central arch, forbidding access to all but the select few.

"Sto-o-o-o-p!" I scream. We do. And when the plume of black smoke from Black Betty's tyres disperses, I can see it's a British-made Draper padlock pat.pen. that clinks gently against the windscreen in the light breeze.

Graham gathers himself. A swift three-point turn in Park Lane and we follow the Pug away from the Triumphal Arch before an international incident occurs.

Past the Attorney-General's chambers (three tiny kid goats playing in the parking bay) and Andy Morgan asks directions, this time from a young beautiful female in khaki drills carrying what looks suspiciously like a Kalashnikov (if only I knew what one looks like). We follow them past the Ombudsman and "Uncle Sam's Security Office" back along the Atlantic Highway, sharing a can of sparkling pineapple juice, a gift from Ali Jarreh.

The Safari Gardens (Springtime) Hotel is unassuming, comfortable, mid-range, bijou. Its rooms are set on the ground floor around a small swimming-pool and terrace restaurant. It's situated in a suburban backstreet, which in Banjul means a sandy track. Graham parks at the back gate, between the Pug and the Wookies' Ford Escort. We're 3878 miles from Long Lane Farm, and our part in the Challenge is at an end. I'm not sure what I expect really. To be decked with garlands and flowers, with wreaths festooned from our necks? A jeroboam of champagne showered on us by adoring crowds? Hugs and kisses from beautiful leggy blondes? A brass band, perhaps, playing triumphal marches? Well there's none of that. The celebrations for our successful completion of the Challenge are anti-climactic to say the least. We have a couple of cold beers at the Safari Gardens, register completion of the Challenge with a spotty 14 year-old youth, and make off.

The Safari Gardens couldn't accommodate us. All rooms were taken by Challengers arriving before. We were quite glad. Having studiously avoided the laddish, beer-swilling behaviour of some colleagues down the West African Coast, neither Graham nor I relished the experience at close quarters in cramped accommodation. We were required to submit a condition report for Black Betty, so she could feature in the auction on the following Sunday. We'd also be requested to surrender all relevant documentation, and the keys. But we could hang on to her for the few days left in the Gambia, and there'd be plenty of time for the formalities.

So we took off for Kololi, a few miles away, and collected tickets for the return flight. Dumb and Dumber followed. Their flight was not due until the 27th., more than a week away. But in the offices of the Gambia Experience they were successful in securing a flight to Bournemouth on the 21st. Dave would be in time for the start of his course.

The standard of cars was a significant improvement over those seen in Mauritania and Senegal. Driving standards however were about the same. It seems a home-made L-plate is all that's necessary to take to the roads in the Gambia as a provisional driver.

We needed accommodation. There are many hotels along the Atlantic coast, mainly catering for English, French and Dutch holidaymakers. We tried the Kombo Beach, but it seemed inordinately expensive, and had just one room available, and that for one night only.

We settled for the Bungalow Beach Hotel, between Banjul and Serekunda and took a self catering apartment on the first floor. With air-conditioning, a shower room and a kitchen diner with cooker and fridge we felt quite at home. From the balcony we could take in the smells of the trees, the grass and the bougainvillaea. The swimming-pool, restaurant and lush green lawns made our choice one of unashamed luxury for our short time in the Gambia. Black Betty would enjoy a few days well earned rest in the shady secluded car park with her own security guard.

A dinner of elephants ear (thin steak) and chips with Dumb and Dumber followed, to the accompaniment of "traditional" Gambian drummers, acrobats and dance.

"Hello love. I'm on the Sat Phone, so can't be long. It's the first time I've been able to speak in over a week. How are you?"

"Relieved you're safe. Sorry I was a long time answering. I was changing a tyre. Good news about the Costa Blanca Dons."

"Why? What happened?"

"Didn't you know? They were lost in the desert for four days. Ran out of petrol and water. Surrounded by bandits. They were eventually lifted out by helicopter. The other members of their group had a whip round to pay. The Jeep and contents are still in the desert. It made the national dailies."

"Any news of the camel?"

"Tit!"

DAY NINETEEN
BUNGALOW BEACH

Graham and I soon slipped into a routine of idyllic domesticity in our luxury apartment on the Atlantic coast. We awoke on this Tuesday in February still sandblasted from the experience of the Barra Ferry, discussing how we, the great social reformers of our time, could make things better for Africa. We had of course been setting the world to rights for weeks, but a latter day Burton and Speke we're not. Although I'd some sort of rudimentary Schweizerian pretensions with the first aid kit and distribution of its contents among the poor and needy, even I had to admit that acts of humanitarian kindness were likely to be limited. I felt demob happy. Our major challenge now over, we could relax, and enjoy the local culture, free from responsibility.

We reverted to Albert and Harold Steptoe mode and I prepared a breakfast of bread, cheese, jam and coffee from ingredients left by the house boy. Our last tin of fruit cocktail would provide the "five a day" Graham was convinced would stave off scurvy and other remarkable diseases.

The complicated property negotiations going on in Gloucestershire were coming to a head. He was anxious to get home and sort matters out, but since all attempts to bring our flight forward had been abortive, we had three days to kill in the Gambia.

The plan today was to return to the Springtime Hotel (Safari Gardens) to secure accommodation for the last two days if available, the Bungalow Beach only able to guarantee a room for tonight. We could also unload some of the gifts at Challenge Control, particularly those no longer needed to grease palms. There were arrangements to be made for the sewing machine, and we'd need to seek out Elizabeth Touray. Tomorrow we'd sort through the remaining contents and arrange for someone to drive Black Betty back from Yundum airport where we'd leave her to fly home. Meanwhile we could enjoy the peace and the air conditioning of our luxury apartment. And the intermittent resonance of the drums. And the menacing grunt of the giant bullfrog in the pond below. And the incessant chatter of the crickets it feeds upon. At least that was the plan.

First, some exploration of our surroundings. Now, the plush hotels of Serekunda are havens of Britishness. The guests, well pensioned and cushioned, come to the Gambia year on year to lounge in the sunshine on their balcony or by the pool. Generally the same pool and often the same balcony as they've lounged on for the past twenty years. They don't often venture beyond the hotel compound otherwise than in sanitised tour coaches and tourist taxis. A white face in Banjul is a rarity indeed, only found on the shoulders of an expatriate administrator.

So when Graham and I strolled, bold and fearless into the minimarket just outside the Bungalow Beach, we caused a stir. Our first encounter was with Mama, who told us excitedly he was responsible for the finest wooden carvings and artefacts in Africa, and these were on display at the Fajara craft market, a few minutes' walk down the beach. His was stall 20. We should visit him for "good price".

"Fajara" rang a distinct bell in the old subconscious. Wasn't that the location of Elizabeth Touray's (Mrs Sewing Machine) stall? It'd be strange and fortunate indeed to find her at such close quarters. We'd take a stroll along the beach to investigate.

We're walking in the fine yellow sand next to the spray of Atlantic rollers. The beach is lined with hotels magnificent and modern and the simple thatched umbrellas which signify beach bars. A sprinkling of British tourists, mad in the midday sunshine, bask on towels, drink at the bars, brave the waves. Horses, some riderless, canter in the shallows.

The craft market is three hundred yards along the beach from our hotel. It's a breeze block compound with a simple entrance gate and an unpretentious sign stating "Fajara Craft Market". We amble around the concourse of buyers and sellers. In fact we're the only buyers, but I don't feel intimidated. They aren't so frantic or insistent as those further north. It's not many minutes before we come across Elizabeth's stall, No. 11, in the corner. She's not there, but the neighbouring stallholder, Omar Darboe, kindly summonses her on his mobile. She agrees to meet us at our hotel in one hour. We stroll back to the beach, promising to return to the market and sample some of the wares one day.

"You want good time mister?" I don't see her at first, because I am arrested by her beauty. Somehow my mouth won't work.

"I give you full body massage. What you want? "

She's about 18, nubile and delicious in a diaphanous floral print strapless beach dress, with, I fancy, nothing underneath.

"I think she fancies you Keith"

"Well, it's only natural isn't it? Only to be expected," I stutter bravely. "I think she must be some kind of beach therapist."

"We'll catch you on the way back," Graham lies, as he drags me away from the dusky nymphet, and I drag my bottom jaw from the sand.

"We have some business to attend to just now, but we'll be back," Graham lies again "and sample your therapy."

Back in the safety of the apartment, recovering from my brief encounter, I reflect on how chilled out we're becoming in the first few hours in this country. During our walk in the Fajara craft market we were pressed to make purchases, sure. But I felt welcomed rather than threatened or nervous. And the beach therapist was, if anything, coy about her services. I'm unwinding and feeling more relaxed by the minute. This is a pleasant place to be. We've bought our last postcards, probably, and a few mementoes, and made contact with Elizabeth Touray. Graham's just taken delivery of his freshly laundered and ironed smalls, left with the house boy this morning, at a modest cost of 125 Dalasi (£2.50). All's well with the world.

Elizabeth's a charming forty something lady, plump, mumsy but attractively so, with bangles on both arms. I recognise her instantly from the photo Cathy Karniewicz gave me with the sewing machine. We shake hands and hug, as I imagine Stanley greeted Livingstone. Clearly delighted with the machine, which travelled in the rear seat foot well for nearly 4000 miles, and two mobile phones from our treasure chest, she gives me her current mobile number for future reference.

She tells me she's the second of her husband's four wives. She and wife number one have ten children between them. Wife number three has just four and wife number four is nursing her second. I ask her, what her husband does for a living that enables him to support this menage à cinq and a brood of sixteen.

"He is supported by his wives and children. As most husbands in the Gambia, he likes to sit around drinking mint tea all day. And talk about sport and politics."

"So you and your children work hard for the right to support a quarter of your shared husband?"

"Yes, that is so. The sewing machine is for Omar, my eldest. With it he will be able to start his own family."

"What, as a mogul in the rag trade?"

"Yes, that is so. Until he has enough wives to support him. Then he will drink mint tea and talk politics."

She insists we accept gifts in return, and we opt for a set of tablecloths and napkins fashioned from bright cotton prints. We'll let her know our colour preferences tomorrow.

Dave and Andy return from handing in the Pug and its contents at Challenge Control in the Safari Gardens Hotel. They were less than impressed with the reception they encountered, and the haphazard way their gifts and belongings, jealously guarded in the back seat since Europe, were treated. Anything left in the car that doesn't specifically relate to it, they were told, is stored in a lock-up for eventual sale or disposal. The lock-up is full to bursting with such items, leftovers from previous years challenges, and there's no guarantee or even expectation of their ultimate destiny. Graham and I are dismayed at this news. We'd both like to think we've done our best for the people of the Gambia, having travelled so far to do it. Graham strikes upon the brilliant idea of making a few people quite comfortable, rather than spreading our beneficence thinly across the whole country. We'll make it our final mission to give away whatever we can to whomever we think will make the best use of it. We'll seek out Elizabeth Touray for advice. Perhaps her village could use some of our booty.

We scurry back over the sand to the craft market. Our second encounter with the beach therapist is not so daunting, although she's brought several of her nymphet assistants with her. Elizabeth's not there, but we're befriended by a number of other stallholders. Still the lone customers in this concourse, getting away is difficult. Every stallholder insists we at least inspect the wares. I buy a "Thinking Man", from Omar of the Alpha Company, at stall 22. Omar's famous for the design, which is rather finely carved and utterly unique. He knocks them out by the dozen. Graham selects a mother and child gazelle, carved from a single piece of wood. It looks beautiful, and very realistic. But it won't stand up. Omar modifies it with a hatchet, sandpaper and stained varnish. Now it stands very well. Now it is truly unique.

Leaving the craft market for the second time today we're approached, for the third time, by the beach therapist, this time in a skin-tight green silk number, which accentuates the nubility, at least to my imagination. Graham and I are becoming seasoned professionals at the bargaining lark by now and we carry our carvings proudly before us as we trudge doggedly through the sand.

"Sorry, darlin', we're all spent up", I chance, for some reason adopting again the vernacular and demeanour of the Eastender. "We'll catch you again. Be lucky". She replies with a grace and a smile that are devastating. I'm ashamed of my cockney deceptions.

Back at the hotel we're still looking for takers for our cornucopia. Just outside the compound I mingle with the tourist taxi drivers and locate Assan Njie, mechanic, who'll take the tools and car fluids. In Black Betty we leave the spare plugs, distributor cap, rotor arm and inner tubes. Our famous cooker, the one that exploded in Western Sahara, together with spare gas canisters and our memories of that event, we pass to the security man at the gate. Now he can make his mint tea in peace.

Our evening meal is the last we shall spend with Andy and Dave. Pasta Carbonara for me, peppered steak for Graham and Dave (the steaks have become worth eating again). Andy passes on dinner. He's got a touch of Montezuma's Revenge, this late in the Challenge. We return to the boys' apartment with beer and the brandy I've smuggled through Africa in a hip flask for "medicinal purposes", and carouse the evening away.

Andy and Dave leave in the morning. For the UK. We shall miss them.

Still the bullfrog rivets.

DAY TWENTY
CROCODILES!

"I remember distinctly Keith Pugsley inviting us to his house in the summer to drink his beer. Keith said, and this is clear in my mind, come around to our place in the summer, I have lots of beer for you to drink." Dave Barrow is so convincing in his assertions, even I believe him.

"Yes, I think I remember that. Anyway, you're very welcome. And I'll throw in a session on no-smoking, gratis."

"Excellent, yes, I'll get my head in order and see you in June."

We're on Dave and Andy's balcony, reminiscing and bidding our faithful companions farewell. They're leaving on the midday flight from Yundum.

Graham and I have become tourists now, almost fully-fledged. We've two days left and are going to spend them wisely. This morning we're visiting the Kachikaly crocodile pool and museum in Bakau Town. Our combined taxi driver and tourist guide, Tijaan Faal, collects us at ten in his Happy Dad taxi, a comfortable if well-worn and beaten-up Japanese tour bus.

There are two types of taxi in the Gambia. The yellow and green cabs, seen frequently in the towns, are for general local use, licensed to trade all over the Gambia, but not allowed within the immediate vicinity of tourist hotels. They're cheap transport, but the drivers aren't particularly knowledgeable. Many don't speak English. The tourist taxis don't bear the standard green and yellow livery and are more individualist. They're more expensive, but you can expect drivers fluent in several languages, with detailed knowledge of the more interesting tourist spots. Such a one is Tijaan, an engaging professional with a broad smile and an easy manner. We both feel immediately at ease in his presence. He tells us he's Mandinka, like eighty five per cent of the population of this tiny country.

"Wolofs account for another ten per cent, and the balance are Jola. All tribes co-exist in a comfortable harmony, though each has its own customs and peculiarities. Wolofs, for instance, may be recognised by their distinctive coiffure, high piled and sculpted. Jolas are timid people. The Serahulis, who are much thinner in numbers, are the descendants of immigrants from east Africa."

In Bakau Town. A squad of hotel security police jog along beside us. On the left, the Timbuktou bookshop, a blacksmiths, fabric shops, all from the tin shack school of architecture. It's a town of alleyways and dirt roads with open sewers, lined with corrugated iron. The Happy Dad picks its precarious way through busy ruts and craters. And yet amongst the filth and decrepitude of tin town, the inhabitants of Bakau have an outward appearance of hope and prosperity. No beggars, no starving fly-blown children with distended bellies and bulging eyes. We bump by the offices of the Observer newspaper and the Swedish embassy.

We take a left, passing an artisan carving wooden ornaments, sitting in the dust of the sidewalk. Weaving between sewer and shack, under a corrugated iron awning, the Happy Dad bursts through a curtain of washing straddling the road and there in front is the modest clapperboard entrance to Kachikaly.

The pool and museum are set in twelve acres of lush tropical rainforest, undisturbed for over four hundred years. It's a mystical place, the shady paths winding through palm, baobab and elephant tree. Thick layers of fallen leaves, twigs and flowers cover the forest floor and deaden the sound of feet. A giant elephant tree, festooned with creepers that brush the skin. Here a small monitor lizard, there a snake hangs from a tree (harmless, I'm assured by Tijaan).

A carpet of green slime covers the pool. Crocodile nostrils break the meniscus, causing concentric eddies in the otherwise still, unbroken, surface. This is Gambia's take on IVF.

"Women who wish to conceive come to this pool in the early evening and bathe with the crocodiles," Tijaan recounts. "Ninety days later they should be pregnant."

I assume some human intervention's necessary in the interim. Would-be mothers have indulged in this aquatic crocodilian caper for five hundred and thirty eight years, Tijaan tells me, since some legendary event the precise details of which escape him. But it's been 538 years. Exactly.

I see at least six crocodiles in the pool. Many more on the bank, basking in the sun, covered from snout to tail in the murky green. Having a lung capacity of two litres enables your average croc to stay submerged for eight hours. There may be many more on the bottom. In any event, I've no hankering to join them and investigate. But I admire the stalwart would-be mothers of the Gambia who travel here to bask and bathe, and then shower in cold water, ministered to by the older women of their tribe. I take the opportunity to stroke Charley, one of the older and tamer crocodiles. She seems quite docile, but the expression on her mazzard is deceptive. Is she smiling? Or is that the natural curvature of her considerable jaw. Perhaps a touch of indigestion. So my display of affection is casual and fleeting rather than effusive. But I've stroked a crocodile, and lived to tell of the tail.

The Kachikaly museum is small but fascinating. Opened as a private venture by the Bojang family in 2004, it consists of three round huts containing between them over a thousand exhibits. We're greeted by a life-size statue of a Fula maiden in full ceremonial dress and all the associated paraphernalia of a wedding. There's an array of calabashes for water, cream and palm wine. Jujus, witchcraft charms for successful circumcision and procreation. Musical instruments from tabala to belafon and Mandinkan board games. There are claps, for rattling, a three stringed Fula fiddle and bongo drums made from calabash and stretched animal skin. Tijaan guides and commentates with skill and great professionalism.

Our dose of culture over, we're travelling back through Bakau Town, past the military barracks and United Nations House, with its egrets in the front garden. In this part of town are housed the ambassadors of most nations. Impressive two-storey mansions interspersed with the ubiquitous tin shack. Tijaan points out the headquarters of the Medical Research Council UK and the British embassy, the Gambian President's country retreat. Next door, the American embassy, secreted behind a tall white wall.

It's harvest time in the market garden and fruit, vegetables and flowers are sold on the road side. Cattle graze on the verge. We pass the Bombay Chowpatty ("genuine Indian restaurant") and the Palm Beach Hotel, and suddenly we're home. Well, at the Bungalow Beach at least.

There's time before lunch for a stroll. We take the left to avoid another encounter with the beach therapist. Unfortunately it's more typically west African in this direction and we're pestered by a man peddling leather belts, and a greengrocer. Walking close to the water, the proprietors of beach bars ("the best bar in Gambia. I give you good price") lurk at the edge of the sand. They scuttle from their domains and try to inveigle us in with the promise of fine cuisine and ice-cold beer. I can't blame them for trying, but it does get a tad boring, particularly if you're strolling and chatting to your mate. In fact, we're pestered off the beach and have to leave the sand, the palms, the horses and the Atlantic rollers to scuttle ourselves back to the safety of the hotel restaurant.

It's fish and chips again for Graham. Foccaccia with cheese and mushrooms for me. But then I always was a poncey bastard.

This afternoon I'm a used car dealer. I need to complete a vehicle condition report for submission to Challenge Control with Black Betty when we surrender her tomorrow. So I don the camel coat and trilby, specially packed for the purpose, and kick the tyres.

Black Betty is, at sixteen years, elderly, and has been well used. But she can be submitted as virtually blemish-free, with no important dents, scratches or cracks. No visible oil leaks, and in all-round good mechanical condition. I reveal the missing piece of rear bumper that fell off in Western Sahara and the fog light that came to grief along the Diama Road. They're still in the luggage compartment. But I don't feel the need to mention her skittishness at the Senegal border, after all that was a protest in response to our treatment at the hands of corrupt officials. And she comes complete with the spares purchased in the UK, the plugs replaced in Okehampton, two inner tubes, a spare rear view mirror and the radio I shoved in to replace that given to Mohammed. As to documentation, the V5, MoT, tax disc and international motor vehicle certificate are all current.

Invited to give some suitable sales pitch, I carwax lyrical as follows:-

"Extremely reliable and a pleasure to drive. Long MoT, taxed for the UK, economical for size of vehicle (making 31 mpg on a run). Comfortable, secure on ferries and through minefields. Air-conditioning in good working order. With new battery, fully serviced 4000 miles ago, modified and improved braking system fitted by Okehampton Motors. Just completed 3878 miles of trouble-free motoring from Plymouth in England using no oil, water or other fluids (apart from a little petrol!). Affectionately known as Black Betty (wham-a-lam) Betty comes to you complete with her own customised paint job commemorating her world famous part in a life-changing humanitarian adventure. She will be sorely missed."

My duties on the forecourt complete, Graham and I take a trip to Sainsbury's. Well, it's not exactly J.S., but he calls himself Alex Sainsbury, and sells his own wooden artefacts poolside in the Bungalow Beach and other hotels along the Atlantic coast. He has a card which says "Alex Sainsbury", so I suppose he's at least a distant relative of the chap who's got the shop in Barnstaple.

"What do you want for the pelican?" asks Graham. The wooden bird is rather nicely carved, and will make a fine present for his sister.

"I give you good price," says Alex.

"Yes, what do you want for the pelican?"

"You make me offer."

"No, you tell me what you want. If I like it enough, I buy. Okay?"

"I make it myself. It takes many hours."

"Yes, I'm sure it does. It's very nice. What do you want?"

"I say 500 Dalasi."

"Fine. I'll take it. Here's the 500."

Graham's more decisive and assertive than I've ever seen him. Encouraged by his lead, I buy a fruit bowl and stand, immaculately carved from a variety of woods and highly polished. I pay the asking price. Alex is startled by this unusual approach to bargaining. Graham and I, however, are pleased with our purchases, and even more so with the little time it's taken to conduct the business. Has the Gambian learnt from his experience? Probably.

One other matter to finalise. I must plant the purple turkey wishbone I've reserved for our last country. I bury it in an herbaceous border in the grounds of the Bungalow Beach Hotel, close to the bullfrog, who guards it to this day. Probably.

For dinner (chicken and chips, spaghetti bolognese, we're getting less adventurous as the days wear on) we're seated close to the entertainment stage. Rather too close as it transpires, as we're treated to a repeat of last night's dancers and drums. If asked to give a review of this particular combo of traditional dance and display, I'd sum it up as "colourful and cacophonous. Not good for the digestion". It's with some pleasure that our meal is interrupted by a visit from Elizabeth Touray, bearing gifts.

I'm not sure Elizabeth's prepared for what happens next. We take her to the back of Black Betty, open the tailgate, and offer her the entire contents. She takes two king-size duvets, four blankets, two pairs of shoes, a mobile phone with charger, a box of stationery including a ream of paper, six toilet rolls, two tents, two sleeping bags and rubber mats, the inflatable mattresses, in short everything moveable.

There are tears.

"You have made me a very rich woman," she sobs, and I have to admit to a moistening of my own eyes. For me, and I think for Graham too, this is one of the highlights. This is the experience that makes all the others worth while. We share hugs and tears. We've made a small difference. We say goodbye to Elizabeth, and help her to her taxi with her new wealth, certain she'll make a good use of everything we've given her.

It's later now. We've had a few beers. As we lie in our cots in the apartment at the Bungalow Beach Hotel we reminisce, retracing the whole of this incredible journey.

I call Gilly on Graham's mobile. She's missing me terribly. It's time to go home.

DAY TWENTY ONE
THE MANGROVE DELTA

I'm good at finishing things, me. What I start, I finish. I'm known for it. Today seems to be the day to finish things. Tie up any loose ends. Say my goodbyes. Because tomorrow we leave for home.

The first to be finished is Colin Dexter's *Last Seen Wearing*, the *Inspector Morse* novel borrowed from the Auberge Sahara in Nouakchott and used to fill the odd pedestrian moment along the way. That's finished, and although I'm none the wiser about the plot, I'll leave it here in the Bungalow Beach Hotel's sparse library to alleviate the boredom of some future British tourist.

We still have a few gifts to dispense on this morning's excursion. We've booked the Happy Dad taxi again. Tijaan has promised a visit to Lammin and a fishing lodge set in the mangrove swamp.

On the outskirts of Serekunda, a crowd of young children in blue and white uniform, satchels on their backs, capped or beribboned, jostle for position. They can be no more than five or six years old. I ask Tijaan to slow down so I can throw them gifts.

"One each, no more," instructs Tijaan, as I attempt to shower them with pens and pencils. "They are greedy. They will fight over them."

I follow instructions and try to make sure they get one pen or pencil. Each. They're orphans, Tijaan tells us, brought up by the state from zero to seven. Then they may be adopted. Usually only the males are successful.

On the left a landfill site, in the process of redevelopment as a glass factory. Piles of firewood for cooking, bales of grass and chaff for fodder. A donkey takes a dust bath. A breakers yard set amongst piles of twisted and defunct cars and bicycles. Heaps of builders' sand. Lock-up shops on both sides. Amidst the miles of concrete and corrugation, the ladies of Serekunda laugh and shop in their bright greens, pinks and yellows. We skirt around a burnt-out wreck. Everything's in disarray, but it all seems to work. Except for the roads, as I'm reminded by Tijaan. We're experiencing the driest time of the year. In the wet season, these roads are swiftly turned into impassable swamp.

Abouka. The National Livestock Showground. Donkeys, goats, cattle and a few sheep line up to go under the hammer. The sheep and cattle chew on fodder bags. The goats help themselves to the cashew nut trees. Agriculture rubs shoulders with industry, commerce with manufacture, and all are intermingled in the residential quarter.

Lammin village is set in a forest of kapok and baobab, a favourite haunt of the naturalist, particularly the bird watcher. A vulture and chicks nest in the high branches of a kapok.

As we turn into the car park children are collecting water from the village standpipe in huge drums, two children and a stick to each drum. At the sight of the Happy Dad taxi, drums and sticks are abandoned, and they crowd around. We're hurling stationery with wild abandon, through the open window.

The lazy boys greet us. Otherwise known as bumsters or hustlers, these unemployed youth of the Gambia live in a state with no welfare system. They're opportunist, and will sell anything, including their bodies, for a few Dalasi. One offers me his visitors' book to sign. There are three columns; name, nationality, and donation.

The lodge is a unique structure of wood, dried reeds and elephant grass thatching a corrugated iron roof. Set on stilts in the mangrove swamp, an elaborate four-storey tree house, with a bar restaurant and top floor lookout giving panoramic views in all directions. The timber floors slope crazily, and access from one floor to another is by a system of madly shifting wooden ladders. The whole structure creaks and groans in the offshore breeze. The unglazed windows and crude plank floors permit you to observe what's going on in the floors above and below. A small object, such as a coin, would, if dropped, fall through all floors into the swamp below. It's surrounded by mature mangrove, populated by green velvet monkeys. A fantasy building with a practical use, it's a cross between Hogwarts and a Tudor shed.

We join some British tourists for a soft drink in the shade of the first floor bar. I take one pull on my Vimto and set it down to photograph a green velvet monkey carrying its baby. The monkey jumps through the glassless window and sits three feet away, gazing at me with soft appealing eyes. And before I can snap the shutter, the little bugger's grabbed my Vimto and leapt back into the mangrove. She sits and finishes the bottle, far out of reach and much to the amusement of all present.

The map suggests we're in the middle of the Tanbi Wetland Complex. A stunning habitat for the diverse wildlife of the Gambia, this area also has a more practical and ecological use. From where I sit in the uppermost lookout, it looks like a large peaceful lake, lined and sprinkled with clumps of the vigorous mangrove bush. In fact it's tidal, a salt water tributary of the Gambia River broken into a maze of rivulets. I expect to see Humphrey Bogart wading chest deep through the river mud towing the upright Katherine Hepburn in the stalled African Queen. As I utter this thought, so the real *African Queen* comes into view, anchored midstream. Tijaan explains this *African Queen* is owned by the village co-operative and used for barracuda fishing.

Tanbi is the site of three mutually supportive and sustainable industries. When the tide's low and the mud's dry, fishermen dig for oysters, cockles and mussels in the flats. They learn their trade at an early age and must be both able to swim in the pools left behind at low tide, and understand how the tides work, if they're not to be caught out. Oyster preparation is the women's preserve. They (the oysters, not the women) are boiled and then graded for sale. The largest are reserved for the tourist hotels where they're used in omelettes and more exotic dishes. The medium go to the market in Serekunda and are a staple of Gambian households. The smallest are taken home for the family.

Oyster shell has its uses too. It's crushed, burnt for twenty four hours to reduce it to ash, and then mixed with salt water to make lime wash. Mixed with sand it becomes a form of homespun cement, to supplement the imports from Senegal and Spain. We saw the shell being burnt just beside the lodge. Again it's women's work. The men concentrate on the more important task of passing around the visitors' book.

Tijaan's guided tour includes a trip up Oyster Creek in a canoe. So for the last time Graham and I take to the water, this time the Gambia River, in a dugout. I take my usual seat at the pointy end and scan the water for hippos, snakes and crocodiles. Tijaan, sitting behind me, assures me there are none such in Oyster Creek. Graham sits aft with our captain and our motive power, Mustafa. I was hoping to meet a Mustafa.

As we glide the maze of winding passages through the mangrove, I wonder at how very peaceful it is, away from the business of the Barra ferry, the fearful Diama Road, the corruption of Senegal and the thievery of Marrakech. Here there's nothing but the lap of the water, birdsong and the gentle instructive voices of Mustafa and Tijaan, educating us in counterpoint.

A kingfisher darts into the undergrowth. Two heron flap their soundless prehistoric way above. There are bee-eaters, sandpiper, pelican, cormorant, cuckoo and wood pigeon.

"Cuckoo and wood pigeon?" I'm a little surprised to hear these last two, in quick succession, apparently from the depths of the mangrove.

"Yeah. Would you like a dove?" smiles Graham. He's been amusing Mustafa with his impressions.

Mustafa is even more knowledgeable than Tijaan in the matter of local flora and fauna. As the dense thick leaved bushes glide by, I'm thinking what use can this be put to? Surely it's just a tangled nuisance. Not so.

"The mangrove depends on the shellfish for its stability. Its roots grapple with the subterranean shells and this is how it anchors itself in place. Mangrove is a good source of firewood and used domestically for cooking, but also on board the fishing boats to smoke out the mosquito. Unfortunately the mosquito, driven inland by the activities of smoking fishing boats, causes a malaria hotspot. Lammin village is the headquarters of the malaria protection programme for the whole of the Gambia." Mustafa could be writing his thesis. I'm impressed.

"Mangrove is also encouraged because it provides a haven for fish and prevents soil erosion. Quite simply, the more mangrove, the more fish. It grows out of the thick mud on the river floor and has to grow to a height of four feet before foliage will appear. Dried mangrove is used with elephant grass for roofing. As termites do not like salt water this doubles as a pest control measure." I'm looking for his script now.

"Mangrove leaves are used locally in the tie dye printing process. They come in green, yellow and red, their colours changing with age. The thicker mud in the middle of Oyster Creek makes for a taller, thicker mangrove branch. These are used for fencing and the stouter roofing cross-members. On the outside edge the mangrove is much shorter, used for firewood and thatching." He's a mangrove encyclopaedia. I'm doubly impressed.

The swamp's a haven of peace and cool tranquillity, tinted with birdsong and the busy little green monkeys. But as we disembark and tread through the broken and burnt shell, I'm reminded again how hard some of these people work to combine their skills and resources into a few Dalasi.

Tijaan takes us back in the Happy Dad taxi, past the celestial Church of Christ (approximately 20 per cent of Gambians are Christians, he tells me, five per cent pagan and the rest, like him, Muslim). Within minutes we emerge into the busy thoroughfare of Serekunda, where tin shack shops of all descriptions ply their haphazard trades. Here a shop selling carpets, lino, hardware. There one peddles garden rakes and building materials. There are phone shops, a store specialising in rear axles, a bicycle mechanic. A truck lumbers by in the opposite direction. I count eighteen passengers. Chickens and dogs sleep under cars in the early afternoon.

Tijaan's looked after us well and made our holiday for the last two days. I'm sure I've paid more than the going rate for his services, but he's been both entertaining and informative. He accepts a present of two denim shirts and a jumper.

The house boy's in our apartment when we return. It seems he's a royalist. We engage in conversation about our royal family, but he's way ahead of me and Graham. He has all the dates and details of the kings and queens of England back to Alfred the Great and can recite Winston Churchill's wartime speeches. He's looked after us well too, and I'll be leaving him my remaining clothes.

It's four o'clock in the afternoon on our last day here, and time to submit Black Betty to Challenge Control. We've disposed of most gifts. The chambermaids and bar staff had the jewellery and cosmetics. It was fun being Father Christmas.

Graham's repacked Black Betty for the last time. Everything in her now will go with her, in the hope it'll be auctioned or otherwise find its way to good causes. We have to trust Challenge Control.

At the Safari Gardens, Black Betty is parked alongside other Challenge vehicles. I hand in the keys and documentation to the same spotty youth we met a couple of days ago. He doesn't seem to have much clue or many social graces. I've never given a car away before, and I've become quite attached to Black Betty. But we say our last goodbyes, and she disappears into the past. She's due to be auctioned on Sunday. In a way, I'm glad I shan't be here.

We also bid farewell to some of the characters we've met on the road over the last three weeks. Ian and Dan of 2 in a 4. The lads from Rattle and Hum. Dumb and Dumber's little Pug. Hugh Jarse and the Iveco van. A hand painted Triumph driven by two girls we've not set eyes on before today.

Walking away from the Challenge now, down a long and sandy lane to the main road, I feel a strange lightness in my step. Black Betty's behind us. For three weeks she's been our security, our fortress and our home. But I've always felt a certain responsibility for her, and what she carried. That load is gone now. I feel somehow relieved.

"How d'you feel Graham?"
"OK. Lighter, I think. Younger."
"Yeah, I know what you mean. Let's have a beer."
"Or an All Butter Shortbread Selection. Probably."

Back at Bungalow Beach we celebrate the end of the Challenge in our own way, I with a club sandwich, Graham with burger and chips. I take a dip in the pool. Ten lengths. My spirits are more buoyant than my body.

Later. It's dark now. We've been sitting at the table, drinking beer and talking for what seems an age about Graham's complex property deal, the drainage problem he's shortly to inherit, and the roof which is likely to collapse at any moment. Then we're on to how we miss our loved ones and the routine of relative normality at home. It's clearly time to ship out of here.

I know we're being soothed by the gentle buzz of the beer when we suddenly drift on to matters nostalgic. Our parallel lives in the village of Eaton Bray in Bedfordshire where we met, my early career as a bus conductor and market porter in Luton, Graham's as a farm labourer. Sledging on Totternhoe Knolls. We've talked ourselves into a wistful self-indulgent reverie.

A knock at the door. Who can that be? Andy and Dave have left and nobody else knows we're here. Must be the houseboy. Perhaps he has more news of the royal family. Graham opens the door to reveal a couple of British tourists. He's mustachioed, distinguished with grey-blonde hair and safari jacket. She's a pleasantly plump sixty something, blue rinse, twinset and pearls.

"Are you the Animal Ambulance chappies?" enquires Colonel Blimp.
"Er, yes. Sort of. What's the problem?" Graham is stalling them, playing for time. Behind the door I'm swiftly donning my Animal Ambulance T shirt and cap.
"Well, there's this little cat in the grounds. It's obviously unwell. But we don't know what to do. We can't catch it."

"Where is the location of said feline domesticus?" I intervene, adopting my best, homo sapiens bureaucraticus.

"It's in one corner of that garden. There are a lot of cats about the place. We feed some of the little dears. This one's a poor old chap. Looks a bit beady. But he can move when he wants to. We've already paid two of the waiters here 250 Dalasi to catch him. They ran about like loonies for half an hour or so, and we haven't seen them since." Blue-rinse.

"Yes, then we saw you chaps and your ambulance. Can you help?"

"Of course. We'll have a look anyway. We're actually on a cultural mission, bringing an awareness of animal welfare to the Gambia. Or something. But we'll certainly take a look." Graham's caught a bad dose of bullshit from being in close proximity to me for three weeks.

"We'll just pick up our equipment," I suggest, "Be with you in a tick."

I have a bent coat hanger, a corkscrew and a tea towel. I'm not at all sure what I'm going to do with them, but I figure I look more professional. Graham's grabbed one of the hotel's bath towels and a fearsome looking bread knife. Thus equipped we sally forth, intrepid cat rescuers, representatives of Diana Lewis's North Devon Animal Ambulance in this far flung outpost of empire.

Finding the cat's not difficult. Several British tourists are supporting us in our quest, and they point to a shrub in the middle of the lawn beyond ours. Graham suggests a pincer movement. We creep up on all fours from opposite directions and descend upon the bush.

I'm on my stomach now, peering inquisitively, if a little nervously, under the foliage. I wield the coat hanger in my right, tea towel in my left, the corkscrew (whatever am I going to do with a corkscrew?) gripped between my teeth. I meet Graham under the bush. Our noses almost touch. The cat appears curious, but unperturbed. It bears the expression of a cat which has experienced a mixture of success and disappointment in its lives, and has had some difficulty forming lasting relationships. But now it's just plain sick, and a bit angry.

"Er, Graham, what are we going to do if we catch this little bugger?"

"Dunno mate. Looks like it's had enough. If we catch it we should kill it."

"What with? I forgot me lethal injection."

"Yeah, and I don't suppose a stamp on the skull would go down too well here, d'you?"

"No. We could take it to a vet. If we can find one."

So we withdraw, strategically, and tell the onlookers we're going for more specialised equipment. But of course we can't find a vet. The Maitre d' looks at me blankly when I try to explain what an MRCVS does. Although there was an informal organisation called Gambicats for a while, set up by the British to minister to the needs of these unfortunate creatures, it's long since folded. The concept of animal welfare just doesn't exist in the Gambia. We have to leave the moggy in its distress and I feel woefully inadequate. I leave a bowl of water and a little lightly poached chicken in case it recovers and feels peckish. Both are still there in the morning, but the cat has moved on.

DAY TWENTY TWO
HOME AGAIN

Our bags are packed and we're ready to go. We're leaving, on a jet plane. Don't know when we'll be back again.

Graham's used his packing skills to good effect one final time and the three part tajine's in my bag, cushioned between three dirty shirts. I hope it'll survive baggage handling.

I'm leaving all my other shirts, towels and other effects for the houseboy. They're neatly folded in a pile on my bed. He can take his pick of the saucepans, plates, knives and forks, and the coffee, sugar, tea, frankfurters and other packaged horrors in the apartment. I'm travelling light, with only the cameras, journal and a few gifts to prove I've been here.

Half past ten. I've settled the bill at the Bungalow Beach. €150 for the second two nights. Expensive, but we've lived in well-earned luxury for the last days. Blue Rinse gave us a bottle of wine last night in recognition of our efforts with the moggy. I've unloaded it on Devon Maid in the apartment next door. Now Graham and I are regaling Devon Maid and her tiny husband with tales of our adventure. She's suitably impressed. He's indifferent.

Eleven o'clock. We're out of the apartment in the car park now, passing the time of day with the security chief. I give him a mobile phone, fully charged, with charger. He's grateful, but not overly impressed. It's not a current model. Gambians are nothing if fashion conscious.

The Road To Banjul

In the Happy Dad taxi for the last time. Tijaan at the wheel. We're heading through Serekunda for Yundum.

ooOoo

Banjul International. The jewel in Gambia's crown. When I was last here in 1984, the airport was three chicken sheds, a ladder, a trestle table and half a dozen disaffected staff, who shuffled around the concrete weed strewn runway chalking cases, touting for tips and absorbing bribes. The operation was affectionately known as Gambia Stairways. The new airport building and concourse was built within the last ten years. It's a vast white concrete and glass lozenge, and it grins welcome at you, with big teeth.

Tijaan drops us in the empty car park. We say our goodbyes and promise to return. We've barely enough Dalasi for the fare between us. A porter takes a mobile phone as his tip for carrying our modest belongings the few yards into the concourse. The last of the Dalasi and Bututs go on a shared diet coke at European prices. I'm carrying five or six mobiles, chargers and assorted telephone paraphernalia, which will have to pass as currency for the last few hours in the Gambia until our scheduled flight. I realise I've become a serial briber, institutionally corrupt.

We're going through baggage check and customs. Though the queues are long, there's more than a semblance of order and we're moving quickly. I'm in the queue, my holdall in one hand, camera bag and All Butter Shortbread Selection in the other. Graham's just behind.

"What about those mobiles?"
"There's only a few left. And some chargers, plugs and bits of wire."
"They'll look good then, to the customs man. Have you any other electronic devices to declare? Any detonators perhaps? Plastic explosive?"

I see his point of course. I've guarded these items, throwaway in the UK, jealously, since I learned their value to your average west African in Tangier. But from here on they're quite worthless. An encumbrance in fact. I wish I'd made better use of them. I leave the queue and thrust the carrier bag full of mobiles at an uncomprehending security guard. He's clearly delighted, if bemused, with his good fortune.

We're in the departure lounge. It's clean, cool and spacious. It's like any other airport departure lounge in the world except, maybe, for the outdoor buffet barbecue and creole music. Duty free shop. Gifts of silly nonsense that no-one ever needs. Ian and Dan, formerly of 2 in a 4, and the lads of Rattle and Hum join us. But we're just tourists now, awaiting our return flights. The real adventure is behind us. I'm surfacing to normality. I send my last text.

"Wot's 4T?"

ooOoo

"What do you think of it so far? What were the highlights of the trip, and what are you going to do when you get home?" I'm back to Alan Whicker mode, and perhaps over-excited, as I point the movie camera in Graham's face. It's a bit snug in the airplane seats, so this has to be an extremely intimate interview.

"I've learnt a lot, seen a lot of things I never thought I'd see. Some of them I wish I hadn't. Looking forward to getting home now. And a decent cup of tea. Oh, one other thing, it's 35 degrees out there. A bit warm for February."

This is to be my first flight in 15 years. They haven't changed much. I anticipate the six hours ahead of mind-numbing boredom as I huddle in my tiny quarters, nose jammed against the seat in front, surrounded by the paper, plastic and other detritus associated with the compulsory in-flight meal. The movie is some squid-brained sex comedy. On my left, Graham snoozes fitfully. On my right, Victor Meldrew in a frock whinges on about how her husband hasn't managed to get premium flight tickets this time.

"It's just a hundred pounds per head and you get much more comfy seats. And at Banjul you get to sit in the premium passenger lounge. On your own settee. Free wine and water. I've been coming here twice a year for fifteen years, and this is the first time we haven't been premium passengers. It's too bad. I'm not coming again, not if he can't be bothered to make sure we get premium passenger. Blah-dee-blah-dee-blah."

ooOoo

Gatwick on a wet Friday in February. I'm waiting for the touts, the hustlers and the bumsters. I'm waiting for the cries for "cadeaux". I'm expecting the inexplicable delays, the bribes, the scowling bureaucrats. But of course there are none of these. Our passage through the customs hall, passport control and to baggage handling couldn't be more swift or smooth. I don't even spot the police and the armed response unit, until Graham points both out. Something's going down at Gatwick and I'm totally oblivious. I'm looking for Gilly and Derrick Hamly, who've come to pick us up in Graham's car.

The reunion is, I'm not ashamed to say, emotional. But then I was the only one to cry at our wedding, and my reactions haven't changed in the intervening years. I'm so glad to see her. I present her with the All Butter Shortbread Selection and tell her I shall never leave her again. Derrick's visibly touched. Graham is understanding, but his reunion with Sally must wait until tomorrow. There's still a way to go.

ooOoo

Graham's at the wheel again, this time the wheel of his black BMW estate, taking us home to Long Lane Farm. It's a four and a half-hour trip from Gatwick, but the time flies by in an exchange of stories. We drop Derrick in Ilfracombe. On the way home to Long Lane Farm I'm sitting next to my old rally buddy, navigating our way through the North Devon country lanes in dead of night.

Two miles from home I remind him that we drive on the left in England. Homesick for Morocco, he's reverted momentarily to the driving habits of that country.

At Long Lane Farm. It's 4.35 a.m. An owl hoots over Maddox Down. I'm home.

POSTSCRIPT

It took several weeks to settle back into the routine at Long Lane Farm. I felt disorientated and outside the normal comfort zones. Pushing a wheelbarrow around the waterlogged fields of the donkery, scraping up dung for the muck heap, collecting wood for the log burner, all seemed to have a relevance once. I'm ever so slightly dissociated, as if a part of me has fallen off and remained with that fog lamp in Western Sahara. The sign pointing to Africa is still at the front gate, still pointing the wrong way. Sometimes, just sometimes, I believe Africa lies just beyond that gate.

Graham returned to a fond reunion in Gloucestershire the following day, after a hearty full English with us at Long Lane. He still hasn't had the roof fixed, or the drain sorted, but he lives a life of splendid isolation in the palace he moved into with Sally while still in Africa.

Dave never did visit in June. I expect he's still smoking. The beer's getting warm.

Andy e-mails me occasionally.

Black Betty fetched £1500 for good causes at auction, and as far as I know can still be seen parading the streets of Banjul proudly proclaiming her support for North Devon Animal Ambulance. She also made about £10,000 for the Ambulance itself, and if you've bought this book, she's made a few quid more.

The tajine was smashed beyond repair by some fumbling baggage handler at Banjul or Gatwick. Gilly made a new one.

And whatever happened to all the other characters who made this, for me, the trip of a lifetime, I shall never know. I can only list them all for you, and wish them all long life and happiness.

A CAST OF SEVERAL
(IN ORDER OF APPEARANCE)

Dave Trickett, landscape gardener and ex-smoker
Gilly Pugsley, Lady Mallens of Bedfordshire, sponsor and editor-in-chief
Jack Sparrow, wherever he may be
Neil Caley, mechanic extraordinaire
Keith Lamprey, indulgent cousin
Graham DeMeur, excellent friend, faithful partner, who drove most of the way
Paul Wilson, excellent friend, but with whom I'd still be lost in France.
Phil Carter, excellent friend, with good advice on left hand drive
Derrick Hamly, excellent friend, in at the start and at the end
Diana and Mick Lewis, who had Black Betty sign written
Kate Helyer of the North Devon Journal, who helped find Black Betty
Frieda and Heidi Whittaker, who posed for photos
Robbie Herrick, who nearly found me an ice cream van
Jeff at the pool, who thought of breakers' yards
Lance Ginns of Freelance Motors, Black Betty's former owner
Black Betty, Cherokee Jeep, where are you now?
Julian Nowill and Drew, the Disorganisers
Sister Marlene, deadly with a needle
The ladies of Ilfracombe High Street Post Office, long may they stay open
The Ilfracombe High Street photographer
The Manager, Nationwide Building Society, Ilfracombe branch
Mfanwy of Swansea
Sally, Emily and Rosie, who hosted me on the embassy jaunt

Gary and Kate, who were there for Graham at Plymouth
Kirkhams, of Barnstaple, who helped with the tyres and battery
Guy Morton of Idam Signs, who reminded Black Betty where she was going
Rick the Dick who helped in Muddiford
Alf Doody, who knows a bit about Gambia
Cathy Karniewicz, Mrs. Recycle
Jack the Back, who sorted it out
The staff and swimmers at Ilfracombe Pool, who supported us
Steve Pam and Helen Parkin who looked after the Missus
Hetty Wainthrop, Gilly's confidante and bessy mate
The Wests of Indicknowle who did likewise
Dame Slap of Leighton Buzzard
My little tiny baby sister Linda
Laraine and Tony
Beryl and Joan, who linedanced and took an interest
Dobby, house elf
Mr. D'Arcy and Hufflepuff, Gilly's faithful companions
Jill and Rob Hunter, helpful in hysteria
Norman Bussel, there to see us off
Gareth Davies of Okehampton Motors, who saved the trip
Madeleine of the Hotel Louisiane, Biarritz
David of Gibraltar
Ian and Dan, Team 2 in a 4, the clockmenders
Officer Mohammed Jaroo
Ahmed, Graham's friend in Tangier
Tajines-R-Us, just outside Meknes
Tony and Harry, Team Hugh Jarse
The candlelit policeman
Sakina of the Palais Didi
All the petrol pump attendants of west Africa
The bog police
Mohammed, the hotel agent
Ali the Scam, and his many cousins
Grizzled car park guard in the Medina
Staff of the Tiznit Post Office

Keith Pugsley

Simo Mohammed of "Le Marin"
King Hussain of El Marsa
Alan and Graham, Team Old Gits
Andy Morgan and Dave Barrow, Team Dumb and Dumber, pals in adversity
The plucky Pug
Mohammed Abdullah, black prince among men
Ivan Beaman, and his elusive wife
Mohammed Bomba, the guide we did not choose
Team Crazy Larry's
The Costa Blanca Dons, who were lost and then found
Team Turbo Tortoises
Lord of the Sands
Team Norfolk 'n Chance
The CliC Sargents
The Reservoir Frogs
Rattle 'n Hum
Team Flapjack
Beauty and the Beast
Mrs. Mohammed
The reporter on the Nouadhibou Gazette
The man from the Pru in Mauritania
Mohammed's nephew in the desert emporium
Bette Davis
The Creole cleaning lady
Our taxi driver in Nouakchott
French Paul
Odious Ali
The Sleeping Policeman
The Reluctant Bureaucrat
The Ayotollah
The man from the Pru in Senegal
The Laughing Policeman
The Special Constable
Martin, host of Zebrabar
Team USIMW, the Wookies Trevor and Scott

The captain of the *Ursula Samira*
Biggles and Algy
The street hustler in St.Louis
The Black Venus
Mr. Fixit
Edith Piaf
Seek, our escort in Senegal
Sergeant Dixon
The Barra Ferry Ticket Official
Del Boy
Junior water vendor on the Barra Ferry
Beef Farmer on the Barra Ferry
The Bull
Ali Jarreh
Mama of the Fajara Craft Market, stall 20
Omar Darboe of the Alpha Company
The Beach Therapist
Elizabeth Touray
Assan Njie, mechanic
Tijaan Faal and his Happy dad taxi
Charley the croc
Alex (not J.S.) Sainsbury
Captain Mustafa at Lammin
Our House Boy at Bungalow Beach
Colonel Blimp
Blue Rinse
Devon Maid
Victor Meldrew in a frock
Pauline Smith who made Day Seven so much better than it was
Terence Sackett who made it even better
Laurence Shelley, who taught me that "a little bit of too much is often not enough". Thanks Laurence, and thank you all.

Printed in the United Kingdom
by Lightning Source UK Ltd.
132035UK00001B/58-273/P